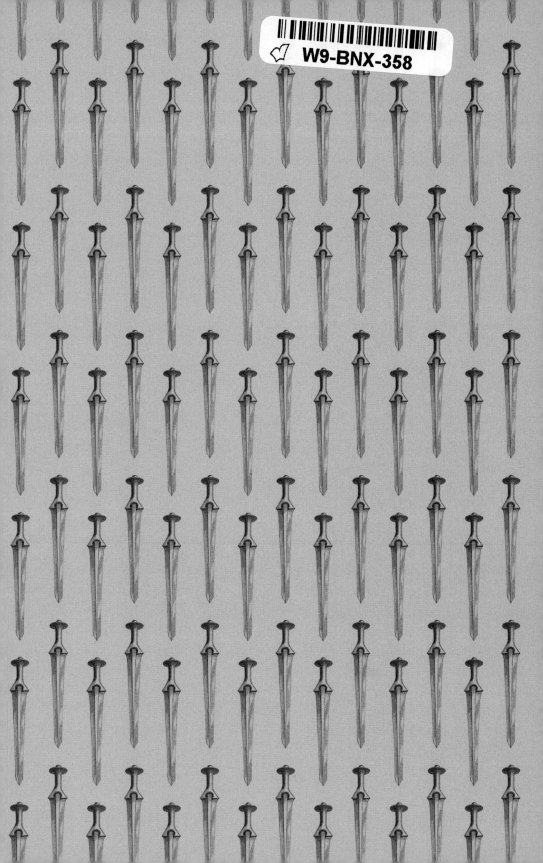

A FATAL THING
HAPPENED ON THE WAY
TO THE FORUM

Also by Emma Southon

Agrippina: Empress, Exile, Hustler, Whore
Marriage, Sex and Death: The Family and the Fall of the Roman West

A FATAL THING
HAPPENED ON THE WAY
TO THE FORUM

Murder in Ancient Rome

EMMA SOUTHON

ABRAMS PRESS, NEW YORK

Library of Congress Control Number: 2020944849

ISBN: 978-1-4197-5305-3
eISBN: 978-1-64700-232-9

Printed and bound in the United States
10 9 8 7 6 5 4 3 2 1

Abrams books are available at special discounts when purchased in quantity
for premiums and promotions as well as fundraising or educational
use. Special editions can also be created to specification. For details,
contact specialsales@abramsbooks.com or the address below.

Abrams Press® is a registered trademark of Harry N. Abrams, Inc.

ABRAMS The Art of Books
195 Broadway, New York, NY 10007
abramsbooks.com

'Right and wrong is not absolute or relative: it is geometrical.'

Mark Cooney, *Is Killing Wrong?*

'The army might teach us to kill,
but it doesn't teach us to murder.'

Casefile, Episode 90

For Amy-Elizabeth, Jess and Kate: my murder pals

Contents

Prologue

Picture the scene: an idyllic hill in central Italy, a group of men sit, silently watching the afternoon sky. In the distance, though easily within sight, on another hill are another group. These men are all shepherds and followers of twins who had risen from nowhere to kill the king of Alba Longa and seize the throne for their own, declaring themselves the sons of Mars. Under their rule, Alba Longa had welcomed fugitives and runaway slaves and vagabonds of all stripes until it had grown so large that the twins had decided to found themselves a city. And here they reached, for the first time in their lives, a point of irreconcilable conflict: for reasons unclear, the city had to be named after only one twin; the other would have to submit to his brother. Neither willing to back down, they agreed to let the gods decide between them by sending an omen. The omen they requested was vultures, and now they, with their followers, sat, waiting and watching, glowering across the valley. You already know the names of these twins: Romulus and Remus.

After god knows how long, a cry went up from the Aventine Hill where Remus and his pals waited. Six vultures had appeared. A sign the gods favoured Remus as the founder of the new city. Elated, he set out with his closest allies to the Palatine Hill where his brother Romulus was grimly waiting. Remus gave his news to Romulus, but at that moment another sign appeared. *Twelve* vultures flew over the Palatine. The gods had decided that Romulus would be the founder.

Each group hailed their preferred twin as the chosen king, which was awkward. Both groups began building their city.

Tensions rose. Eventually, in an act of ultimate contempt, Remus leapt over one of the rising city walls on the Palatine, inciting Romulus into an uncontrollable fury. He attacked his brother and stabbed him to death and declared, unrepentant, that this was what would happen to anyone who ever breached his walls. And thus, in murder, Rome was founded.

By 510 BCE, Rome was a flourishing city under the king Tarquinius Superbus. Something, however, was rotten in the state of Rome and another act of violence soon changed everything. Tarquinius' son Sextus Tarquinius raped an aristocratic woman named Lucretia. Lucretia responded by calling a family meeting, explaining what had happened and then driving a knife into her own heart. Her family saw this as honourable and praiseworthy in the extreme, and, full of righteous rage and grief, they took to the Forum and displayed her body as that of a murder victim. They demanded Tarquinius and his son be overthrown and exiled. The people of Rome agreed and, with a remarkable unity of purpose, swiftly abolished the monarchy and established the Roman Republic. The Romans designed the Republic to deny power to individuals and to prevent, through the means of shared power, checks and balances, any single man from becoming a tyrant. It was the Romans' proudest achievement and it was founded in the unjust death of a woman.

The glorious Republic of Rome lasted 450 years, and the moment of its demise was also marked by murder. That moment came on the Ides of March 44 BCE when Rome's sole ruler entered the Theatre of Pompey and forty of his friends administered twenty-three stab wounds, leaving Julius Caesar, perpetual dictator of Rome and proto-emperor, bleeding to death on the floor of the entrance hall, and opening the path for his nineteen-year-old great-nephew Octavian to become the glorious, deified emperor Augustus.

Introduction

Whenever there was a transformative moment in Roman history, there was a murder. A person died, usually bloodily, and, in the space where they once lived, something entirely new emerged. Rome was built on the blood of Remus; the Republic was born from the death of Lucretia; the Empire grew from the assassination of Caesar. Rome was an unusually murder-y place. But for most of Roman history murder was *not* a crime. And for all of Roman history, killing in the gladiatorial arena was a literal sport. The symbol of the Roman state was the *fasces* – a bundle of sticks containing an axe. The sticks represented the power of the state to beat its citizens, and the axe represented its right to kill them. The *fasces* were carried by guards known as lictors who accompanied all Roman officials whenever they left their houses, so the message was never forgotten.[1] Few other societies have revelled in and revered the deliberate and purposeful killing of men and women as much as the Romans. The Romans were, frankly, weird about it.

But then, we as a Western society are also weird about murder. We absolutely love it. We consume it with a passion. Right now, in the US and the UK, one in every three books purchased is a crime novel, which inevitably opens with a pretty woman found dead. The crime novelist James Patterson has been the world's bestselling author for about five years. The amount of money he makes a year knocking out thrillers about gruesome murders (eighteen of which are about a 'Women's Murder Club') is so enormous my brain can't comprehend it. The joint biggest-selling English-language author of all time is Agatha Christie, selling between two and four *billion* copies of her murder mystery novels.[2] But it's not all fiction. True crime is also booming. In 2014, the podcast *Serial*, about the murder of a high school student, was downloaded forty million times in three months, and things have only got better for murder podcasts and associated media from there. You, dear reader, have picked up a book called *A Fatal Thing Happened on the Way to the Forum*, which promises (and will deliver) lots of good death and gore. I'm not judging, though. I wrote this book. Because I love murder too. I was a *Serial* fanatic. I am an Agatha Christie obsessive. I am fascinated by murder. I'll talk about my (many) serial killer opinions a lot if you listen to me for long enough.

Our Western obsession with murder as a titillating and enormously entertaining outlier makes us extremely odd in the grand cultural scheme of things. No other society has built media empires on such mountains of dead and mutilated women. But, to us, the Romans look like the weird ones because they were fascinated by murder in a different way. We have our mountains of dead fictional girls. But they had mountains of dead real men. Murder was a very literal sport. They took enslaved men and prisoners of war, forcing them to fight one another in an arena until one died violently in front of a screaming crowd of highly entertained people. Regularly. This was the number two sport in Rome (number one: horse racing) and it somewhat skewed how Romans perceived murder in the rest of their lives, along with how they viewed the fundamental notions of life and death and what it means to be a human.

The Romans also had an institutionalised, domestic and utterly pervasive form of slavery that is hard to get your head around as a modern person who believes that every person is equal. Enslaved men, women and children were everywhere in Rome. Aristocratic homes had hundreds of people living in them who had been enslaved by the Romans. Even poorer homes might have had one enslaved member of the household. The Roman state ran on the labour of enslaved men doing the administrative and physical labour necessary to run a huge empire and build massive marble buildings covered in pretty paintings every four hundred yards. No inhabitant of Rome went without contact with enslaved persons and no one ever questioned it. No Roman ever looked at their slaves and at their freed slaves (who remained part of their household) and thought, 'Hang on a minute. These are people!' Instead, they treated these men, women and children with whom they shared their houses as though they were chairs. Things that could be abused and kicked and disposed of without, for the most part, any consequence. And everyone agreed that was fine and normal and right. And that also rather messed with their notions of right and wrong and life and death too.

What is murder?

I suspect that everyone thinks they know what murder is, but I also suspect that most people don't, really. Until I started researching this book, I – like you probably – used murder and homicide interchangeably. It turns out that they are not the same thing. Homicide is the act of killing someone under any circumstances. Any time a human kills another person, that's a homicide. Some of those are legal, such as the death penalty in the hundred countries that still have capital punishment laws (wow, that's high). That's a hundred countries in which one person can inject another person with poison or shoot them or hang them by the neck fully intending to kill them with the support of the state. Soldiers killing one another on a battlefield or with a big drone is another form of legal homicide. As a soldier, you can try your hardest to kill as many people as possible and get nothing but medals and complex PTSD in return.

But most forms of homicide are illegal, and there are lots of them. The lowest forms are called involuntary manslaughter in English and US law, and culpable homicide in Scottish law, and a bunch of other things in other places. They are incidents where maybe the perpetrator didn't mean to kill that other person, but still someone died and it was definitely their fault. This is for when parents accidentally leave their babies in hot cars or healthcare workers accidentally give the wrong drug. That kind of thing. Then there's voluntary manslaughter. This is when you meant to hurt the victim but not to kill them. Maybe you meant to punch them in a fight but when they went down they cracked their head and died. Maybe you were provoked and lost control. Maybe there is diminished responsibility because you were really high or in the middle of a psychotic episode.

After all these – and gosh is English law very specific and detailed about these – comes murder. Murder is defined in England and Wales as 'where a person (1) of sound mind (2) unlawfully kills (3) any reasonable creature (4) in being (alive and breathing through its own lungs) (5) under the Queen's Peace (6) with intent to kill or cause grievous bodily harm'. All six conditions have to be met in order for a homicide to be considered a murder in an English court. In Scotland, simply intent and 'wicked recklessness' are required. In American federal law, murder is 'the unlawful killing of a human being with malice aforethought'. I bet you never knew that murder laws had such lovely turns of phrase.

Americans like to complicate this further by separating murder into first and second degrees, and then adding extra complications by letting each state decide what constitutes first- and second-degree murder. Generally, first-degree murder is intentional murder that has been premeditated or planned, while second-degree murder is intentional but unplanned. So, if I go out and buy a gun and then go to someone's house and shoot them, that's first-degree murder. If I am Ted Bundy and I am pretending that I hurt my arm so a woman will help me lift my canoe up so I can beat her to death with a hammer while she's not looking, that's first-degree murder. I planned that. However, if I am arguing with someone and then I pull out my gun in the middle of the fight and shoot them, that's second-degree murder. Some states also have third-degree murder, which covers all forms of manslaughter. In New York State, first-degree murder only refers to the murder of police officers, multiple murders, murders involving torture or being a paid assassin (!). So if I buy a gun and drive to someone's house and kill them in Glenville, NY, that's second-degree murder unless I am being paid or they are a cop. But, if I did that same thing in Pottsville, PA, that would be first-degree murder. If I did it in Lancing, UK, it would just be murder. Furthermore, I'd be liable for the death penalty in Pennsylvania, but not in New York because only capital (first-degree) federal murders are death penalty murders in New York State. Which means, in Pennsylvania, a second homicide could occur as a result of the murder, this time in a nice state-sanctioned cell.

What I'm getting at here is that murder is a constructed act. The only black-and-white part of a murder is the bit where one person killed another, and that's actually the homicide bit. Homicide is clear cut, but murder is a label we apply to some forms of homicide, and that label changes over time and across space. What is clearly murder in one state is manslaughter in another; what is legal homicide to one person is obviously murder to another. Murder is the interpretation of an event, interpreted by individual people, which makes murder an emotive label, no matter how much legalese it is couched in. It is not a binary category. It is not a single or simple descriptor. Murder is complicated.

During the writing of this book, I had one quote above my desk, from the sociologist Douglas Black: 'Right and wrong is not absolute or relative: it is geometrical.' This is why I have used a very comprehensive definition of 'murder' to include basically all killing. Rightness and wrongness are products of social space, where gender, status, race, location, means, time, wealth and infinite other variables shift and move and come together to create rightness and wrongness that are never static. Because of this, I have interpreted the concept of murder very (very) broadly.

And I want you to keep all that in mind as we leap into the world of Roman homicide.

Murder on the Senate Floor

Like a band playing its biggest hit first, we start with the reason you probably picked this book up. We start with that colossus bestriding the narrow world, the big hitter of Roman murders, a big hitter in all-time murders, burnt into our consciousness by two millennia of thinking about him: Gaius Julius Caesar. The problem with Caesar's murder is that everyone thinks they already know it. They have seen Shakespeare's tragedy in some community theatre or BBC adaptation or that film version with Marlon Brando as Antony, or they've watched a box set of HBO's *Rome* or read a Robert Harris or Conn Iggulden novel about it. There's no shortage of fiction about Caesar bleeding out on the Senate floor. Everyone in the West knows the meaning of the Ides of March even if they don't actually know when the Ides are.[†] Everyone has an image of what they think forty men stabbing Caesar looks like and all of them come with Shakespeare's 'et tu, Brute?'

There are a few reasons why we know so much about Julius Caesar's murder. The first is that the Romans themselves wrote about it a lot, and left us pleasingly detailed descriptions of the Ides of March and its aftermath. The second is that, in hindsight, as Caesar died, he took the Republic with him, which they made quite a big deal about. And, of course, the story is fabulously dramatic. The arrogant general, who has announced himself dictator for life, ignores the soothsayers and his wife's dreams and weeping and walks to his own death; he dies on the

---

† It's March 15.

Senate floor at the feet of a statue of his greatest rival; his final conscious realisation is the dawning horror and humiliation that his own closest friend has killed him and that no one will come to help; his final act is to cover himself, and his dignity, with his toga, always the showman to the last. All this means that Julius Caesar is more myth than man; he is a story that is told. His murder is not remembered as a bloody human act conducted by forty frightened dudes in ungainly dress who were so confused that they only got twenty-three stab wounds in (an almost fifty percent fail rate if you think about it). But Julius really was a man who lived and breathed and blinked and then one day felt a punch in his side that was suddenly cold and wet and very pain-ful. And his murder was not a standalone incident. It was one of a series of astonishing political murders in the late Roman Republic that, together, show us how very odd political murder was in the Roman world at this time, and how it changed. So I'm going to confess that I teased you a little. I've played the opening chords of a familiar song. But now I am going to take you back almost a century before JC breathed his last and introduce you to Tiberius Gracchus, whose murder was even more of a horror show than this one.

Tiberius Gracchus

Tiberius Gracchus was a genuinely extraordinary man, mostly because of his death. His death marked the demise of the Roman Republic as much as Caesar's, because it was his death which started almost a hundred years of open warfare in Rome. And I don't mean that metaphorically. I mean that senators took to stabbing the hell out of each other with disturbing frequency for almost a century – very frequently in the centre of the city. It was a knife crime epidemic among the very richest and most powerful in the Roman Empire. It theoretically ended when Caesar fell, or perhaps when Octavian got the better of Antony and Cleopatra at Actium. But really, senators never stopped trying to kill each other; they just got sneakier. Before we get there, though, we need to see how murder became so central to Roman politics, and I'm sorry but it involves a lot of politics and chat about land reform policies and it's awful. We can get through this together; I believe in us.

From the day the Romans drove their king out of Italy (notably not killing him) and constructed their beautiful Republic of shared power, they were at war with one another. It began with patricians versus plebeians, but it swiftly became the landed versus the unlanded, and eventually the *populares* versus the *optimates*. The *populares* were populist politicians who courted the people's vote with handouts, while the *optimates* were high-born patricians and wannabes who literally called themselves the 'best men' and believed that the people should be kept as far away from government as possible. Italian land was desired by everyone because ancient wealth was based entirely on the ownership of land. Land equalled money in the same way that property in London and Dublin and New York equals money. So, the poor wanted half an acre to call their own, rather than having to rent a single room with a shower in the kitchen, while the rich wanted places to grow massive vineyards and frolic without having to look at the poor. As Rome expanded its power and influence into Italy throughout the fifth century BCE, the poor saw each victory as an opportunity for them to claim some land of their own – after all, they were fighting in the armies that were conquering these Italian neighbours. Unfortunately for them, they had no power and the patricians just gave themselves all the land. Or, even more cruelly, pretended to set aside land for 'public use', and then rented it to themselves for ludicrously low rents, leaving the landless Romans still landless and adding to their ranks those poor Italians who had suddenly been conquered by these fighty bastards from Rome. They kept that land and cultivated it and passed it around the family and bought and sold it.

As generations passed, this 'public' land became the patricians' inheritance given to them by their grandparents and the patrimony they'd leave their children. It was their dowry and their daughters' dowries, and the fruits of their hard labours, and they were absolutely not giving it up.

We can yada yada yada the lead-up to Tiberius Gracchus because this isn't a book about Republican politics, but, basically, tension over this land ownership issue seethed constantly in Republican Rome and there was a very real split between the power held by the people of Rome in their tribes which they exercised through voting, and the power held by the Senate of Rome which was exercised through senatorial decrees. It's all deeply uninteresting but, by 133 BCE, the land ownership thing was causing not just tension but very real, pragmatic problems for the growing Roman Empire and the city of Rome. The city was losing its ability to feed itself. So much of the land in and around Rome had become leisure land for aristocrats and pretty gardens and immense villas that Italy's food production had dropped. Rome was coming to rely more and more heavily on imports, which is a bad plan. The expansion and maintenance of the now significant Empire was also threatened. By 133 BCE, Rome had conquered Italy, destroyed Carthage and colonised North Africa, and had just conquered Greece and Macedonia. It had been fighting expansionist battles for a solid two centuries and was not planning on stopping for a long time, which meant it needed Roman bodies in the army and newly built navy. Lots of Roman bodies. But there was a problem: service in the army was technically supposed to be a privilege limited to property-owning

Roman citizens and Rome was running out of disposable men who owned land. The third problem, from the perspective of the Roman ruling classes and citizens, was that rich Romans were using the immense influx of enslaved labour to work their personal land rather than renting it out or employing free labourers. There was a sense among Roman citizens, one which was almost certainly false, that enslaved foreigners would eventually outnumber Romans and were an existential threat to Roman supremacy. This is almost the same as when a taxi driver told me that there were so many Eastern European people 'flooding' into the UK that 'England would sink', except slightly worse because the people 'flooding' the Roman countryside were enslaved people forcibly removed from their lands. Such concerns caused real problems, though.

So that's three problems facing the government of Rome. The easiest way to resolve these issues, as far as our protagonist Tiberius Gracchus was concerned, was to redistribute the land. Settle landless Roman citizens on Roman land to farm it and basically all three problems were solved in one fell swoop, with the added benefit – for Tiberius Gracchus – that Tiberius Gracchus would be a hero to the Roman people for the rest of time. He was far from the first person to suggest land redistribution. The first had been the consul Spurius Cassius Vecellinus in 486 BCE – the people of Rome were delighted; the Senate, horrified. His co-consul and all other senators acted as though he were trying to cut off their legs. They accused him of being far too popular and trying to destroy their liberty, and eventually his own father held a household trial, found him guilty of something, had him scourged through the streets of Rome and then publicly executed him.[1] That, unsurprisingly, put a dampener on land reform for a while.

Tiberius Sempronius Gracchus was the son of, of course, Tiberius Sempronius Gracchus and his wife Cornelia Africana.

Tiberius the Elder was not of patrician stock but was highly distinguished. He was consul twice, a successful general and became Tribune of the Plebs, during which time he used his veto to prevent the great general Scipio Africanus from being prosecuted after he was accused of taking bribes from the Seleucid king Antiochus III. Scipio was so delighted he immediately betrothed his daughter Cornelia to Tiberius without bothering to consult either his wife or his daughter. Tiberius the Elder and Cornelia allegedly had twelve children, of which three survived to adulthood, one of which was a girl so she didn't count. The boys were Tiberius Gracchus the Younger and his baby brother Gaius Gracchus. Tiberius the Younger was, as it happens, a remarkably boring Roman. He's even the most boring member of his family. His mum got statues dedicated to her for being, essentially, the best Roman mother ever. The dad was the subject of a famous story: one day he found two snakes in his house, a male and a female (apparently he was an expert at sexing snakes because I've just Googled it and it's hard. It involves the words 'probe' and 'cloacal vent'.). He did the first thing that any good Roman chap did when confronted by an unusual situation and found a fortune teller to explain it. The fortune teller told him that he had to kill one snake and release the other (it is unclear why; fortune tellers never explained themselves). However, if he let the male snake go and killed the female, his wife would die, but if he released the female and killed the male, he would be killing himself.[2] Being terribly fond of Cornelia, Tiberius chose to kill the one connected to his own fate and shortly afterwards he died of unknown causes. So that's a good story. Tiberius' brother Gaius was an absolute riot, said to be the first person in Roman history to pull his cloak open and expose his shoulder while speaking, which is both pointless and a bit sexy. He also had a full-time personal musician who would follow him around and play music: calming when he was getting too angry and excitable if he was getting too sleepy. What a guy! Even their sister Sempronia, who by virtue of being a woman in Roman history is basically invisible in the sources, got to be accused of murdering her husband Scipio Aemilianus (who was also her cousin). Tiberius, on the other hand, has nothing. No good anecdotes at all. An absolute personality vacuum. Until he became Tribune of the Plebs in 133 BCE.

Tribunes held enormous power in Rome; they were supposed to be the elected representatives of the non-patrician people of Rome and Tiberius apparently took that seriously. Having identified land redistribution as the solution to Rome's problems, he got stuck in and proposed a commission. The commission would find and confiscate land which rich people were, technically, squatting on and redistribute it in parcels of five hundred *iugera* (about 350 acres) so that every (male) Roman citizen owned no less and, ideally, not much more than that five hundred *iugera*. Everyone would be equalish. To make matters worse, he very selfishly followed the normal protocol for Tribunes and, instead of presenting his proposal to the Senate, he called an assembly of the people (which explicitly excluded patricians) and, standing on the Campus Martius in front of thousands of urban and rural poor, made his proposal there first. Basically, he called together all the disenfranchised of Rome and offered them the chance to vote on whether they wanted to be given some free land or not. Both the city tribes and the rural tribes – unsurprisingly – voted enthusiastically for Tiberius' brilliant proposal.

At first the Senate shrugged. Attempts like this had been made before and the laws had either been ignored or the rich had just bought back the land that was being 'redistributed'. Unfortunately for them, Tiberius Gracchus knew his history and he had built into his law a commission that would actively confiscate land, and a clause forbidding land from being resold. It could only be redistributed. Once they worked that out, the rich became hopping mad. He may as well have proposed a commission for the redistribution of wives and daughters. Their dinner parties became rage-fuelled pity parties as they outlined their grievances to one another. The Greek historian Appian, writing many centuries later after the winners had been conclusively declared, outlines the complaints of the rich alongside the complaints of the poor and suggests that they are equal, which makes for some fun reading. Appian tells us that the rich were hugely upset that the land that they had worked very hard on, and dedicated many enslaved people to, was going to be stolen from them so they'd lose all their work. Also, some of them had bought that land fairly from neighbours after the neighbours stole it from the state and people of Rome, so they were definitely being treated unfairly. Others had inherited their stolen land from their parents or had received it in dowries and yet more had taken out loans against the stolen land – and what were they supposed to do?! Their prestige and inheritances were being cruelly attacked and they were weeping into their cups.[3]

A date was set for the Assembly to vote on the law and, as word spread, people began to flood into the city. The rich, suddenly concerned that they might lose, resorted to the Romans' favourite insult: they accused Tiberius of wanting to be a king. Sadly for them, again, Tiberius Gracchus was convincingly not a tyrant. He was too virtuous for that. But he gave great speeches which roused the people to believe in a better future for themselves. One is quoted by Plutarch and it makes you want to rise up and start singing 'The Internationale':

> The wild beasts that dwell in Italy have their homes,
> with each having a lair and a hiding place, but the men

who fight and die on behalf of Italy have a share of air and light – and nothing else. Without houses or homes they wander aimlessly with their children and wives, and their generals deceive them when they urge the soldiers on the battlefield to drive off the enemy to protect their tombs and temples; not one of these Romans has a family altar, not one an ancestral tomb; instead, they fight and die to protect the luxury and wealth of others. They are called masters of the earth yet have not a single clod of earth that is their own.[4]

The day of the vote finally dawned. Rome was heaving with rural men who had travelled to vote and crackling with the rage and fear of hundreds of landowners. Everyone congregated in their thirty-five tribes on the Campus Martius. The Tribunes and officials began. First, according to Appian, Tiberius stuck to his strengths and gave a long speech in which he attempted to please everyone. He emphasised that this law was for the good of Rome – the glory of the Roman people! – because everyone would be able to join the army and fight then come home and farm a few acres for the rest of their lives. What a life! He encouraged the rich to see this as a gift from themselves to Rome and to all the future Roman babies that would be born on the lovely Roman land. He went full Centrist Dad to be honest. No one was won over. As was immediately demonstrated by his colleague in the Tribuneship, Marcus Octavius. As he concluded his speech, Tiberius stepped aside and ordered an official to read aloud the law to be voted on. Octavius stepped forward and ordered the official not to. He vetoed the vote. There was a screaming row between Octavius and Tiberius and the Assembly was adjourned. Everyone was sent home to reconvene the next day. No one comments on how the crowd reacted, because by the time anyone was writing histories about this, no one cared about the people, but I can't imagine it went well.

The next day, the Assembly convened again. Thousands of men again massed into the Campus Martius and waited. The Tribunes appeared and this time Tiberius brought a guard to protect himself. Thankfully, he didn't make a speech. The official launched into the reading of the law, and Octavius shouted at him to stop. This time there was uproar. The Tribunes screamed at one another and the Assembly collapsed into a mob. Before things got out of control, Tiberius shouted that he would recon-vene the Assembly yet again and this time he would be asking the people to impeach Octavius and 'decide whether a Tribune who acted against the interests of the people should continue to hold office'. So he did. And he won. Octavius was voted out of office and meandered off into obscurity and Tiberius' agrarian law was passed. A commission would confiscate land and everyone would be given some. Joy was unconfined.

The Senate were not delighted but, in the end, they were going to be in charge of the commission so they worked on hobbling it from the inside in a manner that is too tedious to contemplate. Tiberius had technically won, but a technical win wasn't going to bring land to most Romans or hurt too many senators. It seemed that, despite all the drama, Tiberius' reforms would go the same way as every other attempt. They would die in committee. Except then, all of a sudden, Attalus Philometor, the king of Pergamon, died and made the people of Rome his heirs. Pergamon was a very rich and large city in Turkey, where Roman rule was beginning to creep in violently. Attalus had watched the long horrific wars in Greece and Macedonia and had seen the Romans brutalise everyone in their path so he hoped to spare his city and his people. He knew that the Romans would come for Pergamon soon enough and, by surrendering rule of the city to the Romans in his will, he gave them control of Pergamon without any bloodshed. It sort of worked. Technically, no blood was spilt there. But it was Tiberius' downfall, because he leapt on it. Here was a lot of land which could be immediately distributed to Roman citizens by his commission without upsetting anyone. Here was a lot of money which could be given to Romans to run their new farms. Thank you very much, Attalus, said Tiberius, I'll take this from here and the Senate doesn't need to be involved.

By this time, Tiberius had been Tribune for a year and it was time to run for re-election. The rich desperately wanted Tiberius out of office so they could kill his commission and ideally exile him for being annoying. Tiberius desperately wanted to stay Tribune to protect himself and his work. Both sides worked furiously. Tiberius paid to bring in voters from the countryside and personally accosted voters in the city to beg for their vote, a move which Appian considered to be somewhat embarrassing, while his opponents were running on an 'Anyone But Gracchus' platform, a simple but effective strategy. When voting day dawned, the atmosphere in Rome was tense. Voting in Republican Rome took place on the Campus Martius where all eligible voters who could be bothered had to show up in person, line up in their tribes and spend basically the whole day voting – orally one by one. It took ages and was boring, unless something went wrong. This day, things went wrong. The first attempt at voting was interrupted when Tiberius appeared to be winning and his opponents got in the way. The votes were erased and everyone started again. Now Tiberius appeared to be losing, so his supporters interrupted and the whole thing was called off. Tiberius returned to his house, where people congregated shouting lamentations and encouragement through his window all night.

The next day began badly with a series of omens. First, the sacred birds of Rome refused to eat their breakfast, which definitely signalled bad news. Then, when Tiberius was leaving the house, he badly stubbed his toe on the doorframe, breaking the nail and filling his sandal with blood. This might have been because people had kept him up all night with the shouting and lamenting, but doors and doorways had great symbolic significance for the Romans, and they saw this as the gods telling Tiberius to go back to bed. Tiberius wasn't listening. He kept going, only to have a tile thrown at him by a murder of crows fighting on a rooftop. It was all very ominous, but still Tiberius didn't stop. After the previous day's activities, voting had been moved to the Capitoline Hill where people might be expected to behave themselves a bit. It didn't work. By the time Tiberius arrived, the tribes had devolved into two restless mobs, each furious that their vote had been erased the day before. When the other Tribunes tried to prevent the vote from going ahead yet again, a riot inevitably broke out. The *fasces* were snatched from the hands of the lictors and used as weapons by Tiberius' followers, and his opposition were driven out of the Capitoline enclosure. The monumental centre of Rome was in chaos, and Tiberius and his friends were trapped on the Capitoline Hill by a mob waiting for revenge . . . Now, well done if you've made it this far through this thoroughly awful rundown of Republican politics, for which I'm very sorry and really I did my best, because this is where it gets good. And, for once, all the sources are remarkably consistent on what happened.

In the Temple of Fides, the Senate were in session and they were having a debate that would change the face of Roman politics forever. They were discussing whether to kill Tiberius Gracchus. In fact, many members of the Senate, the most grand and august body of Roman government, were trying to persuade the consul Publius Mucius Scaevola to use his *imperium* (supreme power) to kill Tiberius and officially execute him, without trial, for trying to take their stolen land. Mucius Scaevola refused. Killing a Roman citizen, a Tribune no less, without a trial was an abominable act, regardless of how much trouble he'd caused. The senators argued back and forth, while Tiberius tried to find a plan. Something was going to break somewhere, and one side was going to have to front up or back down. Appian, being of Greek descent and always slightly bemused by Republican Roman mores, says that he's surprised that they didn't take this opportunity to declare a national emergency and appoint a dictator, but suspects that they were so riled up, they completely forgot that appointing a dictator and legally suspending democracy was possible. That would have been a better plan, but then hindsight is always 20/20. The person who finally broke was, astonishingly, the Pontifex Maximus, the head of the college of priests who oversaw state religion. Admittedly, the priesthood wasn't exactly a spiritual calling in Rome, but it was still a bit like the Archbishop of Canterbury going full Rambo when Scipio Nasica lost his patience, stood up in the temple and shouted, 'As the consul is a traitor for letting the whole Empire and its laws collapse, I'll fix this.' (I'm paraphrasing a bit, but so were the Roman historians, who weren't there either.) He then threw his toga over his arm and bellowed, 'Let anyone who wants to save the country come with me!' The senators roared and, as they were not allowed their swords in a Senate meeting, they tore their wooden benches apart and armed themselves with the planks of wood. Everything had gone awry.

One senator ran to the Capitol to warn Tiberius that the Senate were armed and dangerous. People surrounded Tiberius to protect and remove him from the literal theatre of conflict as the mob of senators approached. It was not a long walk from the

Temple of Fides to the top of the Capitoline and there weren't many ways out. As the supporters of the Senate and the rich surged forwards, Tiberius' supporters tried to hold them back and the Senate began to swing their homemade clubs. This had got out of hand. It had transcended a simple riot as soon as the Senate themselves came in and started hitting. As wood shattered bones and blood began to flow, the Republic was being inexorably mutilated along with the faces of a lot of Roman people. As Nasica swung his chair leg into the heads of those trying to protect Tiberius, he shattered the façade of democracy and republicanism that allowed the people of Rome to believe they had a voice and power in their government. Bodies fell to the ground, some dead, some injured. People were trampled. The air around the temples was filled with screams. Tiberius was fleeing to the east side of the Capitoline area when someone grabbed his toga. A long, heavy, woollen blanket wrapped around you is a real hindrance when fleeing for your life. He let it fall, but tripped. As he went down, someone took their chance. Plutarch says that it was Tiberius' fellow Tribune, Publius Satyreius, who threw the first blow and Lucius Rufus threw the second. Appian says that Tiberius fell at the feet of the statues of kings; Valerius Maximus simply says that he got what he deserved. Wood came down on his head and Tiberius died. He, along with hundreds of others, was beaten to death by a mob of the richest men in the West. He hadn't reached his thirtieth birthday. Murder had been introduced as a solution to Roman political arguments and it could never be taken back.

It would be easy to imagine a kind of political hangover affecting the Romans the next day, that they were filled with shame and disgust at what had happened the day before. Instead, the Senate doubled down. Tiberius' body and those of his supporters were defiled and thrown in the river. The Senate exiled several of his surviving friends, and killed some more. Plutarch claims that one, Gaius Villius, was punished as if he had killed his father by being sewn into a sack with some angry snakes. The bad guys had won and they weren't going to back down. And they were absolutely the bad guys. For all the weaselly attempts by later Roman historians to make Tiberius into some kind of deranged traitor to the Republic, it's pretty clear that what they mean is class traitor. He tried to undermine the controlling power of the rich and force some limited form of equality on them and they hated it. They hated it so much, they were willing to kill him. They ripped apart the chairs they sat in and beat his head to a pulp to stop him and then they threw his body in the river. It was an outrageous moment in Roman history and not one person complained because everyone suddenly knew the consequences of complaining. Everyone knew that there was no power balance between the Senate and the people of Rome. Democracy was a charade. There was just the Senate and they would kill to keep it that way. And there would be no consequences when they did.

From this point on, violence was always a possibility in Roman politics. It took a generation for murder to really take off as a strategic approach to political problems, but the elephant very firmly moved into the room as Tiberius' blood splattered onto the statue of Romulus. At that moment it became OK to murder someone designated an 'opponent of the Republic' even if that designation wasn't legal or official. At first, no one really believed that this was as important a moment as it turned out to be. In the moment, no one ever realises that they're living through historical turning points. People thought that it was a bad thing but a one-off. It would never happen again. Until it happened again.

Tiberius' little brother Gaius was nine years younger and significantly more lively than Tiberius. As soon as Gaius entered political life, he was subject to scrutiny from both the people and the Senate. The people pressured him, through overt appeals and calling at him in the street and writing graffiti on the walls, to take up his brother's cause. The Senate, meanwhile, eyeballed him like the police eyeball an abandoned bag in an airport: they were ready to engage in a controlled detonation at the slightest sign of popularity. After being badgered with irritating lawsuits designed to annoy and exhaust him – because litigation really was a way of life for the Romans – Gaius eventually cracked and announced his candidacy to be Tribune in 123 BCE. Obviously he succeeded, to the fury of the Senate who, to a man, opposed him. Gaius was as confrontational and disruptive as his brother was conciliatory and compromising. He immediately started throwing out policy proposals designed to upset all the wrong people. He wanted land redistribution back on the agenda. He wanted new rules about magistracies. He wanted the people of Italy, known as the Latins, to have Roman citizenship. He wanted more money for public works and poverty alleviation. According to Plutarch, he really wanted long, straight, aesthetically pleasing roads with mile markers and special stones so that people could get on and off their horses easily. He loved a long, straight Roman road. He wanted a lot and the people loved it, while the Senate didn't want him to have any of it. There was a great deal of politics happening to stop him from winning, all of it interminably dull, but eventually, after a good two years of squabbling, in 121 BCE, violence kicked off again.

This time, proving his combative nature, it was Gaius' fault. After his supporters stabbed a rude lictor to death with their pens (!) and Gaius' main complaint was that it looked bad for him, it became clear that violence was now part of the Roman agenda. Gaius decided to lead an armed insurrection against the Senate, despite no longer being Tribune or having any justification for it, and tried to occupy the Aventine Hill. It went badly.

Fulvius, a supporter of Gaius' and consul at the time, was found hiding in some baths and brutally slaughtered; Gaius was forced to flee the city and got his enslaved attendant, Philoctetes, to stab him. When the Senate found Gaius' body, they cut off his head and a man named Septimuleius (say that three times fast) impaled it on a spear and carried it back to Rome. He was rewarded with the head's weight in gold. To be fair to the Senate, Gaius did rather ask for it by trying to mess with the Senate with a rag-tag army of pals and knives, but it was another violent blow to the Republic and another blood-soaked disaster that put an end to the idea of democratically reforming the government of the Roman Empire pretty much forever. It's hard to call Gaius a good guy (even though he did pull open his toga like an absolute flirt) but his death, the death of the consul and the grotesque display of his head (which weighed 17.6 pounds) really hammered home how much the bad guys were winning and loving it. And how much murder was rapidly becoming business as usual.

Publius Clodius Pulcher

The best example of how mundane political murder became in the late Republic is the somewhat pathetic street murder of Publius Clodius Pulcher by his political rival Titus Annius Milo.

Publius Clodius Pulcher is probably my favourite ever Roman. He was a colossus of a personality. If I had had to live during his lifetime, I would undoubtedly have despised him and the horse he rode in on but, with the benefit of two millennia's distance between us, I am able to gaze at him with delighted awe. He was simultaneously a theatrical, nose-snubbing, aristocratic, cape-swirling, pantomime villain, the people's hero and an absolute anecdote machine. Wherever he went, glorious stories followed. And the rest of his family (who were all called

Publius Claudius Pulcher) were the same. His great-great-great-grandfather, the first Publius Claudius to be called Pulcher (which means handsome), was the author of one of my top five best Roman anecdotes during the First Punic War against Carthage in 249 BCE. As the head of the Romans' fledgling navy, created specifically to fight the Carthaginians, our hero Publius was the handsome consul charged with winning the war. To do this, he sailed the entire navy to Drepana in Sicily for an epic showdown between the two Mediterranean powers. As the sun came up, Publius prepared to fight. For the Romans, this preparation included reading the omens by checking in with the sacred chickens. The sacred chickens were a Big Deal in Roman religious practice, a way of hearing the desires of the gods, and decisions were made based on when and how they ate. So Publius asked the chickens, 'Should we go into this battle? Will we win?' and waited for the chickens to eat their food in the correct way to give him the green light. Unfortunately for him, the chickens were on a boat and absolutely not in the mood. Or, the gods were sending a message. Either way, the chickens would not eat. No matter how much the consul wanted them to, or how badly he wanted to attack the waiting Carthaginian navy. So Publius, in a fit of sacrilegious rage, launched the chickens into the sea, screaming, 'If they won't eat, let them drink,' and stormed head-first into a catastrophic defeat, losing 93 of his 123 ships. When he eventually limped home, covered in shame, he was prosecuted for 'activity hostile to the state'. Today's lesson: don't fuck with the sacred chickens.

Anyway, that's the lineage our Clodius is coming from. It's an ancient and magnificent one with a lot of history to live up to. He was the youngest of six in his generation, so he had youngest child syndrome and a real need for attention. This compulsion regularly manifested itself in causing immense amounts of trouble and pissing off Cicero. He really, really loved annoying Cicero as much as possible, a position with which I empathise. Cicero had the pompous, easily pricked ego that is absolutely irresistible. He also cared very deeply about the sanctity of Roman government, while Clodius cared about absolutely nothing.[5] Once upon a time, Clodius *had* cared about Cicero and they had been enthusiastic allies in the extrajudicial murder of Lucius Sergius Catilina, better known now as Catiline. Catiline was also a troublemaker during a time of troublemakers. By the 60s BCE, Roman government had effectively broken down. Pompey, Caesar and Crassus were coming up to full war, while every aspect of government was poisoned with bribery, violence and uncertainty. In the middle of this, Catiline was a low-level rapscallion who wanted to make a name for himself by somehow violently overthrowing the consulship and perpetrating a lot of murders in the name of the disenfranchised people of Rome. Unfortunately for him, Cicero was the consul and Cicero was no Mucius Scaevola. As soon as Cicero found out about Catiline's conspiracy, he had Catiline executed without trial. Most people were at least a bit horrified that consuls were now willy-nilly executing patrician citizens based on hearsay and without allowing them a defence, but Clodius was firmly on Cicero's side. I think he just liked the chaos.

Their relationship broke down over a very Clodius scandal. In December 62 BCE, the same year that they murdered Catiline, Clodius got hornily curious about the ladies-only religious ceremony for the Bona Dea festival. Bona Dea was a specifically Italian goddess whose festival was held at night, in secret, in the house of the Pontifex Maximus. His wife led the ceremony, accompanied by the Vestal Virgins. It was a big thing that men weren't allowed to participate, so obviously Clodius wanted in. Being precisely thirty years old and an idiot, he thought he might look young and feminine enough to pass so he disguised himself as a woman – presumably by putting on women's clothes and some make-up – and climbed in through the Pontifex Maximus' window. The Pontifex Maximus at the time was Julius Caesar, so the house was pretty large and Clodius immediately got lost. According to Plutarch, he was found by a maid who instantly saw through his bad drag costume and started screaming. Despite his brilliant attempt to hide in a nearby room, he was found and prosecuted for sacrilege. In a move of extraordinary ballsiness, Clodius went full Shaggy in court and declared that it wasn't him in Caesar's house because he hadn't even been in Rome that day. He claimed he'd been miles away. At which point Cicero stepped forward and testified that Clodius had definitely been in Rome because he'd been in Cicero's house. However, Clodius was immensely popular and cultivated a gang of supporters who liked to beat the living daylights out of people who looked at him funny. He was also enormously rich, so he was able to use that classic combination of bribery and intimidation to get himself acquitted. And that was the end of 'Cicero and Clodius: Best Friends Forever'.

Clodius, who was technically called Publius Claudius Pulcher, then got himself adopted by a plebeian family in 59 BCE, meaning that he was no longer part of the patrician Claudian family, and changed his name to Clodius so he could run for election as Tribune of the Plebs. As a move, this was unprecedented and truly audacious. But this was the time of the first Triumvirate, where Crassus, Pompey and Caesar were openly ruling Rome as a basically illegal cabal, so all bets were off. It tends to get brushed over a little in comparison to the sexy scandal of the Bona Dea situation and the stabbiness of Clodius' later career but it was, I think, a real turning point in the battle between the *populares* and *optimates*. Until this moment, the point of gaining prestige and power and winning elections and victories for Roman men was to honour the family name. Every elite Roman man wanted to live up to his grandfather's greatness or create a greatness to bequeath to his grandchildren. The family was supposed to be honoured by personal glory. But Clodius gave up his family and voluntarily surrendered his family name in order to be able to take an office to which he had no right, to be able to court the favour of the people of Rome and increase his personal prestige. He technically took the glorious patrician name of Claudius away from his children in order to hold a little more power in his grubby little hands.

As Tribune, Clodius proceeded to annoy the Senate, provide a perpetual corn dole to everyone in Rome, and, specifically to ruin Cicero's life, he passed a law to prosecute consuls who had executed citizens without trial. And got Cicero exiled. Then burnt Cicero's house down. And then, in 58 BCE, he created an armed gang of free and enslaved men to protect his interests. This is where things started to go really bananas because once Clodius effectively had a personal paramilitary force ready to beat the life out of his opponents, everyone wanted one. Organised violent gangs became the must-have accessory of 58 BCE. In particular, Titus Annius Milo got himself a gang of enslaved men and gladiators and, before long, political meetings became brawls. Every election was now a battleground. Rome was in chaos. For years. By 52 BCE, gang violence had become as normal a part of political life as bribery and prosecuting one another for gang violence. In Cassius Dio's words, murder had become an everyday occurrence and by this he means open murders in the street. It was impossible to hold elections without them turning into bloodbaths so no one was holding elections. As someone who has been lucky enough never to have experienced civil unrest, it is tough to imagine what life is like when something that is supposed to be as tedious, staid and controlled as politics becomes a perpetual street brawl, where lives are genuinely under threat during elections and violence has become normal. Where Mark Antony chasing Clodius around the Forum with a sword, screaming bloody murder and forcing Clodius to lock himself inside a bookshop, was not the world-shaking drama it should have been – because an ex-consul chasing a Tribune around with a sword is wild – but a minor footnote of an anecdote.[6] I have to sit and think hard about the mobs that Clodius inspired because the Roman sources are always keen to dehumanise these people, who were the urban middle and working classes. The Roman sources were all written by the one percent so they pretty overtly depict the urban plebs as an unwashed mass of disgusting subhumans when really they were people like you and me. The shop workers and builders and bakers and tanners and all the rest. These are the people who were being beaten up if they voted the wrong way in the elections, and whose homes and businesses were damaged every time a street fight broke out between two political gangs, and who were more and more alienated from the running of the Empire. And Clodius, odious though he was, was the only person offering them anything. The corn dole is presented by the Roman sources as a cynical ploy, which it probably was, but for the people in Rome it meant that no one ever had to go a day without eating. In effect, Clodius gave every citizen in Rome a universal basic meal plan, and for that reason they'd love him forever. So when he was murdered, it was a problem.

On 18 January 52 BCE, Clodius was travelling with his entourage of gladiators and enslaved men, thirty enslaved men with arms according to Asconius, when he met his arch-nemesis, Milo, at Bovillae. After Milo had leapt on the armed gang bandwagon so enthusiastically, he had emerged in the politics of the

50s BCE as a real problem for Clodius. The two of them spent years having gang fights over whether Cicero should be allowed to return to Rome and taking it in turns to unsuccessfully prosecute one another for said gang fights. Their relationship was one of vehement antipathy. So when Clodius and his entourage met Milo and his on the Appian Way that day in 52 BCE, the violent clash was tediously inevitable. Except, this time, one of Milo's gladiators went too far.

Clodius and Milo, being senators, did not engage in violence themselves. They hired and bought men to do it for them. They were generals, not soldiers, and so they did not expect to be the ones injured in street brawls. So on this day, when one of Milo's men drove a knife into Clodius' back, it was a surprise to everyone. Reports differ on what precisely happened. Cicero, speaking in Milo's defence at his trial, minimises the murder and makes the whole thing sound like Clodius selfishly threw himself on Milo's slave's dagger on purpose while Milo was looking in the opposite direction. Appian claims that Milo may have given the order to attack, and that he certainly gave the order to make sure Clodius was dead. Cassius Dio, writing almost two centuries later, states that the initial wounding of Clodius was an accident, while the final stab to ensure he was dead was deliberate, with Milo believing he would be more likely to get away with murder than he would assault. Mark Antony, according to Cicero, went around telling everyone that Cicero had asked Milo to kill Clodius, which is a version I like a lot.[7] Cicero did occasionally write letters dated 'x days from the battle of Bovillae', which suggests that he held the date of Clodius' death close to his heart.

Asconius, who wrote commentaries on Cicero's published speeches as absolutely rubbish but quite sweet presents for his sons during the reign of Nero (oh thanks, Dad, you wrote me a school book. Thanks.), gave the most detailed account. He

portrays Milo as a killer without remorse. In his telling, the gladiator Birra attacked Clodius for giving him a threatening look,
and Clodius' entourage then dragged the wounded man to a
nearby wine shop. There he lay, bleeding but alive while the
brawl (though the Romans do insist on calling it a battle) between
sixty enslaved men raged outside. Milo, when he heard that
Clodius was injured, sent his men to find him and finish him. In
Asconius' telling, Milo's men dragged Clodius' injured body
from the wine shop and threw him onto the road where they
proceeded to stab him over and over and over until he stopped
moving. They then finished killing the rest of his enslaved entourage and left the Tribune and his men in piles on the side of the
Appian Way. Another senator, Sextus Teidius, travelling along
the side of the road later in the day, came across the carnage and
brought Clodius' corpse back to Rome.[8]

Whatever the truth, Clodius ended up dead on the side of
the Appian Way with a knife in his back and the people of
Rome were appalled. This was a step too far. Clodius' entourage carried his body to the Forum where they laid it on the
rostra. He suddenly became a martyr for the Republic. He may
have been an incestuous, sacrilegious, violent, horrible patrician
co-opting the power of the plebeian Tribune, but he was *their*
incestuous, sacrilegious, violent, horrible patrician co-opting
their plebeian power and they were absolutely not OK with
other senators killing him. It's a truism that only good things are
ever said about the dead, but Clodius embodied this. Suddenly,
all his obnoxious behaviours were forgotten. Suddenly, he was
the beloved Tribune who gave the people the corn dole and
punished the Senate. He was their hero and they mourned him
and they built him a pyre right there in the Forum. They built
him a pyre of benches and wood ripped from the Senate House
and then, at the appropriate hour, they burnt his body and the

Senate House with it and held the funeral feast in the shadow of its flames. It had stood for five hundred years, built by the king Tullus Hostilius, and now, with the body of yet another murdered Tribune, it burnt. It took with it another slice of the Republic, and the Senate, in a panic, gave sole control of the Empire to Pompey.

Pompey created a special court to try Milo for Clodius' murder, chose the judges himself, sat himself in the courtroom and surrounded the court with armed guards. Cicero spoke for the defence. His speech was significantly curtailed by the sheer number of Clodius' supporters who packed the room and the power of Pompey, sole consul and sole ruler of Rome, looming over the room. Pompey's intimate involvement with the case meant that the outcome of the trial was decided long before anyone stood up to speak at it and everyone knew it: Milo was going down. Which was a real problem for Cicero. Never one to back down easily, though, Cicero did his best. He powered through a truncated speech which was practically an epigram in comparison to, for example, his all-day thirty-six-thousand-word epic speech for Cluentius. He also, amusingly, didn't even try to convince the court that Milo was innocent. He simply tried to argue that he shouldn't be punished for murdering Clodius. His argument rested on three things: first, that it was self-defence; secondly, that the city was effectively at war so the laws shouldn't really apply (the infamous line: *silent enim leges inter arma*); and thirdly, that Clodius was a villain and, had Milo deliberately murdered him (which he hadn't), he would have been saving Rome from yet another populist leader of the plebs who threatened the stability of the Senate.

The entire city was shut down for the trial and Cicero was the sole speaker for the defence. According to both Plutarch and Dio, the armed guards surrounding the court and

Pompey's watchful gaze terrified Cicero, and even more terrifying were the threatening shouts of Clodius' friends and family. According to Dio, Cicero could barely speak and, when he did, his voice wobbled with fear. These sources can't necessarily be trusted, writing as they were a couple of hundred years after the fact, but there is general agreement that the whole thing was one of Cicero's more difficult days. Milo was, accordingly, found guilty and banished from Rome. He went to live in Massilia, now Marseilles, which is not that bad a punishment for a murderer.

Milo was convicted of murder in April 52 BCE. In the same year, Caesar began his war against Vercingetorix in Gaul. The year before, a Roman attempt to invade Parthia had ended in bloody disaster. Armies were marching across the Empire and the Triumvirate of Caesar, Pompey and Crassus had collapsed when Crassus inconveniently died in Parthia. Without a third person to balance them, tension between Caesar and Pompey became unmanageable. Almost three years to the day after Clodius' murder, on 10 January 49 BCE, Caesar crossed the Rubicon and marched his army on Rome. In the grand sweep of history, Clodius' murder seems like a footnote. It's not got the cultural cachet of Caesar crossing the Rubicon or the formation of the first Triumvirate, and Clodius, as even his own modern biographers argue, left no stamp on Roman history except as a rake and a power-hungry dandy.[9] But Clodius was another in a long line of magistrates who were on the side of the people of Rome, who were loved by the people of Rome, who tried to address their needs and alleviate their poverty, and who was murdered by men who hated him for it. He is a link between Tiberius Gracchus and Julius Caesar, *populares* who died violent, illegal deaths at the hands of the elite of the Empire to 'save' the Republic and to protect the interests of a tiny number of the richest men. His murder, like those of Tiberius Gracchus and Julius Caesar, caused such mourning that history was changed. In life, Clodius was an abhorrent jerk who thought of nothing but himself and would probably try to put his hand up your skirt. But in death, he was another popular martyr to the cause of Roman democracy.

Julius Caesar

So this is the context of Julius Caesar's murder: a solid century of judicial and extrajudicial murders of senators by senators; decades of senators defining themselves as representatives of the Roman state and using their own hands to kill to save their status quo. These oligarchs had won every encounter so far with anyone who tried to mess with wealth and power, and they were the men who wrote the histories of their own encounters. And so the senators lauded themselves as saviours of the Republic and as heroes of Rome. Fine, upstanding men willing to kill in the name of the fatherland. A legend emerged in a few sources around this time about the fate of the great and deified Romulus. The traditional story of Romulus' death was that he was suddenly assumed into heaven in a highly localised and very dense thundercloud while parading the troops outside the walls of Rome, to the surprise of everyone. However, there was a second story which we see in Livy's *History of Rome* and in Appian's *Civil Wars*. That version says that Romulus began acting as a tyrant towards the end of his reign, and that the cloud which surrounded him that day on the parade ground was not a divine thundercloud but a cloud of dust raised by senators falling on him with knives. The assumed-into-heaven story was far more popular – and obviously neither actually happened – but the survival of the tyranny version well into the Imperial period suggests that there was at least a strain of high Roman culture that wanted to lionise the killing of even the divine Romulus, son of Mars, in the name of Rome.

We have so much information about Julius Caesar, including his own writings about his activities as a general which – in an unbelievably annoying move – he wrote in the third person, that we almost can't handle it. But we have only five sources for his death, none of them contemporary. An immense amount of information about Caesar's career and rule as dictator of Rome comes from Cicero's speeches and letters, of which he wrote a great many. Pick up any history of the late Republic or biography of Mark Antony or Caesar and look at how much of it relies almost entirely on Cicero's words. He is a historian's wet dream, or he would be if he wasn't so deeply unreliable, but he never wrote about Caesar's death. He wrote about before, and he wrote about what Mark Antony did after, but never about what happened on the Ides of March 44 BCE. Which is interesting, isn't it. Anyway, we are left with five sources from the Imperial period: a fragment of a biography of Augustus by a Syrian philosopher, Nicolaus of Damascus, written between twenty and thirty years after the death of Caesar; a biography of Julius Caesar written by a member of the equestrian class called Suetonius from the emperor Hadrian's household in around 100 CE, 150 years after the murder; another biography of Julius Caesar by the Greek philosopher and moralist Plutarch written at about the same time; a history of the civil wars of the late Republic by Appian, a historian from Alexandria in Egypt, from approximately 180 years after the events it described; and, finally, a history of Rome from the beginning by the Greek-speaking Roman senator Cassius Dio, written in around 230 CE, almost three centuries later. Much as we like to call everything between

753 BCE and 476 CE (when the last emperor of the West was deposed) 'Roman', we sometimes have to confront the fact that things changed over those twelve hundred years and this is one of those times. Apart from Nicolaus, every single one of these was born into a world in which emperors were the norm, where Julius Caesar was a literal god to whom they sacrificed little (and big) animals, who had priests and whose name – Caesar – had become a simple noun to denote imperial power and semi-divine authority. They existed in a world where killing a Caesar was a pretty big fucking deal, and a world that only ever killed emperors in order to replace them with other emperors. The notion of the Republic was an imaginary, near mythical one by the time Julius Caesar's dynasty ended in 69 CE. By the time Dio, for example, was writing, it was ancient history. It's also important to note that almost all the Greek-language sources (with the exception of Dio who likes to remind everyone that he was a Roman senator about once every three lines) refer to the Romans as 'them' rather than 'us'. They are clear that the Romans, or at least the Romans of the past, are other and deeply weird in a lot of ways.

The first source, by Nicolaus, is perhaps the most interesting, as the account of the murder is contained within a deeply sycophantic biography of Augustus which appears to have been written specifically to make Augustus smile. Nicolaus had managed to build himself a distinguished career of being really close to people who pissed Augustus off. He was appointed as tutor to the children of Antony and Cleopatra, which was probably amazing until they fell out with Augustus. Somehow Nicolaus escaped that situation and he took up with Herod the Great, the king of Judea, aka *that* Herod from the Bible with the baby killing. The baby killing wasn't a massive problem for Augustus but going to war with the king of Arabia without permission was, so

Herod had to send Nicolaus off to Rome to try to beg Augustus for forgiveness. This was the lived experience context in which he wrote his account of Augustus' newly deified adopted dad's death. The death, let's not forget, which had launched Augustus' career when Augustus decided that it was a murder that needed to be avenged via the medium of civil war. This leads to some truly excellent lies and misrepresentations from Nicolaus, including calling Julius Caesar, one of the most successful, and most corrupt, politicians in Western history, 'unskilled in political practices by reason of his foreign campaigns', and 'easily taken in', which is laugh-out-loud hilarious.[10]

Caesar's career was long and pretty horrific. He had a single-minded desire for power and several exceptional abilities. He was brilliant with people – utterly charismatic. He was the Bill Clinton or Barack Obama of his time. When most people met him, they adored him and he made them feel like they were the only person who mattered in the whole world. And in particular he made his soldiers feel special and loved and appreciated. Roman soldiers rarely felt these things; like the British army under Wellington, they were considered to be the scum of the earth to be whipped into shape and thrown into battle and then forgotten. But Caesar was an exceptional general, who led his legions to a great many victories across Gaul[11] and into Britain and then he didn't forget them afterwards. His rise had been based on popularism and, like all *populares* before him, on proposals to redistribute land to Roman soldiers and the poor. As a general, he rewarded his soldiers richly, by letting them keep the stuff they stole from the poor Gauls they massacred, and he promised them more and more glory and cash. He promised them that they'd be able to return to Rome with a heavy purse and the ability to boast that they fought with Caesar, and this really worked. To a frightening degree. He was also an extremely hard-working bureaucrat with an eye for detail and the ability to juggle a lot of projects at once, which is just as frightening as his military prowess because it meant there was nothing he wasn't trying to be involved with.

Like all populist leaders, Caesar was always deeply divisive. For every person who adored him, there was another who despised him, who loathed his populism and his constant banging on about being descended from Venus. The *optimates* hated and feared his relentless desire for change and glory, and were terrified of his disregard for things like convention, propriety and the law. Because Caesar was astoundingly corrupt. He bribed his way into his first official job and didn't stop from that point on. Always remember that he took his troops across the Rubicon not to save Rome, but because he had refused to give up his job as governor of Gaul as it protected him from being prosecuted in Rome for crimes he had committed. Imagine if your least favourite world leader just refused to stop being in charge when their term ended because they just didn't want to and that they also had an enormous personal army. When the Senate – correctly – said he was committing insubordination and treason, he invaded Rome and chased Pompey for a few years. And that was all pretty controversial, to put it mildly.

Once he finished beating Pompey, he made himself dictator and started rejigging the entire system, beginning with how the Romans counted time, and allowing petrified minions to vote him more and more honours. The honours he was granted are staggering, quite apart from the dictator-for-life thing. Cassius Dio lists them all and as a list they're pretty tedious, so here are the highlights. He was consul, dictator for life and censor of the Senate. He was called *imperator* and father of the country. He had golden statues built and placed among the statues of ancient kings and among the gods. He had altars and temples in his name. A college of priests was founded to dedicate their whole lives to looking after his temples and praying for him. When he revised the calendar, he changed the name of the fifth month to his own name. He had a golden throne that he could sit in whenever he liked. He was allowed to wear special knee-high red boots which were seen as the stereotypical clothing of the ancient kings and he was allowed to wear the big purple Triumphal robe all the time. He got special lictors and the right to ride his horse in places where horses weren't allowed. Official prayers were given every year for his safety and wellbeing, and on and on and on. These things were all granted to him separately and over a long period, but by the time he died in 44 BCE, he had all of them and he was basically Louis the Sun King in all but name. He was so far above every other member of the aristocracy in every visible and invisible way that the *optimates* found it terrifying. He was ruining *everything*.

The fear that the *optimates* felt watching Caesar being literally worshipped by the people and Senate of Rome, being given more and more honours and wielding his power with increasing confidence was compounded in 44 BCE by three incidents, which are present in all five of our sources.

The first was perhaps the most galling to the *optimates* as it was the most unexpected and actively disrespectful. It occurred one day when the Senate met without Caesar. Caesar was busy, sitting on his most fancy chair on the building site that would eventually become the Forum of Caesar, overseeing some knotty building issues and doing some project management. Caesar was a perpetual micromanager with an unending energy for dealing with things. He'd be amazing on *Grand Designs*. Appian and Plutarch say that he was sitting in front of the *rostra*, which he had moved to his Forum, while Dio and Suetonius think that he was sitting in the atrium of the Temple of Venus Genetrix. Wherever he was, he was working hard with his papers and plans. The senators, meanwhile, had decided to take the opportunity of Caesar's absence to go full sycophant and, for absolutely no reason other than trying to make Caesar like them, voted him a bunch of new and extraordinary honours. Deeply pleased with themselves, a group of senators wanted to break the news in person that he now had an even fancier chair or the right to kick people in the face or whatever, in the hope that he'd reward them. So they put on their best togas – all the sources emphasise that they dressed up for the occasion – and traipsed over to the building site to tell him. They found Caesar surrounded by enslaved attendants and clients and papers and approached with as much dignity as a bunch of absolute nerds in wool blankets could muster. And Caesar ignored them. He was supposed to stand in the presence of senators in formal dress, but he didn't even look up. His friend Gaius Trabatius, obviously dying of second-hand embarrassment, politely suggested that Caesar might want to talk to these nice men who'd come all this way. Nicolaus has Trabatius say, 'Look, Caesar, at these people who have come to see you!' and can't you just feel the awkward in that sentence. Caesar replied, however, with nothing more than a disdainful look and, I imagine, a sigh. Eventually he looked at them and heard them out, though he never stood. When they finished reciting the list of presents they were giving him, he was unimpressed. He replied that he didn't want some of them, but he'd take the rest and then he dismissed them to get back to work. He humiliated the Senate. And they were not men who liked being humiliated. They were supposed to be the best men in the whole Empire. They were supposed to be treated with fawning respect by everyone, including each other. (I really recommend reading some of the surviving letters between

Roman senators because they spend half of each letter talking about how brilliant the other guy is and it's revolting.) Caesar was supposed to be grateful and pretend that he was just like them. Instead, he may as well have spat in their faces.

This tiny act was a shattering moment for a lot of senators and it obviously resonated with later sources because those sympathetic to Caesar try to come up with reasons why he couldn't stand. Plutarch, bless him, puts the blame on Caesar's friend Cornelius Balbus, claiming that Balbus prevented Caesar from standing by telling him that the senators wanted to treat him as a superior and physically pushing down on his shoulder while Caesar tried to get up. A patently ridiculous tale. My personal favourite is Cassius Dio's. Dio is an unapologetic Caesar fan. He shows his hand early in his account when he states that Cassius and Brutus destroyed the only stable government Rome had ever known and killed Caesar out of jealousy and stupidity. Even Dio struggles a bit with Caesar's refusal to stand for senators; he is, after all, and he might have mentioned this once or twice, a Roman senator himself. So he states 'some said that' Caesar had been suffering from diarrhoea that day and had therefore been unable to stand and greet the senators lest he have an unfortunate accident. You really have to know that you have done something truly terrible when the best possible defence that your biggest fan can give you is that you might have shat yourself. Even Dio has to admit that Caesar did get up and walk home a bit later. He's not willing to admit, however, that this was a reasonable reason to murder Caesar because Dio lived in an age that was accustomed to emperors not standing for senators, and accustomed to senators being beneath Caesars. The senators of 44 BCE were not, and some realised for the first time, in that awkward silence between their dignified arrival and Trabatius' little cough, that they didn't rule Rome any more: Caesar did.

The useful thing about having sources which are not traditionally Roman and which are removed in time from the events they describe is that they can be remarkably perceptive about what was going on in 44 BCE between Caesar and the senators, even while they are baffled or appalled by the murder itself. Plutarch, for example, notes that the Senate saw Caesar's dictatorship as a welcome relief from the wars that had raged, and killed so many of them and their friends and family, over the previous decades. It's easy to distance ourselves from the past and write 'the civil war lasted four years' and forget how unbearable those four years were for the people of Rome while half the men were off killing one another, with no knowledge of when it would end. Four years is a long time in the lives of humans. Just try to think about where you were four years ago and you'll feel it. So Caesar's outright win, his admirable forgiveness of those who had fought with Pompey, and the prospect of some peace and healing were certainly a relief to the Romans. But, Plutarch says, when an unaccountable autocrat becomes a permanent fixture, and the reality of living under an unaccountable autocrat sinks in, what you have is tyranny. Tyranny could be tolerated if it was disguised; Caesar kept making it obvious.

Another particularly perceptive note comes from Appian, who had obviously thought long and hard about what the hell was going on in Rome. He struggled to work out why the Senate would voluntarily give Caesar so many honours and privileges and nice shoes and adore him and worship him and then get homicidally mad at him for using them. Appian was not accustomed to the habitual doublethink and hypocrisy of the Senate apparently, but he tried. In the end, he came to a conclusion: it was all about a word for them. The whole problem was not the gold chair and red boots and prayers for Caesar and the rest. It was the word *rex*. Appian remained somewhat baffled: a dictator for life, he says, is exactly like a king. It's just a substitute title. To steal from a different bit of Shakespeare, a rose by any other name would smell as sweet, and to Appian – and virtually every writer in the Imperial period – a king by the name dictator was still an emperor. But to the Romans of 44 BCE, that word *mattered*. A lot. The Senate built their whole identity on the fact that they had overthrown their kings and created the perfect Republic. Yeah, it was a bit broken right now but that didn't mean that they had been wrong to get rid of kings. That was their absolute best cultural achievement. Even better than conquering every city they ever came across. The concept of kings was complete anathema to Romans who had grown up in the Republic and the word *rex* was practically a curse. So it was upsetting for the *optimates*, and a large number of the *populares*, when things started happening that suggested that Caesar might grant himself the title.

First, Caesar was about to go off with his army again to try to conquer Parthia for the seventy-eighth time.[12] Marching off against Parthia was a good sign that a Roman general or emperor was getting too big for his boots, but this time a very specific anxiety arose. The Romans had a book of prophecies called the Sibylline Books which had been sold by a Greek female prophet to the last king of the Romans, Tarquinius Superbus. They were highly sacred and considered to be the true and very clear words of the gods.† They were kept in a vault beneath the

---

† The Sibylline Books were an incomplete set of vague prophecies allegedly written by a divinely inspired Greek female prophet, in Greek. The story of how the Romans got the books was that a Sibyl appeared one day on the doorstep of the last king, Tarquinius Superbus, holding nine books of prophecies which she offered to the king for a high price. He took one look at the old Greek lady and told her to piss off. Which she did, and she burnt three of the books and came back the next day offering him the six remaining books at the same price. Now vaguely irritated and also a tyrannical king, Tarquinius told her to double piss off, this time throwing in some mocking at the same time. The Sibyl wandered

great Temple of Jupiter, heavily guarded and consulted only at times of extreme distress. In 44 BCE, a rumour arose that the books contained a prophecy that the Parthians could only be defeated by a king of Rome and that Caesar was going to use this information – which no other Roman would be able to check – to get the Senate to grant him the title of king, possibly king of one of their provinces. This wouldn't be the first time Caesar manipulated Roman religious beliefs for his own ends, and the rumour scared people.

Then the Tribunes Marullus and Caesetius started causing trouble. The first incident occurred when a diadem was found on a statue of Caesar. A big golden statue of Caesar. A diadem is a traditional Roman crown – a wreath of laurel leaves and white ribbon. It was the ultimate signifier of kingship. But it's on a statue, you might think. Big deal. Who cares! The Romans cared; very much. Statues were a public space in which the inhabitants of Rome could express their opinions about political figures. It was common for anonymous people to respond to the actions of politicians, celebrities and even emperors via the medium of graffiti on statues. A rude couplet on a golden statue was the *Saturday Night Live* or Twitter outrage machine of the time. One of the things raised by all the sources as prompting Brutus to join the conspiracy against Caesar was a series of insulting lines written on his statues suggesting that he was letting down his family name by

---

off again and burnt three more books, then, the next day, returned once again to Tarquinius and offered him the final three books for the price of the original nine. Tarquinius was by this point a bit weirded out. She hadn't heeded his mocking at all, but had remained steadfastly sure in the ever increasing value of her books. He called in his soothsayers and asked their opinion, and they replied, 'Good god, man, what have you done! Oh my god, get the rest of them immediately! Bloody hell, why didn't you call us earlier!? What is wrong with you?' So he bought them, and then the Romans relied on those three books for the next few centuries.

allowing Caesar to rule. Statue graffiti was a way of learning public opinion about a person or issue. So, finding a diadem on Caesar's most golden statue was a disturbing sign that certain people within Rome might actually *want* Caesar to be king. Marullus and Caesetius were not happy. They found the person who had put it there – whose name was sadly never recorded – and imprisoned him. This is how much Romans hated kings – it was illegal to shout 'king' at people in the same way it's illegal to do the Nazi salute in Germany. This alone would have merely added to the general atmosphere of uncertainty around Caesar's ambitions and status, and Rome's future. But then there was another, similar incident. Caesar was riding around on his horse one day when he was hailed by some adoring fans – politicians were a bit like boy bands in the Roman world – as Rex. Rex is both the Latin word for king and a Roman name, so Caesar, extremely smoothly and demonstrating why he was generally so good at his job, laughed and replied, 'I'm not Rex, I'm Caesar!' as if the crowd had merely, somehow, got his name wrong. An impressively quick response. Again, problem handled, until Marullus and Caesetius heard about it and went out to hunt down these Caesar fans and punish them. This time, Caesar lost his temper and screwed up.

Caesar called the Senate together and dragged the two Tribunes in front of them. Tribunes, you'll remember from Tiberius Gracchus' murder, were sacrosanct. They were supposed to have equal power to a consul – the highest Roman rank – and to be protected from the interference of other Roman offices. But Caesar accused the two men of plotting against him. He claimed that they had fabricated the two incidents in order to frame him. He basically thought that they were complex false flag operations in which the Tribunes, his enemies, set up people to call him a king in order to make it look like he wanted to be a king. A weird and complicated thing, but not unthinkable for Roman senators. Dio, for example, believes that this is exactly what they did; the other sources hedge their bets. Caesar shouting at Tribunes, however, looked bad. And then he really went too far. He stripped them of their Tribuneship and their powers and barred them from the Senate House. This was tyranny. This was Caesar showing off his power over the government of Rome and his disdain for the constitutional norms of the Senate. He could strip even the most sacred and powerful of the magistrates of their office and have them thrown out. Anyone who hadn't been freaked out by the sitting incident was freaked out by this.

Then came the famous Lupercalia incident. The one everyone vaguely knows about: when Mark Antony, Caesar's best friend in all the world and partner in crime (literally), knelt in front of Caesar and offered him the crown. There are two versions of this story, the one Nicolaus tells and the one everyone else tells, but the basic details are consistent. It was at the festival of the Lupercalia, held on 15 February, which culminated in the brilliant spectacle of all the most famous men in the city getting naked, slaughtering a sheep, oiling up all shiny, and then running through the city hitting women with bits of leather. For fertility, of course. People loved it. Everyone came out to watch and cheer and be hit by a nude senator for luck. A fantastic day out for all the family. And of course, Julius Caesar was there, sitting in his gold and ivory chair, raised above everyone else in the Forum where the run culminated, wearing his bright purple toga and his bright red boots. He sparkled above the crowd and glowed against the backdrop of senators in their ordinary white. He was obviously special. This is where the accounts split slightly. Nicolaus has another friend of Caesar's called Licinius pull out the diadem (though he thinks a diadem and a laurel wreath are different things so maybe he's not totally on the ball with Roman things). Caesar saw this and pushed a dude called Lepidus to intercept Licinius. So, a third guy, Longinus, grabbed the diadem from Licinius (I'm sorry, they all have virtually the same name) and placed it in Caesar's lap. Caesar pushed it off, so Antony leapt up – nude and oiled – and put it on Caesar's head. Caesar snatched it off in horror and lobbed it into the crowd. I find this version very funny, because it's essentially Caesar fighting off all of his friends trying to put a crown on his head. One of whom has his dick out. The crowd, in Nicolaus' version, beg Caesar to take the crown. Thus, Nicolaus paints Caesar as an innocent in this, while virtually everyone Caesar knows and the Roman people are desperately trying to force a crown on him.

None of the other four sources drag all these other men into it. They have the scene play out between Antony and Caesar alone. In all these, Antony completed his run through the city in the Forum and produced the diadem from somewhere on his nude body (probably best not to think about it). He then approached Caesar and placed it on his head. In Dio, the latest of our sources, Antony says, 'The people offer this to you through me,' to which Caesar replies, 'Jupiter alone is king of the Romans.' Thus, Dio's Caesar is also an innocent who behaves impeccably. In Plutarch and Appian, who are the most hostile to Caesar, there is an extended back and forth between Antony and Caesar where Caesar waits to see how the crowd reacts to him wearing the diadem and then to him rejecting it. In Plutarch, the crowd is quiet when he receives the diadem and explodes with joy when he rejects it; this happens twice, just to be sure that the people definitely didn't want a king. In Appian, the people boo when he receives the crown and clap when he rejects it. Twice. Their versions of the incident are that Caesar and Antony were testing the people of Rome. Much like when governments 'leak' new policies in order to test a reaction without embarrassment,

Caesar was 'leaking' the idea of him being a king.

Whichever interpretation you want to go with, the incident happened and it made the *optimates* sick to their stomachs. The diadem had been rejected but they had seen, with their own eyes, a man – a friend and enemy – sitting on a golden throne in red and purple wearing a royal crown, and they were deeply alarmed. Caesar was due to leave the city in just a few weeks to go to war again. He had already decided who the consuls and magistrates would be while he was gone. He would expect to continue controlling events in the city from a distance. He seemed unstoppable. He was a king in all but name and he had, for just a second or two, had the name. The *optimates* were desperate.

It's important to stop here for a second and think about what the *optimates* wanted when they began to formulate their plan. There were three leaders of the conspiracy: Marcus Junius Brutus, Gaius Cassius Longinus and Decimus Junius Brutus Albinus, otherwise known as Brutus, Cassius and that other Brutus everyone forgets about. Cicero wrote a letter to his best friend Atticus (it's cute that they all have best friends) on 8 June 45 BCE – ten months before the murder – from Marcus Brutus' holiday home in Antium and already the beginnings of a plot are obvious. Brutus was already concerned that he was unsafe and Cassius felt the same. The men and their wives (who, as an aside, are always cut out of the story) discuss whether Brutus and Cassius should ever return to Rome. Cicero's letter ends with him celebrating getting a five-year job but lamenting, 'But why am I thinking about five years? If I am not much mistaken, the end is not far off.'[13] The mood among the senators was already glum. They saw themselves as being in constant danger because their careers now relied on Caesar's mood and whims, rather than their own political actions. By the time of the Lupercalia incident in February, the mood was one of despair and reckless-ness. The conspirators needed to save their careers in the Republic and regain their liberty, and they were ready to do *anything*.

But Roman aristocratic liberty is not the same as our liberty. Our liberty is freedom for all from oppressive restrictions on our lives and behaviours. Roman aristocratic liberty was the free-dom to fight among one another, according to the rules, to achieve political power. These were men who owned people as slaves – loads of people – legally kept women as minors and made legal distinction between the invented categories of patri-cian and plebeian. They did not want freedom; they wanted the right to become Caesar. As the excellent Gretchen Weiners once said, 'Brutus is just as cute as Caesar, right? Brutus is just as smart as Caesar, people totally like Brutus just as much as they like Caesar, and when did it become OK for one person to be the boss of everybody because that's not what Rome is about!'

And so a plot was formed. There was never a meeting of all sixty (or eighty if you want to believe Nicolaus) conspirators. Instead, they were set up like true revolutionaries in little cells. Few people in any cell knew who was in the other cells, and they met in their houses, as normal meetings of friends, to discuss ways in which Caesar could be bumped off. They were also aware that time was tight – Caesar was leaving for Parthia on March 20 and then he'd be untouchable for a few years. They generally vetoed any plan that involved anyone tangling with Caesar's bodyguard or where any person willing to defend Caesar might be available and armed. They were all pretty keen on surviving to live their lives and continue their careers as competitive senators after Caesar died. So, plots to push him off a bridge during a tribal vote, to ambush him on the Via Sacra in the Forum and to surprise him as he entered the theatre were all thrown out as too dangerous. Fortune intervened when Caesar himself called a meeting of the Senate for the afternoon of March 15. The Senate House would be the perfect place: they could get close to Caesar without suspicion; no weapons were allowed inside so other senators wouldn't be armed; and he would have no bodyguard.

They also, according to Appian, believed that killing Caesar in the Senate House, which was a religious space, would make it clear that their actions were done on behalf of the state of Rome and not for personal revenge. It was this too which persuaded them not to kill Antony. They hoped the people would view the murder as the assassination of a tyrant and an attempt to restore the Republic, rather than an attempt to eradicate a rival political party. Cicero would later sigh heavily over this decision, writing that they acted with the bravery of men but the strategy of children.[14] Which is true. It was a desperate and pathetic attempt to make the murder of a popular leader look like an acceptable act and to save their own reputations. In the end, the two Brutuses and Cassius really wanted to come out of the murder looking like heroes who could be given consulships, or at the very least a decent province to govern for a while. It backfired badly, but you can see how they persuaded themselves that it would work.

The Ides of March came and the day ticked slowly towards the time of the Senate meeting. The omens were as bad for Caesar as they had been for his predecessor, Tiberius Gracchus. Each source gives us different omens because they all love omens. Romans were obsessed with omens. Suetonius includes a long one about a tomb being found in Capua which warned that the grave being moved would result in 'a son of Troy slain by his kin and avenged at heavy cost to Italy', which is a pretty suspiciously detailed prophecy. Caesar, of course, liked to tell everyone that he was descended from the goddess Venus, while the Romans believed themselves to be descended from Aeneas, who escaped the sack of Troy. No other sources liked that one, though. Plutarch has a good one about Caesar performing a sacrifice and opening up the beast to find that it had no heart. He clarifies that this isn't normal, just in case his readers thought it might be. Suetonius also includes this one, but in his version Caesar snorts derisively and says that if he had wanted the beast to have a heart, it would have. Which is a pretty baller response to a nightmarish omen. The traditional omen, however, is the fortune teller who warns Caesar to 'beware the Ides of March' in Shakespeare's play. Shakespeare lifted this from Plutarch and it also appears in Appian, Suetonius and Dio. He is called Spurinna. In most, Caesar sees him again on the way to the Senate House and mocks him, saying that the Ides had come and he was fine, to which Spurinna replied that the Ides had come but not yet gone.

All the sources ramp up the narrative tension with Caesar being reluctant to attend the Senate that day. He was feeling sick, he'd had bad dreams, his wife Calpurnia had had bad dreams, there were all these omens and Calpurnia was nervous. Meanwhile the conspirators waited nervously at the Senate House. Decimus Brutus was eventually sent to find Caesar and convince him to come to work. Decimus managed to persuade him that he was needed and they began to leave. In Plutarch's account, an enslaved man tried to warn Caesar before he left but got caught up in the press of people outside the house and was unable to reach him – a delightfully cinematic addition. Finally, as the sun was setting, Decimus, Caesar and Antony arrived at the Senate House. Before anything could happen, it was necessary for Caesar, as the person who had called the meeting, to sacrifice some animals to check that the gods wanted them to hold a Senate meeting at that time. This was traditional. But the sacrifice produced bad news: the gods wanted them to go home. So they killed another animal and looked at its guts. Same answer. Another one was brought out, smashed over the head and slaughtered. None were coming up with the right omens. In Appian's account, Caesar was worried about pissing off the Senate and decided to ignore the omens. In Nicolaus' version, Caesar wanted to go home but Brutus called him a chicken who wasn't man enough to overlook some bad omens. Apparently that was his Marty McFly weak spot because it worked. Caesar entered the Senate House, while Decimus Brutus suddenly pulled Antony aside for a vital private chat. As Caesar walked up the steps, the usual press of people asking for favours approached him. One thrust some paper at him and begged him to read it immediately to save his own life. Caesar continued walking.

The Senate House was attached to the Theatre of Pompey and had in fact been built by Pompey while Caesar was away conquering Gaul. It was a magnificent place, a temple to Roman senatorial power, and at its centre was a statue of Pompey himself. There were around three hundred senators, and they had been waiting a long time. They all rose as Caesar finally entered, and several immediately approached him. The Senate House wasn't the white togas and white columns place of quiet dignity that is portrayed on TV. It was a bustling place full of constant chatter. Caesar kept walking to his fancy chair, unaware that Antony had been detained outside and that the murder plot had already swung into precise action. A man named Tillius Cimber (which is a silly name) approached Caesar and fell to his knees to beg Caesar to bring his brother back from exile. Caesar dismissed him, but Cimber grabbed Caesar's toga in desperation. While this was happening, the rest of the conspirators approached the chair. Cimber pulled Caesar's toga and exposed his neck. This was the signal. In Suetonius' version of the murder,

Caesar was offended by Cimber's tugging on him and shouted, 'Why! This is violence!' and in Appian's, Cimber shouted, 'What are you waiting for, friends?!' but in all the others, the first stab came unannounced. The first man to stab Caesar was Casca. He came from behind and aimed for the neck. He missed and drove his dagger into Caesar's shoulder. The murder had begun.

Caesar's response to the first stab varies across the sources. Nicolaus has him leap up silently, to be felled immediately with a sword to the side, driven into him by Casca's brother. Suetonius' Caesar grabs Casca's arm, still holding the blade dripping with his own blood, and stabs Casca with his stylus before being cut down by another, anonymous blade. In Plutarch's version, Caesar doesn't just grab Casca, he grabs the blade of the dagger like an absolute hero and shouts, 'Damn you, Casca,' before being hit by Casca's brother. Appian's account portrays Caesar standing up, grabbing Casca and whirling around, flinging Casca across the room but exposing his side to another blade. Finally, Dio's Caesar is the most pathetic and gentle. He is unable to react and is beset by attackers instantly. In most, Caesar is presented as a beast, thrown from one knife to the next, bewildered and bleeding until the volume of blood pouring from him causes him to slip to the floor, at the feet of his old enemy Pompey. In Suetonius, Dio, Plutarch and Appian, Caesar's final act is to cover himself in his toga. Only in Suetonius and Dio does he say his famous last words, not in Latin but in Greek: καὶ σύ, τέκνον. This translates as 'You too, my child,' which Shakespeare reworked into Latin (presumably Tudor audiences weren't expected to be up on their Ancient Greek) to give us that saddest of lines: 'et tu, Brute?' Gaius Julius Caesar died having received twenty-three stab wounds in a pool of blood, his own and others', in the Senate House.

The aftermath of the murder was chaos; a brief forgiveness

followed by rage followed by the arrival of Octavian to take vengeance on Cassius and Brutus. The Roman aristocracy were torn apart by their reactions to the murder. Cicero, for example, was vocally on the side of the killers. He wrote, in a much later piece called *On Duties*, that killing a tyrant was no more than the amputation of a rotten limb. It was not murder to kill Caesar, in Cicero's opinion, because the tyrant had given up his humanity. It was an unfortunate and unpleasant act but not murder. Of course, Cicero himself had murdered Catiline as an enemy of the state in 63 BCE, against Julius Caesar's arguments and without a trial, so he is defending himself as much as the assassins. Cicero's friend Gaius Matius was of quite the opposite opinion. Matius believed that Caesar had been the Republic's last hope, asking, 'If a man of his genius could not succeed, what hope is there for anyone else?'[15] Moreover, Matius had no time for Cicero's philosophising. It might be ethically right to kill a tyrant in principle, but in the actual situation in which they found themselves, he did not believe that it was a good idea to kill Julius Caesar. And on top of that, Brutus murdering Caesar was a violation of friendship which Matius found offensive. These arguments were happening in every home and public space.

The public definition of Caesar's homicide changed too. In the first days after the murder, it seemed that the murderers would get their wish: they were granted forgiveness by the Senate led by Antony. The homicide was briefly an assassination for possibly honourable purposes. The killers would be unpunished because they had not committed a punishable act. The peace didn't last. Against the wishes of the murderers, and entirely undermining their aims and goals, the Senate granted Caesar a public funeral. Here, his friends built a wax mannequin of him, laid it on an ivory couch within a gold shrine draped in purple and dressed it in the clothes Caesar died in. His blood-soaked, filthy torn tunic hung in the centre of the glorious shrine. The message was unmistakable: our sacred and beloved Caesar was taken from us. Antony used his eulogy to recite the decree of the Senate in which they had voted Caesar his highest honours and the pledge the senators had made to protect Caesar. In that moment, the mood changed and Caesar's death became, in the minds of the people of Rome, truly a murder. And they were enraged.

What Cassius and Brutus failed to realise, or stupidly ignored, was that the process of senatorial murders, of mob killings on the street sanctioned by the government, of arbitrary death sentences and civil war had changed the world they lived in. They thought that they could be classical heroes like the Brutus who overthrew the kings, forgetting that Brutus overthrew the kings with the help and consent of (almost) every single other senator, having made his case in public in the Forum. That Brutus had not made his plans in whispers in quiet rooms, in secret and fear with a tiny number of equally scared friends. Tiberius Gracchus had been beaten to death by the majority of the Senate working together, and his brother was forced to suicide by even more. Times had changed in the century since senators had been able to kill with their own hands and for it to seem honourable. Even Milo had had to answer to a trial for the pathetic murder of Clodius, and no one even liked Clodius. The Senate were no longer a cohesive whole, and the people were no longer completely downtrodden and disenfranchised. A new world had been ushered in by two centuries of murder and these murderers were the last to realise it.

2

Murder in Roman Law

Once upon a time, in the middle of the second century CE, a ten-year-old girl named Julia Restuta was walking down a street in Salona, the capital city of the Roman province of Dalmatia (now Croatia). Salona had been a Roman city for centuries. Rich and peaceful, it apparently felt like the kind of place where wealthy ten-year-old girls could go skipping off by themselves for the afternoon. We know that Julia Restuta was wealthy because this trip turned out to be her last. While skipping along the street that day, Julia was accosted by unknown assailants who snatched her up, tore her jewellery from her neck and wrists and fingers and left behind her little body, broken and bleeding. Julia Restuta died that day, murdered by anonymous robbers. Her parents, rich and heartbroken, did the only thing they could: they raised an enormous headstone for her which outlined the whole sorry story. Under a tiny bust of Julia's face, the inscription reads: 'To the spirits of the dead and to the most unfortunate Julia Restuta, murdered at the age of ten on account of her jewellery. Her parents, Julius Restutus and Statia Pudentilla, [set this up].'[1]

This kind of death never troubles the annals and books from which we draw most of what is now called Roman history, and would have been completely swallowed by the murky blackness of the past if it hadn't been for Julia's rich parents who could afford to buy a lump of stone and pay a man to inscribe their daughter's story on it. The same can be said for Prima Florentina, who was sixteen when her husband Orpheus threw her into the Tiber, or Domitilla who was fourteen (and just four months married) when she was kidnapped, assaulted and killed by some 'men from Pontus', or Grattius who was murdered by muggers on the Via Salaria between Rome and Castrum Truentinum.[2] These people weren't senators or the children of senators, they weren't important in the politics of the city of Rome, or descended from ancient, aristocratic families, or owners of immense estates in Ameria, or friends with consuls. They were those who, in George Eliot's words, 'lived faithfully a hidden life, and rest in unvisited tombs'.[3] Their parents were *just* wealthy enough to raise a memorial to them and leave a little snapshot of them to history. And the snapshot they chose to immortalise in stone was the manner – and sometimes the perpetrator – of their death, which may seem, to us looking at them from here, a little bizarre. The only thing we know about Prima Florentina is that her husband murdered her. The only thing we know about Julia Restuta is that she died in a mugging that went horribly wrong. Their epitaphs seem to exist simply to draw attention to the terrible manner of their deaths and that is probably exactly their purpose.

There's a very good chance that these epitaphs were the only justice that the relatives of Julia and Grattius and Prima ever received. The only way their parents could force the indifferent universe to hear their agonised howl of grief was to inscribe it into stone. Prima's parents were able to name and shame the man who took their daughter from them, but he was probably never tried or punished. The men who attacked Julia Restuta and the gang who murdered Grattius likely disappeared into the setting sun never to be seen again. The Roman world had no official police force to do investigations, and no Child Protective Services to prosecute a case. It had no long-term prisons and no state-sponsored public defender. All it had was a self-help system that forced the families of the victims to investigate, prosecute

and – sometimes – punish crimes. These tragic murders high-
light two significant legal issues in Rome that we need to take a
quick look at. The first is that murder was not a crime in the
Roman legal system for a surprising amount of its history. By
this, I mean that the state of Rome had absolutely no interest in
when, how or why its citizens were killing each other. Actively
disinterested, if anything. But gradually, over centuries of social,
cultural and legal change, it was forced to develop an interest.
The second issue is that the Romans never developed a concept
of manslaughter or murder committed in the act of another
crime. So, even if the men who killed Julia Restuta *had* been
identified and captured, they probably wouldn't have been prosecuted for murder anyway if they hadn't actively *meant* to kill her.
To untangle these two issues, we need to take a little stroll through
the history of murder in Roman law.

The Twelve Tables

Way back in the semi-mythical mists of Roman time, for the first
three hundred years of Rome's existence, there was no written
law. What was and wasn't legal was up to the king, and then,
when kings were booted to the kerb, to the priests. In 451 BCE,
however, it was decided, for whatever reason, that this situation
was not a sustainable or useful way forward for Rome. Romans
being Romans, a fundamentally pragmatic people, they decided
to set up a committee to deal with the situation. This committee,
of ten men with consular *imperium*, put together ten tablets of
laws and then bolted on another two tablets the following year.
These were known as the Twelve Tables and they were carved
into either ivory or bronze and hung in the Forum Romanum so
that every Roman citizen would know their rights and obliga-
tions. These were the Romans' Ten Commandments, and they

are primarily concerned with the administration of debts and courts. As far as anyone can tell, the first law the Romans wrote down, on tablet one of their epoch- and civilisation-defining law code, the basis for Western law for millennia, was: 'When anyone summons another before the tribunal of a judge, the latter must, without hesitation, immediately appear.' As I say, they were a remarkably pragmatic people.

The Twelve Tables are now almost completely lost, existing in fragments scattered across about five hundred years' worth of Latin literature. While the internet likes to suggest that you can read the Twelve Tables and offers a number of lovely extant-seeming translations, what we actually have is numerous decon-textualised snippets and allusions to the Twelve Tables, most of which are considerably more cryptic than is ideal. The fragments that survive are of a law code that avoided the abstract and the communal and focused almost entirely on relations and interactions between individuals, with a very strong focus on property rather than morality or ethics. They're full of mundane things like how debts have to be paid within thirty days, judges have to make decisions before the sun has set on the court, women mustn't scratch at their faces during funerals, a tree is worth twenty-five asses[†] if it's illegally cut down, and so on. At a gut level, it seems that murder would count as an interaction between two individuals and would require legislation, but that is not the case. In the fragments of the tables that remain, the lawmakers instead appear to have been more interested in emphasising when homicide was lawful rather than delineating when it was unlawful. For example, one of the clearest fragments

---

† An ass being a little stumpy bronze bar which rapidly stopped being worth anything when the Romans adopted proper coins. It was broadly (and reduc-tively) equivalent to a penny.

states that if someone is caught while in the process of theft and killed, then that homicide is lawful. The Twelve Tables also emphasise that fathers have the power of life and death over their legitimate sons (more on this later) and have the right to kill any children born as 'monsters' (this too). We also see a number of ways in which the Roman court, as representatives of the Roman city-state, were allowed to kill their citizens, including by throwing them off a big rock, scourging them, throwing them in the Tiber in a bag, something odd that no one understands involving a dish and a girdle that may or may not be a death penalty, being burnt to death, being sacrificed to Ceres, or being beaten to death with rods (that last one was the punishment for writing mean poems about other people). Giving false testimony was punished by being thrown off the Tarpeian Rock (the afore-mentioned big rock, which is the cliff of the Capitoline Hill). Punching a free man's teeth out, however, just cost three hundred asses.

We have just two mentions of what we might now call murder in the Twelve Tables, but which actually refer to unintentional and intentional homicide. The difference between murder and intentional homicide is, of course, moral judgement. Murder is a moral outrage; intentional homicide is just a legal thing that happens. The death penalty is intentional homicide; it is not murder. It's reasonably safe to say from the two extracts that we have that the Twelve Tables didn't really contain a murder law. The first part of what it did have is extracted from two oblique references from Cicero, primarily a defence of a man called Tullius which manages to break off in the middle of the signifi-cant sentence. It reads: 'Who deserves to be pardoned more than a man who has killed by accident . . . for there is a law in the Twelve Tables "if a weapon escapes from a hand . . ."'.[4] There it ends. This is the kind of inconvenient survival of source that I take as history trolling us. Thankfully, we also have a deeply tedious treatise called the *Topica* in which Cicero wangs on about Aristotle for ages and then suddenly says, 'For to shoot an arrow is an act of intention; to hit a man whom you did not mean to hit is the result of fortune . . . if a weapon has flown from the man's hand rather than been thrown by him.'[5] From this, we can infer that the Twelve Tables said something along the lines of 'it's only murder if you mean it', which is very similar to our own differentiation between murder and manslaughter, but without the concept of manslaughter. This isn't exactly clear, though, or indeed as clearly discussed or considered by later Roman authors as those laws about debt and hair rending.

The second mention comes from a fragment of a commentary on the Twelve Tables written in the second century CE – that's a full six hundred years after they were written – by a borderline anonymous legal expert known only as Gaius. This states that there was something to do with poisons in the eighth book of the Twelve Tables, which most people have taken to mean that poisoning people was illegal and probably, maybe, punishable by death.[6]

The Republic

That was it for murder as far as the earliest Roman law code was concerned. The Ten Commandments are ten sentences long and even they've got more in them about murder.† The Ten Commandments have somewhat misled modern readers into thinking that written law has always been interested in moral

---

† For wider context, the Code of Hammurabi, which is the oldest law code in the world, doesn't have a law on murder either and is remarkably focused on property, so the Romans weren't totally unique on this.

issues like murder and adultery, when really only religious law is interested in those things. Roman law had no particular interest in legislating morality at the beginning.

That was the situation until sometime in the third century BCE, possibly around 286 BCE, when a Tribune named Aquilia got the Lex Aquilia passed via a plebiscite (basically a referendum). We know of this law because it survives in a text from late antiquity called Justinian's *Digest*. Justinian was the Byzantine emperor from 527 to 565 CE and he is mostly remembered for building the Hagia Sophia in Istanbul, being accused of being a literal demon by a contemporary historian and for the corpus of civil law that he put together. So a mixed legacy. Essentially, Justinian got fed up with a legal system based on a series of badly recorded, often contradictory and usually obscurely worded laws, judgements and imperial edicts dating back to the Twelve Tables, so he asked a set of legal experts to take a look at that one thousand years' worth of material and tidy it up a bit. The *Digest* is one of the products of that astonishingly successful project – the success of which really demonstrates the occasional efficiency benefits of a monomaniacal dictatorship – a collation of thousands of legal commentaries on the actual application of laws in the later Roman Empire. From this, we have access to the application and perceived meaning of many laws which, themselves, have been lost. The Lex Aquilia is one of these and it dealt with property damage. It was concerned with the circumstances under which someone who damaged someone else's property had to pay compensation, which seems unrelated to murder until you look at section one of the law, which goes like this:

> Where anyone unlawfully kills a male or female slave
> belonging to another, or a quadruped included in the

class of cattle, let him be required to pay a sum equal
to the greatest value that the same was worth during
the past year.[7]

Do you see what's happened here? The law deals with enslaved
people, who the elite Roman lawmakers considered to be identi-
cal to four-legged animals that hang out in herds. The Lex
Aquilia deals with sheep and cows and goats and enslaved
people. To the modern reader, used to seeing every person as a
person, therefore, it deals with murder because the commentaries that follow this section consist of over seven thousand (Latin)
words of Roman legal scholars imagining hypothetical ways in
which enslaved people and children could be killed and debating
whether the person who killed them was liable to pay compensation to their owners. (There are also a couple of sentences on
whether an elephant counts as cattle. Conclusion: no.) These
hypotheticals go like this:

> A shoemaker, while teaching his trade to a boy who
> was freeborn and the son of a family, and who did not
> properly perform the task which he had given him,
> struck him on the neck with a last, and the boy's eye
> was destroyed. Julianus says that, in this instance, an
> action for injury will not lie because he inflicted the
> blow, not for the purpose of causing him injury, but of
> warning and teaching him.[8]

What is happening here is that a kid is hit on the neck with a
replica foot and his eye is destroyed. How did the eye get involved
here? It is very disturbing but not, note, illegal under the Lex
Aquilia.

The Lex Aquilia will apply where anyone who has been too heavily laden throws down his load and kills a slave; for it was in his power not to be overloaded in this manner.[9]

I like this because it suggests that Roman lawmakers want everyone to be thinking all the time 'if I fell on an enslaved person or cow while doing this, would it kill them?', much like my personal favourite hypothetical:

> [I]f while several persons are playing ball, the ball having been struck too violently should fall upon the hand of a barber who is shaving a slave at the time, in such a way that the throat of the latter is cut by the razor; the party responsible for negligence is liable under the Lex Aquilia. Proculus thinks that the barber is to blame; and, indeed, if he had the habit of shaving persons in a place where it is customary to play ball, or where there was much travel, he is in a certain degree responsible; although it may not improperly be held that where anyone seats himself in a barber's chair in a dangerous place, he has only himself to blame.[10]

What a wonderful imaginary series of events for multiple legal scholars to have worried about!

This is what the commentary on the Lex Aquilia is: a series of nasty and brutal ways in which men, women and children unlucky enough to be enslaved to the Romans could be maimed and killed, both accidentally and on purpose. In the Lex Aquilia enslaved people are beaten while ill, thrown from bridges, poisoned, stabbed, strangled, starved, trampled by mules, eaten by dogs and burnt. Reading it is like finding Patrick Bateman's diaries: a sickening litany of violence committed casually, and this is why the Lex Aquilia has been seen as a murder law. It describes a lot of killings. It even usefully defines killing as something 'done either with a sword, a club, or some other weapon, or with the hands if strangulation was used, or with a kick, or by striking him on the head, or in any other way whatsoever'.[11]

To a Roman reader, though, reading the Lex Aquilia is akin to reading a list of ways in which tables might be damaged. Because this isn't a murder law, it's a property damage law. To the Romans, enslaved people weren't people who can be murdered any more than cows and sheep were people. This law deals with intentional homicide because Rome survived on slave labour and enslaved people were everywhere, and sometimes people deliberately killed them for no good reason so it was necessary to ensure that their owners' losses were repaired in these circumstances. This is intentional homicide, not murder. A person who kills an enslaved man, woman or child has to pay their owner their value. It is the owner who has been injured by their death and the owner whose loss must be made good. The life of the enslaved person is not the loss; their labour is.

That's it for homicide laws for another two hundred years, until the dictatorship of Sulla in 81 BCE changed the landscape of Rome forever. Sulla led a decade of civil war between him and Gaius Marius which he eventually won. His prize was that he got to be dictator, an emergency short-term position within the Roman constitution, basically a version of martial law, held absolute power for a year and was able to make all the laws he liked. His main aims as dictator were threefold: reduce democracy; centralise power on the Senate; and kill as many enemies as possible. And so he executed four hundred senators and sixteen hundred equestrians and simultaneously enacted the first true murder law, known as the Lex Cornelia de Sicariis et Veneficiis, which (very) roughly translates to the Cornelian Law on people who carry swords and also magicians. These two simultaneous acts introduced a radical new relationship between the state of Rome and the people: Sulla centralised power and this included the power to kill. For the first time, the Roman state decided that it could interfere in what had previously been private interactions between families. For the first time, the Romans legislated the lives and deaths of free citizens. Murder was invented.

That is a little hyperbolic (sorry not sorry). Technically, there had been a standing court against *sicariis* – men who carried swords with the intent to kill – since the time of Gaius Gracchus in 122–124 BCE. Standing courts had been invented in 149 BCE because enormous numbers of people from the provinces were turning up in Rome complaining that the men who had been sent to 'govern' these conquered places were not the upright moral guides and administrators they had been promised, but were in fact venal thieves and extortionists who were taking every imaginable opportunity to steal, kill and enrich themselves at the expense of the inhabitants. So much so that having temporary courts for individual cases had become untenable. So huge were the numbers of complainants, with their gripes about Roman governors stealing from their temples and raping their daughters, that a whole new judicial arm of the government had to be set up for them. Obviously, this created a precedent that allowed later Tribunes to establish permanent courts for other issues deemed pressing and important. For Gaius Gracchus, a pressing and important issue was apparently dudes with knives who intended to kill.

There's quite a lot of academic debate over whether this court included 'amateur' murderers or just 'professional ones' but it is enormously technical and very, very boring. It exists because whatever law was being enforced by Gaius' court is lost completely and we have no records of any of the trials that took place there so we have simply no idea what they were for or what they did. So, for the purposes of this quick overview, we're going to ignore them. As far as the legal record is concerned, which is Justinian's *Digest*, Sulla invented murder. And the murder he invented was oddly specific.

If you cast your mind back to the Introduction, you'll remember that we looked at the wording of some modern Anglophone murder laws and they are all mostly about what the perpetrator intended and whether they were of sound mind and not so much about the specifics of the act itself. Sulla, on the other hand, decided it was only important to be very, very clear on the precise acts that he was legislating against, and so he explicitly outlawed killing people on purpose with arson, by giving false evidence or arranging for people to give false evidence in court, by presiding over a criminal trial with the intent of executing someone, by taking bribes so that some-one will be found guilty, or – weirdly – by poison, and ruled that it was no longer legal to carry a knife or weapon in Rome with the intent of killing someone. This is, I hope it's safe to say, not a recognisable murder law to us. It is a murder law which is very clearly and specifically aimed at the elite ranks of Roman society who were, in the aftermath of a brutal decade of war, using the civil courts and armed gangs to harass each other and rid themselves of people who pissed them off. Sulla needed it to stop, because he wanted to be the only person using the legal system to kill people.

The Lex Cornelia paints a picture of a scared and vengeful segment of society who had spent ten years killing one another on battlefields and absolutely were not over those wartime resentments. It exposes a legal system that appears to be completely rotten with false evidence, corrupt magistrates and vindictive judges, and a Rome that is riddled with mysterious deaths by poisoning and plagued by gangs of armed men roaming the streets, all of which Sulla needed to fix. It is not the kind of abstract law which can be applied to a wide variety of different scenarios in order to sort the murders from the accidental homicides. It is a highly specific law designed for a highly specific moment in Roman history that just so happened to continue to be useful as the Republic crumbled and the imperial system was built, because it – along with Sulla's other laws and constitutional amendments – planted the idea that the state could legislate private actions.

The Empire

In terms of legal provisions around murder, it was not until Hadrian (117–138 CE) that anyone bothered to say anything official. Neither Julius Caesar, nor Augustus, nor Vespasian, nor Trajan got around to saying 'hey, don't kill people on purpose' because that was, quite simply, not their job. Hadrian's edict was a very casual but very significant encroachment of the Roman state into private lives and actions. He wrote:

> he who kills a man, if he committed this act without the intention of causing death, could be acquitted; and he who did not kill a man but wounded him with the intention of killing ought to be found guilty of homicide.[12]

And thus he invented attempted murder for the first time in Roman history, for which he's really not given enough credit.

All that covers several hundred years of Roman history – pretty much all the famous bits are included in there, and almost all the murders that we are going to look at for the rest of this book. The difference is that, until Hadrian, the Roman legal system considered the individual to be the victim of a violent, personal crime, not the state. I can practically see you, dear reader, rolling your eyes at this brutally obvious statement because in modern vernacular we also see the person who has been killed as the victim and their relatives as the victim's family. But that is not how the state sees them. Or, at least, as far as the modern Western state is concerned, there are two victims in every murder: the person who bled out on the floor and the dignity of the state. The person with a knife in their chest suffers violence, but the state suffers a challenge to its power to control the behaviour of its citizens and therefore it is the state that brings criminal cases. The victim of a murder or attempted murder cannot decide not to press charges against a perpetrator because, although they are *a* victim, they are not the *only* victim and they are unable to define what is and isn't a crime worth prosecuting. Also, they are usually dead. Instead, it is the state that decides whether or not to prosecute and it is the state that appears as the plaintiff in court because, in criminal law, it is the state that has been harmed by the crime and the state that defines crime.

In Rome, however, murder was not technically a crime, in that it was not investigated or prosecuted by the government. No senators were spending their days gumshoeing around Rome and there were no state prosecutors or criminal prosecution service employees. The Roman state, at least until the dawn of the Imperial period, did not consider itself to be harmed, threatened or challenged when a man strangled his wife or stabbed a rival. That was their personal business. And it was the personal business of the victim's family to sort out the harm done and make things right either by having a chat with the perpetrator or by employing an advocate and taking the perpetrator to court. Dealing with a murder in the Roman world was less like *CSI* and much more like dealing with an uninsured person driving into your car, forcing you to take them to the small claims court to get them to pay for a new bumper. The responsibility for investigating, prosecuting and punishing a murder was entirely on the family and friends of the deceased.

What we see in these surviving laws is the evolution of the idea of murder as a crime, as something which harms the state and is to be regulated by the state, in parallel with the evolution of the Roman state into a centralised, military-backed absolute monarchy. This is not a coincidence. As the power of the state came more and more to rest on just one man, the emperor, the state slowly took control of the power to kill and reduced the power of the family and the individual. As violence became a threat to the smooth running of the Empire, violence gradually became the sole domain of the emperor and his government. This does not mean, however, that Romans were cool with killing during the early years. It just means that they didn't think it was the state's job to police it, except in extreme circumstances like when someone very rich or very famous was involved, or when a large number of people died. The rest of the time, it was the victim's family's responsibility to deal with it however they wished or had the resources to enact.

There is just one curious exception to this rule, which is parricide. Often misinterpreted as patricide (killing one's father), parricide refers to the killing of any ancestor – any member of the family of a generation above the murderer – but in Roman law it applies to any family member, including patrons. Romans were weird about parricide, in that it is the only form of murder we know that was definitely included in the Twelve Tables, deriving from a law believed to have been set by the second king of Rome – Numa. Romans, unlike virtually any modern society, had little to no legal interest in stranger murder but a unique and deep-seated cultural horror of murder within the family.

3

Murder in the Family

Roscius

The Roman fear of being killed by their kids – and Roman here is short for 'Roman men of the aristocratic classes' – is so well discussed among historians that it almost feels a cliché to write about it. A very famous French historian called Paul Veyne claimed in 1999 that the Romans had a 'national neurosis' about patricide and that's pretty representative of how most people think about parricide in the Roman world.[1] The *Digest*, citing a law created by Pompey when he was ruling Rome, is incredibly and tediously clear about what parricide refers to. It is the killing of one's:

> father, mother, grandfather, grandmother, brother, sister, first cousin on the father's side, first cousin on the mother's side, paternal or maternal uncle, paternal [or maternal] aunt, first cousin (male or female) by mother's sister, wife, husband, father-in-law, son-in-law, mother-in-law, [daughter-in-law], stepfather, stepson, stepdaughter, patron or patroness . . . And a mother who kills her son or daughter suffers the penalty of the same statute, as does a grandfather who kills a grandson; and in addition, a person who buys poison to give to his father, even though he is unable to administer it.[2]

That's a pretty exhaustive list. It is, you'll note, significantly more exhaustive than the laws concerning bog-standard non-familial murder, which worked hard to be as useless as possible.

Outside of the law, however, we don't really see people killing their first cousins on their mother's side or their grandmothers. I'm sure it happened, it just didn't really make the news. It's most likely that parricide meant patricide in common usage like homicide means murder in general to us. One day our vernacular interchangeable use of murder and homicide in comparison to the careful wording of our laws will confuse the hell out of future historians. At the very least, when the term parricide was used it was almost always describing someone who killed their real or metaphorical dad. And it was used to describe the absolute worst people that Romans could think of. Also, in a twist that is one of the more irritating of Roman behaviours for your historian here: the Romans sometimes also seem to use parricide to mean treason. Just for fun. For our purposes here, though, we're going to pretend that parricide meant patricide, which meant killing one's parents and, at a push, siblings and patrons, and we're not going to look too hard at the laws. If we get started on it we'll all be here for twenty thousand words of hand-wringing over what *precisely* a lot of Latin words mean, and honestly it's both stressful and dull. Like getting a filling. So let's not. Let's move on.

The main problem with patri/parricide is that the vast majority of Roman sources for what parricide was and what it meant come from the late Republic, that very narrow period of history when Romans were struggling a lot with their culture and politics and when all those people who had styled themselves as fathers of the country kept stabbing each other in the streets. Problem number two is that just about every single written mention of parricide comes from rhetorical or hypothetical sources. Sources that only barely pretend to be describing any kind of reality. This is a problem for the assertion that Romans were, as a cultural group, terrified of parricide in the way that we are afraid of Ted Bundys and Golden State Killers lurking outside our bedroom windows.

At least part of the evidence for the arguments that patricide was a 'national neurosis' for the Romans was the punishment that they came up with for it. Perhaps one of the most notorious things the Romans ever devised, it is technically known as the *culleus* or *Poena Cullei*, and is fairly regularly the subject of clickbait articles with titles like 'This Roman Punishment Will Make You Sick!' It's also a really good factoid to pull out in pubs with people you barely know, so take notes. According to the *Digest*, it goes like this: a person found guilty of parricide was beaten with 'blood-coloured rods' (presumably they painted them, I guess), then put into a sack. To the sack was also added a dog, a cockerel, a monkey and a snake. And then the sack was thrown into the sea.[3] I'll let you sit and think for five seconds about the horror of being trapped in a bag with a terrified dog, and then we'll move on to the added chaotic tangle of terror that the cockerel, monkey and snake bring to the process of drowning. It is a point of unique horror for Roman writers, and when Romans think something is bad, it's bad. Seneca the Elder wrote that he 'kept imagining the sack, the snake, the deep'[4] and I actually recommend that you don't follow his example because you won't sleep. There's some question over whether the animals were ever actually used or whether the punishment in reality was just ('just') being sewn into a sack and drowned. Or if it even existed, which is really wishful thinking from old men who identify too hard with Cicero to be honest with you. For me, though, those lines of Seneca's, along with the fact that Cicero's own brother claimed that he had done it to two people (not even Romans) in the space of a one-year governor's term in Smyrna, leave open enough possibility that it did happen at least a few times. Also the Romans ritually crucified dogs every year so I put absolutely nothing past them.[†] They were horrid.

The point of the animals is, to be honest, utterly obscure. God knows what they were thinking there. The point of the sack is outlined for us by Cicero in a defence speech. It was not for pure sadistic pleasure, but to prevent the profane and polluted body of the murderer from contaminating the earth, sky and water that it would otherwise touch. The point was to protect the very elements from contact with something so obscene and defiling as the body of a parricide. At the same time, the person themselves would be deprived of those base things which represented freedom and goodness and purity: the fresh air, the life-giving earth and the cleansing water. Even their bones, says Cicero, would be denied the support of the shore when they washed up. They would never receive the veneration given to the dead in their afterlife. They were, for eternity, isolated from every good and natural thing because of the all-encompassing horror of their deed.

The punishment for parricide was, apparently, so abhorrent because Romans thought that parricide was abhorrent. It was monstrous to a degree that they simultaneously could barely conceive of it and couldn't stop talking about it. Parricides were to the Romans what Adam Lanza is to us.[5] According to Cicero, they violated the rules of human life for the Romans at a deep, fundamental cultural, personal and religious level. Parricide didn't just upset them, it offended them; it was almost a blasphemous act to kill one's parents. There are multiple histories of Rome written in the late Republican and Imperial periods

---

† This is also a good one to bring up in pubs if you quite enjoy horrifying people. Google *supplicia canum* if you absolutely must but do try not to think about the logistics too hard.

which, in the middle of describing a lot of tedious wars and politics, suddenly record the first person to be punished with the sack
in 101 BCE. His name was Publicius Malleolus and the only thing
we know about him is that he, with the help of some enslaved
men, killed his mother. His crime appalled Rome to such an
extent that they kept recording it over and over again, though
naturally they are highly inconsistent. Livy says that Malleolus
was the first person to be punished with the specific sack punishment, while a Christian historian called Orosius quite sweetly
and unconvincingly claims that Malleolus was literally the first
person in the whole of Roman history to murder his mother.[6]
Hundreds of years and not one suspiciously dead parent!
Apparently, the whole city was upset that such a thing would
happen, and this upset never really went away.

However (there's always a however), the Romans didn't like
to talk too much about the specifics of people who killed their
parents. It's almost like it didn't happen very often, or at least
didn't make too much of a splash when it did. One of the best-
known cases of parricide is that of the Cloelius brothers who
were tried for murdering their father in his bed. The method of
the poor man's murder isn't noted but Valerius Maximus, who
records the case in his delightful book of memorable words and
deeds, states that there were gruesome wounds and a lot of
blood, which suggests that it wasn't a quiet pillow smothering.
Cloelius Senior's body was found in the morning when someone
opened the bedroom door to find a blood-soaked scene on one
side of the room and the two brothers peacefully sleeping in
beds on the other. Aside from the fascinating insight into sleeping arrangements in the Roman world, where two well-heeled
adult men apparently shared a bedroom with their dad, the
scene caused a bit of a scandal. No one had been into the room
in which the three men slept and no other suspects could be

found. It perhaps seems like a slam-dunk case for the prosecutor, which is why we should never assume anything about the Roman justice system. The judge decided to fully acquit the brothers on the basis that 'it was not naturally possible' for the men to have beaten their father to death and then gone to sleep afterwards. It appears not to have occurred to anyone that the only other possible interpretation of events was that two men had slept through someone entering the room, brutally attacking their dad mere feet away from them, beating him to death and then leaving again. Call me a cynic but that seems significantly less likely than the possibility of them having a nap after doing a strenuous bit of patricide. But then, I am not the Romans, and the Romans thought that killing a dad was so truly shocking and unnatural that it would be physically impossible to sleep afterwards.

The most famous patricide who has come down to us, though, didn't even kill anyone. He is a guy called Sextus Roscius, which sounds like a skin disease but was really his name. It was also his dad's name, which is going to make this a little confusing so we'll call him Roscius and his dad Sextus. (To make things extremely Roman, there are two other Rosciuses involved, both called Titus Roscius, for which I apologise now.) We know so much about Roscius and his dad because he hired Cicero to be his lawyer and Cicero was so characteristically pleased with his own speech that he polished it up and published it. You'll see why in a minute.

Sextus was a well-respected landowner and small business-man in the town of Ameria in Umbria, now called Amelia. He was your classic big man in a small town: he had enough money and land that he could dominate his area, his estate was worth six million sesterces, and he had a few strong connections in Rome but, by the standards of the city elite, he was basically a bum-scratching hog-farmer. For comparison, Cicero's estates were relatively modest for an elite man and they were worth ten million sesterces. In his home town, Sextus had an ongoing neighbourly feud of unknown origin with a retired gladiator named Titus Roscius Capito and his pupil, Titus Roscius Magnus (I swear the Roman naming system was sent to test me). Roscius was Sextus' only son and – according to his defence lawyer – a modest, hard-working young man dedicated to the smooth running of the Amerian estates and the simple pleasures of country life.

In 80 BCE, the consuls were Lucius Cornelius Sulla and Quintus Caecilius Metellus Pius. Sulla had 'retired' from the dictatorship mere months previously. Rome was still reeling from the war and Sulla's behaviour after the war had sparked savage paranoia. He had enacted what are euphemistically called 'proscriptions': he published regularly updated lists of men who had pissed him off, confiscated all their property and then executed them. The proscribed were hunted across Italy by Sulla's armies. Anyone who had opposed him at any time was a target, but the proscriptions were also a way for Sulla to make money, so even supporting him wasn't necessarily a protection for the conspicuously rich. The atmosphere in Rome was tense and difficult. Suspicion had been cast on everyone still standing after the war and so Sextus was in Rome making sure that every-one knew that he had been enthusiastically on Sulla's side the whole time. All seemed to be going well until, one fine evening, Sextus was walking past the baths on the Via Pallacina after a dinner party at a friend's house. He was perhaps being a little cavalier with his own safety walking around at night but maybe he'd had a little too much Falernian wine. It was only early even-ing – an hour after dark – and perhaps he wanted to enjoy the cool air. Whatever his thoughts as he sauntered through the dark streets of the war-torn city that night, they were cut short as he was ambushed and murdered on the street, a knife driven into his soft, full belly.

Someone found his body and raised the alert and sent a messenger to Ameria, a freedman called Mallius Glaucia, which is a villain's name if ever I heard one. One might expect that Glaucia would go to Roscius and break the news of his father's death immediately, but there one would be wrong. Glaucia, who turned out to be a pal of Titus Magnus', went straight to Titus Capito, Sextus' local enemy. Two things would stand out here to any budding Columbo, or even a half-awake beat cop: first, that Roscius was in Ameria, fifty-six miles away from Rome, when the murder occurred, and second, that Sextus' enemies knew about the murder before anyone else. A third piece of alleged evidence which really seems damning to the modern eye is that Glaucia had the still-bloody knife with him when he arrived in Ameria.

At this point, I suspect you are wondering how the hell this open-and-shut case got into a patricide chapter and that is because you were apparently not paying attention to the previous story.

Immediately following his death, Sextus was posthumously and mysteriously added to the list of proscribed persons drawn up by Sulla. As a result, all of his properties were confiscated from his heirs and sold. They were purchased by one of Sulla's own freedmen, Chrysogonus, who – as it happens – was also in charge of adding people to the proscriptions list, for the knock-down price of two thousand sesterces. To make this really, really suspicious, he then gave half of the properties to the two Tituses. This all happened so quickly that, again according to Cicero, Titus Magnus turned up at Roscius' house on the day of his father's funeral and kicked him out without even the clothes on his back. In the space of a few days, Roscius went from being the son of the lord of the manor to being a nude, bereaved, home-less person. According to Cicero. I'm not sure I believe the nude bit to be honest. Anyway, he ended up living with Caecilia Metella, who was related to Sulla's co-consul and was terribly posh.

The people of Ameria were not happy about all this. Sextus was their local celebrity, their lord of the manor, their Mr de Winter, and he had been murdered in the street like a dog. The treatment of Roscius in particular upset them. So they sent a delegation to Sulla to ask him to intervene. Sulla heard their case and, like a true dictator who had definitely given up the dictator-ship, he agreed with them, removed Sextus' name from the naughty list and said he'd give back all the properties to Roscius. Much rejoicing, right? Wrong. The Tituses wanted those houses; they wanted them a lot. Because Roscius was living with one of the most famous families in Rome, and probably wasn't thick and had security, they couldn't just stab him like they had his dad. So they came up with what Cicero calls 'a maniacal plot': they'd get the state to murder Roscius by accusing *him* of killing his father.

My best guess here is that they thought that the accusation of patricide would be so utterly appalling and so defiling to every-one in the vicinity of it that Roscius would lose all his friends, that no advocate would agree to defend him and that he'd end up a country bumpkin in the big city, condemned on nothing but an accusation. Ludicrous though it seems, it is entirely plausible that the Roman magistrate overseeing the case (a certain Marcus Fannius, whose name I am only telling you because it's funny) would condemn Roscius on the basis that no one would dare to make up such a terrible accusation. In this case, however, it backfired wildly because the Tituses hadn't reckoned with Cicero, whose love of his own voice and people looking at him exponentially outweighed his feelings about everything else.[7] Including parricide.

The case was a chance for the young Cicero to really make a splash in Rome. In 80 BCE, he was just twenty-seven years old and a New Man in the Senate. A fresh-faced provincial newbie senator with a big brain, a massive ego and an insatiable ambition. He had made a minor name for himself as an exceptional student of rhetoric, and he saw in Roscius a chance to punch Rome and its establishment hard in the face and make sure they all knew the name Marcus Tullius Cicero. And he succeeded. His speech, much as it has clearly been rewritten after the fact, is a brilliant and devastating destruction of the prosecution's case from every possible angle. For all his many, many personal faults, Cicero's skill as a rhetorician is really something. Even reading the written version today, 2099 years from the day that little twenty-something Marcus delivered it, it is possible to feel the sting in his wicked barbs against his opponent and feel the reaction of the crowd as he drops bombshell after bombshell, battering his opponent's arguments into a sad, corrupt pulp. It's so good that the two hours it would have taken to deliver (at least) were probably immense fun for the audience who thought they were showing up to watch a provincial nobody get sewn into a sack – a great bit of entertainment for a Roman – only to discover that they were actually getting a political takedown for the ages.

Cicero's speech is, as I say, enormously long. Hours long. It tears the Tituses' case to pieces, exposing their bizarre behaviour and the total lack of means, motive and opportunity presented by the prosecution. Cicero outlines his theory about the criminal conspiracy to steal Roscius' house in a level of detail that deeply upsets the other side. But mostly he talks about how the charge of patricide is so horrific that it stains the accusers to have made a false accusation of such.

Patricide is, he says, a crime so disgusting that it contains within it every kind of guilt. It is a crime so hateful, so unique, so exceptional that its occurrence is a portent and a monstrosity. Only a man of pure savagery, hatred and degradation could do such a terrible thing. Even Orestes, who killed his mother to avenge his father at the urging of the gods, was haunted by the Furies for the rest of his life. The crime of killing one's parents was the worst thing that Titus and Titus could have accused Roscius of, so Cicero forced them and the audience to confront the full horror of what they were saying and the full horror of the punishment to which they were trying to condemn Roscius.

Cicero obviously won, and his name and career were made. And, for all the hints at unnamed people being thrown into sacks, and for all the opprobrium spilt upon it by late Republican rhetoricians, there are no more named patricides in Roman history. What we do have are a lot of legal exercises known as *controversiae* written by law teachers and show-offs to play around with hypothetical court cases. They are all from the century around the late Republic and the early Imperial periods. And they are all, apart from Cicero's defence of Roscius, fictional. They are also all remarkably consistent in their construction of patricide as the worst possible crime that a person could commit and that the punishment was the worst punishment imaginable.

There is a great hypothetical proposed by Seneca the Elder which I desperately wish were a true story because it is soap opera levels of excellent. It goes like this: a man convicted his eldest son for attempted patricide in the family court and handed him over to his second son for punishment. The second son, who we'll call Secundus here to make this easier to read, was supposed to give his brother, let's call him Primus, the punishment of the sack but Secundus found that he couldn't do it. Instead he tied Primus up on a disabled boat and set him afloat on the sea. We will overlook the extremely Austin Powers fact that the father just sent his kid off to kill his other kid and didn't even bother to watch because this is fiction. Skip to several years later, the father went on a trip and was captured by pirates. To his astonishment, he found that the pirate chief who had captured him was his distinctly alive son Primus. The father was extremely cross to find his son alive, and his rage fuelled his return home from captivity, whereupon he immediately disinherited Secundus for disobedience, which Secundus appealed. In the commentary quoted by Seneca, Secundus plays on his father's emotions, wailing: 'You tell me to have my brother sewn into a sack? I cannot do it, father . . . Can you use your eyes and hands for such a task? Can you bear to hear the groans of your son trapped inside?'[8] Meanwhile, another commentary on the fictional case has Primus telling Secundus as he is put in the boat: 'I acknowledge it, I wanted to kill [our father]; but then I realised how difficult parricide was . . . Even now I cannot do it.'[9] This little hypothetical tells us a couple of things. It tells us that Cicero's rhetorical approach of forcing his audience to think about – really imagine in detail – what killing one's father or sewing one's son into a sack to die would actually be like was one that all the orators and rhetoricians used and that this trick was apparently pretty effective in arousing people's sympathies.

Secondly, it tells us the reason we don't see very many parricide cases in the courts: such issues were dealt with domestically. When a violation occurred within the family, even if, like parricide, it was technically a crime, it was usually dealt with by the family *consilium*. The *consilium* was a family council, a group of adults in the family who came together equally to celebrate, support and police one another. The membership of the council (which is how I'm going to very loosely translate *consilium*) would vary a lot and may well have included friends. If you've read Ovid or Livy's account of the death of Lucretia, for example, you'll remember that when she calls a family meeting to tell them that the prince of Rome raped her and then kills herself, she invites a random family friend. That's how they worked. The *consilium* would certainly include Mum and Dad, and dad's parents and siblings; maternal in-laws might be there too. The purpose of the family council was for the family to look after the family, which primarily meant the family name. The individual was always subordinate to the family name and reputation in Rome. And so, the family council would be called upon to give money and support to a young Crispus' campaign to become a praetor or to celebrate little Lucius getting his *toga virilis* (literally his toga of manliness) and becoming a man at fourteen or to choose a suitable husband for Fausta. Or they might be called together because Fausta had tried to run off with an unsuitable boy and needed to be dealt with, or because little Lucius wouldn't stop beating their enslaved household too hard, or, sometimes, because our Crispus had gone to Spain with his father and come home without his dad, and his brother – also called Crispus of course – was pretty sure that Crispus the Younger had committed patricide while no one was looking.† Part of the role of the family council was to deal with this shit so that no one else found out about it, and part of the role was to deal with this shit because there was no other way to deal with it. To go to the courts required both financial resources and status. Without one or both of those things, there was nowhere else to go. Terrible things had to be dealt with in-house, quite literally. And if we believe Seneca and his short story about Primus and Secundus, that sometimes included killing your adult children.

---

† This last is taken direct from a hypothetical posed by Seneca, *Controversiae* 5.4. In this, the dad reappears healthy and happy after his extended holiday to find a family convinced he was dead and in the process of sewing an innocent kid into a sack. Awkward.

Pontius Aufidianus

When it came to tales of parents murdering their kids in Rome, there were two types of stories: fathers who valiantly killed their children for the good of the state, and parents who horribly murdered their children so they could get laid. Gallons of ink have been spilled over the former because they are wild. They are stories, told as parables of idealised behaviour, of a heroic, stoic, patriotic father exercising his *ius vitae necisque*, his power of life and death over every member of the family, by killing his off-spring. They show his responsibility to uphold the sanctity of the city of Rome over the love he felt for his children. If an aristo-cratic man's children fucked up, they couldn't be allowed to live and poison Rome; they had to go. The stories are all pretty simi-lar and are told in that peculiarly Roman style which blends myth and history into something unique. Myth-tory. Histh. Whatever. There's a version for sons and a version for daughters and you're not going to be shocked to find out which one has boning in it. They go like this:

In 509 BCE, the last king was expelled from Rome by Lucius Junius Brutus following the rape and suicide of Lucretia. We've said it before but still, it's important to note that Tarquinius Superbus and his family were exiled from Rome and not exe-cuted. They were just sent away to live their lives elsewhere while Junius Brutus got on with creating a whole new form of Roman government in which he was the first consul. While this was ad-mirable, it caused entirely foreseeable problems because humans are deeply contrary and, at the time, not everyone was delighted that the king had been overthrown and the monarchy eradi-cated. Some people liked kings. Some of those people were Brutus' two sons, Titus and Tiberius. Titus and Tiberius con-spired with some unnamed like-minded individuals to bring Tarquinius and his family back to Rome and place them back on the throne. They were, of course, immediately caught and brought before the new consul, their dad. The story of Brutus' reaction is told by just about every Roman chronicler of that near-imaginary time as evidence of his extraordinary devotion to the fledgling Republic. He, in Valerius Maximus' words, acted the consul, not the father; he would rather be childless than betray Rome.[10] Livy gives the most detailed and obviously fictional account. In his telling, Titus and Tiberius are brought before their father and bound to stakes. There, in front of the crowd and overseen by their father, lictors whipped them with sticks until they bled and then beheaded them. Throughout the whole ordeal, says Livy, the crowd watched Brutus, saw his fatherly anguish at his suffering sons and saw him enduring it for a higher purpose.[11]

Here's another one. Titus Manlius Torquatus was consul in 340 BCE. He was already famous for an act of wild teenage delinquency that was inexplicably portrayed as a heroic act by the Romans. In his youth, his father Lucius Manlius thought that his son was thick and useless and so kept him working on their rural estates and away from politics. Torquatus was sort of the proto-Claudius in Roman history. Except this happened in the early Republic, so someone prosecuted Manlius for keeping his son out of politics (and also for failing to give up his army command on time during a war, like those things are equal). When Torquatus heard that his father was being prosecuted for anything at all, he became furious and rushed to Rome. I like to imagine him grabbing a horse and riding through the night in a melodramatic fury, because he went not to the courts, but to the home of the prosecutor. In the middle of the night. And threatened him and his family with a sword until he promised to withdraw his case. Torquatus enacted a full-on home invasion and terrorised a family until he got his way. This is probably why his father kept him away from Rome. Valerius Maximus tells this story as a wonderful, charming tale of extraordinary filial devotion. Anyway, Torquatus grew up, was a dictator and a consul and fought a Gaul in single combat and generally became a Roman hero of semi-mythical proportions. And his son, presumably inspired by his father, tried to impress him. Rome was fighting the Latins and the Campanians at the time and was in the process of conquering Italy. Torquatus was leading an army in the lead-up to a battle when his son, who was obviously also called Titus Manlius, was goaded by an enemy commander into having a single combat duel, just like his dad. Manlius won by, according to Livy, poking his opponent's horse in the ear. Thrilled with his victory, feeling like he was living up to his dad's legend, Manlius galloped back to tell his father, the great consul and general, all about it. Unfortunately for him, due to some prophecies that are irrelevant here, everyone had been ordered very specifically *not* to engage in fights or duels with the enemy until the formal battle. So, rather than be proud, Torquatus was furious. Well, that's very good, son, he said. I can't fault your bravery. But you did break my rules and so I am going to have to have you beheaded. Which he immediately did.[12]

These are the most famous cases of fathers bravely sacrificing their children but they are not murders in the strict sense. They are executions, carried out while the father was in a position of military or political authority. There is, however, a murkier version of this story, which is the story of fathers who kill their sons for political crimes in family courts. For example, Spurius Cassius Vecellinus proposed the first agrarian law while consul in 486 BCE and, as soon as he was out of office, was taken home by his father, tried in a family court and killed in the home for treason.[13] Aulus Fulvius joined the alleged conspiracy of Catiline to overthrow Cicero and so was dragged home by his father, tried and also killed for treason. These are weirder and more dubious to the modern reader. The idea of a family court and the right to kill one's adult children at home without any kind of checks and balances feels uncomfortable and open to abuse. Which is why these stories have lit up the imaginations of modern scholars.

Similarly, the stories of women being punished for sexual crimes, such as having any sex at all, by their fathers really thrill the modern reader. The most famous and the oddest is the tale of Verginia, the young sexy daughter of Lucius Verginius, who attracted the unwanted attentions of Appius Claudius. Claudius tried to seduce the young girl, who was betrothed to another young man, several times and was knocked back every time. She just didn't fancy him. But in the grand tradition of toxic men through the ages, Claudius was not willing to take no for an answer and he came up with a complex and insane plan to make Verginia his. He persuaded a pal to publicly claim that Verginia was his slave. As the girl was walking to school one day, because she was probably about fourteen, a man leapt out, grabbed her arm, shouted that she was his property and began to drag her away with him. It was the kind of plan that was so astonishingly audacious that no one knew how to react. A scuffle ensued and the man declared that he would take this matter to court. Which he did. The court of Appius Claudius. After much back and forth and the appearance of Lucius Verginius, Appius declared his verdict: the girl *was* a slave and would be sent to the house of his friend. Appalled and terrified, Verginius took drastic action: he grabbed his teenage daughter and plunged a knife into her heart. When questioned about what he had done, he said through his tears that he would rather lose his daughter to death than dishonour. And so Verginia became a second Lucretia: better dead than raped. Better a murdered daughter than a broken one. Better a murderer than the father of a sullied woman.

Here's another: Pontius Aufidianus, an equestrian, came home one day to the news that his lovely daughter had been sleeping with her tutor, Fannius Saturninus. Oddly, the enslaved tutor's name is recorded, but the daughter's isn't. I say oddly, but I don't mean it. Aufidianus' first course of action was easy: he had Fannius executed. He probably sent him off to be thrown to wild beasts as part of the games. Enslaved men who slept with free women couldn't be allowed to live and their punishment should be public. But what to do with the girl, who I'm going to guess was probably called either Pontia or Aufidiana or both. Her virginity was lost, her honour gone. She had brought shame on the family name. Aufidianus used his own hands to execute her and punish her for her crime of getting laid. Or possibly, being sexually assaulted by her teacher. Again, Valerius Maximus tells this tale with smug satisfaction: 'Instead of celebrating a disgraceful marriage, he led a pitiless funeral.'[14] Better a killer than a shamed man. Or how about the story of Publius Horatius and his triplet brothers who fought a mini-battle during a war with the people of Alba Longa in the reign of Tullus Hostilius (673– 640 BCE). Unwilling to have an all-out war between the Romans and the Albans, Tullus suggested that the Horatii triplets fight three-on-three with a set of triplets from Alba called the Curiatii. Last man standing wins the war. Nice efficient thinking. The six men fought and five died. The final man standing, wobbly and drenched in blood, was Publius, his sword aloft in glorious victory. Rome had won, but not everyone was celebrating. Publius' sister Camilla had been engaged to one of the Curiatii (because Alba Longa and Rome were effectively the same city. It's a long story.) and when she saw her future husband dead, she cried. She put her own feelings of loss and grief over the victory of her city and for that her brother calmly walked over and thrust his sword, still dripping in her fiancé's blood, into her chest, shouting, 'So perish every Roman woman who mourns a foe!'[15] Bystanders were understandably shocked by this but his father, also called Publius Fucking Horatius, told the king that, as far as he was concerned, his son had done the right thing. Because Publius was the brother, however, and not the father, the king forced him to do a penance and cleanse himself of the murder. Had Daddy Horatius done it, that wouldn't have been necessary.

This kind of story gives the very strong impression that the Roman father was constantly going around killing his children left, right and centre, telling his mates that they'd committed a crime and being carried through the Forum on their shoulders in celebration of his excellent parenting. Pick up any book on the Roman family or the Romans in general and there's a 2/1 chance you'll find a sentence or two about the *patria potestas* and how Roman dads could kill their kids without repercussion. I just looked it up in the *Horrible Histories* book *Ruthless Romans* and there it is on page 62: 'A Roman father had the power of life and death over his children.' It's one of those inescapable 'facts' about the Romans, like Gaius Caligula making his horse a consul (guaranteed to make me scream with irrational rage) or Nero fiddling while Rome burnt (acceptable only because it spawned a cracking joke in the late 1990s when a German company called Nero made CD burning software and called it Nero Burning Rom, which made me chuckle every time I made a mix CD as a teenager).[16] Academics have devoted entire careers and a lot of sleepless nights to agonising over whether a father could kill his children without consequence and they've eventually come to the conclusion that you might have reached if you were paying very close attention and also looked at the endnotes. All these stories, which make murderous fathers into glorious heroes, able to put their country above their children, are legends. They all originate in the early or mid-Republic, those misty times many hundreds of years before any of our surviving sources were written. They all come from Livy, writing his glorious history to please Augustus, and Valerius Maximus, writing decontextualised anecdotes to please and guide Tiberius, and Dionysius of Halicarnassus, also writing his history to please Augustus. They were all written at the very start of imperial, monarchical rule to please and delight monarchs who based their power on the notion that they were the father of the country (the *pater patriae*) who loved and ruled their Empire as benevolent citizens, not kings. Definitely not kings. Just kindly fathers. Who loved their senatorial children. And had the right to kill them whenever they wanted.

In the real world of actually raising snotty children with their bodily fluids and their learning to walk and say mater and pater for the first time and growing up and being your heart outside of your body, just running around all soft and unprotected, Roman fathers did not go around holding courts and stabbing their children in the heart for the good of the country. Because in the real world people aren't patriotic heroes, and even real Romans would have thought their friends were utterly psychotic for acting like Verginius. When the emperor Augustus had his daughter Julia exiled from Rome for committing adultery and pissing on the *rostra*, the Roman people spent all their time exhorting him to be nicer to her and bring her home. They thought him terribly cruel and unforgiving. He exiled her to what was basically a permanent detox holiday on a tiny island in the Tyrrhenian Sea. Imagine how they'd have felt if he'd executed her. In the real world, when parents really killed their children, they did so for selfish, stupid reasons and were treated as monsters.

There are a few examples of men murdering their children in historical rather than mythical circumstances and, pretty much without exception, Roman commentators got up in arms about the situation, as you'd expect. There's a bit of a trope about the Roman world that they didn't love their children or care if they died, which is obvious nonsense. Love between parents and children was considered to be the most natural and most basic love, the first law of nature, and parents who violated that love were just as egregious as people who killed their parents. Only the worst of the worst killed their kids, especially their adult kids. One of the late Republic's great villains was Catiline, who you'll remember was judicially murdered by Cicero. Even before he conceived of a popular overthrow of the Senate, he was causing trouble. He was prosecuted, and acquitted, for fucking a Vestal Virgin, which was a very bad thing to do, for a start. And then he suffered an unfortunate series of events: his wife died, then his teenage son died, and then he married a beautiful but unpopular woman named Aurelia Orestilla. It was widely believed that he had proposed to Aurelia before the death of his son but that she had refused him. The reason she gave was that she didn't want a stepson. So Catiline poisoned his own son and buried him and, in Valerius' words, offered his childlessness as a gift to his new bride. Both Sallust and Appian call Catiline a madman and a lunatic for such abhorrent behaviour, while Cicero, never one to use one word when eighteen will suffice, says:

> when lately by the death of your former wife you had
> made your house empty and ready for a new bride, did
> you not even add another incredible wickedness to this
> wickedness? But I pass that over, and willingly allow it
> to be buried in silence, that so horrible a crime may not
> be seen to have existed in this city.[17]

Cicero also has a lot to say about another great villain of the late Republic, a man who stalked the small town of Larinum like Blanche Taylor Moore stalked Concord, North Carolina, bumping off person after person, pocketing their cash and getting away with it: Statius Albius Oppianicus.[18] Oppianicus appears to have been a quite spectacularly murderous individual and a real whizz with the poison jar. He was an Agatha Christie wet dream. We have a version of his life from Cicero, who defended his stepson Cluentius several years after his death. We'll get to Cluentius' trial later, but in 74 BCE he had accused Oppianicus of trying to poison him. In the process of that trial, Oppianicus was accused of murdering twelve other people, including two of his own children, one of whom was an infant, and an unborn foetus. His motive for poisoning his two sons, one after another in the space of a week, was that he wanted to marry Cluentius' mother Sassia. Like her contemporary Aurelia Orestilla, Sassia hadn't wanted stepsons getting under her feet and in the way of her access to Oppianicus' money, so she refused to marry Oppianicus while he was a father. Just like Catiline, Oppianicus put his new love (and her fortune) over the lives of his children. One of his young sons was living with his mother Papia in Teanum, eighteen miles away, and only visited on public holidays (he was a bit of a deadbeat dad to this one), but Oppianicus wasn't going to let that stop him. He asked Papia to let his son visit him and, as soon as the kid arrived, poisoned him. The child was, in Cicero's telling, dead before nightfall and cremated before morning. He didn't even get a funeral. Less than ten days later, Oppianicus' tiny infant son was dead under the same circumstances. Only his eldest, who shared his name, managed to survive somehow. Oppianicus then tried to poison his new stepson, Sassia's teenage biological son Cluentius, and was caught, ending a life of quite extraordinary cruelty and cold-blooded murder. In addition to these murders, Cicero also accused Oppianicus of poisoning Cluentius' paternal aunt, Cluentia (of course), his own brother Gaius, Gaius' pregnant wife and her unborn child, and his first mother-in-law, Dinea. But poison wasn't Oppianicus' only weapon. His first murder was an intriguing one. He found out that his brother-in-law (his first wife's brother) had not died in the civil wars between Marius and Sulla as everyone had thought, but had, in fact, been taken into slavery. Oppianicus' mother-in-law Dinea was overjoyed to hear her son was alive but Oppianicus was not. This interfered with his ability to inherit Dinea's money. So he tracked down his poor brother-in-law, and killed him. And then poisoned Dinea. When people found out what he had done, they ran him out of town, led by another of Sassia's husbands (she had five). But when Sulla won the civil wars, Oppianicus armed a band of enslaved men, rode back into Larinum Wild West style, declared he was there on Sulla's orders, and butchered the men who had originally run him out, including Sassia's husband, leaving her open to his advances.

Of course, this all comes from Cicero, from a defence speech that rested very strongly on painting Oppianicus in the worst light possible, but as a series of alleged crimes it is extraordinary. If it happened today, an American newspaper would make a prestige twelve-part true crime podcast about him followed by a Netflix film because the fact that he got away with it for so long, and then was only stopped through an attempted poisoning case, is wild. Most people did not lead such lives of murderous horror. Most people were stopped after the first one.

Seneca, for example, tells of a man named Tricho, an equestrian, who, in the reign of Augustus, beat his son to death. Whether the death was accidental from overzealous corporal punishment or a deliberate act of immense cruelty is unclear.

Nor is the name or age of his son known. All we know is that Seneca remembered the case and that the son died a nasty death. Being flogged with rods was a punishment that was not supposed to be meted out to free citizens; only the enslaved were considered worthy of it, because it was horrendous. Because I am a dedicated researcher, I watched several videos of people being flogged in India and Indonesia and it takes more blows than you'd expect to draw blood. It takes an awful lot of time and effort and, frankly, dedication to beat someone to death with a flexible rod. Like a really long time. Hundreds and hundreds of blows. To your own son. Which is probably why it upset the Roman people so much when they found out about it. When Tricho next appeared in public, he was set upon by a group of furious men who stabbed him over and over with their sharp little styluses. Augustus had to send in armed men to fight off Tricho's attackers and pull him out before he was himself killed by a thousand tiny stabs. No one liked a man who could hurt his own offspring in such a manner, no matter what the kid did to deserve it.

The only real exception to this, possibly, is when dads were killing tiny newborns. There is a very strong belief among lay people that the Romans, like all ancients, spent a lot of their time giving birth to babies and then immediately tossing them out of the window like rubbish. In any general history of Roman life you will usually find a claim that is relatively similar to this quiz question in the *Horrible Histories* book *Ruthless Romans*:

> What could a Roman father do to a baby son he didn't want?
> A. Leave it outside the city to die.
> B. Throw it in the river to swim for its life.
> C. Feed it to the family dogs.[19]

MURDER IN THE FAMILY   95

The answer, apparently, was all of them. The confusion here is one that academics have been battling for at least thirty years, which is the conflation of exposure and execution. It's easy to do because we, as modern people with 2.4 children, see child abandonment occur only in times of desperation and we assume that babies being placed outdoors and rejected from their biological family means that they died. The truth is they mostly didn't. A lot of babies were exposed in local places which were sort of designated baby-abandoning spots. If you had a kid and couldn't look after it for whatever reason, such as you already had seven, then you could place it there and someone would probably pick it up. We have some such places today, protected by what are known as Safe Haven or Baby Moses laws, which sometimes allow parents to give up their parental rights and offer their babies for adoption without being prosecuted for abandonment as long as the baby is left in a hospital or at a state agency. In the ancient world, quite often, these babies were raised in slavery but there are lots and lots of cases where babies were picked up and raised, and sometimes made their way back to their bio-families, causing absolute havoc when it came to inheritance time. The most famous of all of these are Romulus and Remus, the abandoned babies who founded the city of Rome. They were the twin sons of Rhea Silva, a Vestal Virgin forced into the job by her evil uncle. Despite being a Vestal Virgin, and absolutely banned from shagging, she somehow turned up pregnant and claiming the god Mars had raped her, a story that her uncle did not believe one bit. When her twins were born, her uncle ordered the babies to be put into the river. The babies were placed in a basket and gently floated down the river far from the city. When they hit land, a wolf was drawn to the sound of them crying and allowed them to suckle from her, saving their lives. Soon afterwards, a local yokel came across the children, being licked by the wolf, and took them home to raise as his own as he and his wife had just experienced a stillbirth. The boys were raised as happy peasants until fate took its course a couple of decades later.[20]

What happened to Romulus and Remus is probably what happened to most exposed babies, without the gods and wolves. They were probably mostly picked up, and that's what biological parents expected would happen when they wrapped a baby up and put it outdoors. They expected, and maybe hoped, that their offspring would be taken in and raised by someone. They would probably live, even if they ended up enslaved. But not every infant was so lucky.

In 1912, the improbably named archaeologist Alfred Heneage Cocks excavated ninety-seven infant skeletons from graves around Yewden Villa, a Roman villa site in Hambleden, Buckinghamshire, which was inhabited from the first to fourth centuries CE. His team carefully packed each tiny skeleton into a cigarette box, popped them into storage and promptly forgot about them. Ninety-nine years later, an enterprising archaeologist with an eye for publicity 'rediscovered' the burials and went around telling the world's media that Yewden Villa was a brothel where sex workers were constantly having babies and murdering them. The media loved it. She got a whole TV show and everyone was thrilled, except other archaeologists and historians whose cries of 'hang on a minute' could barely be heard over the sound of the media revelling in stories of sexed-up baby-murdering Roman whores. The truth is, you can't really tell anything from a tiny skeleton (only thirty-three of which were found in 2011 incidentally; the other sixty-four having vanished) except that a baby died. We can't know how it died or whether a mother wept or a father laughed or no one cared at all. Modern archaeologists and demographers have estimated that around fifteen percent of pregnancies in the ancient world failed to reach full

term and twenty to forty percent of infants died during their first
year of life.[21] A baby that died of SIDS or was stillborn looks
exactly like a baby that was suffocated once it's skeletonised; a
skeleton baby does not equal a murdered baby.

Unfortunately, such inconclusive archaeology is our best
evidence for infanticide because men didn't write about it very
much at all. Exposure comes up every so often, but the deliberate killing of a newborn very rarely does. The contexts in which
it does appear, though, do tend to support the perspective that,
in most circumstances, infanticide by the family was not considered to be a social or cultural problem that ever needed to be
dealt with. It was a family issue, handled within the family and
what happened there was nobody else's business. Partly this
comes from the echoing silence around infanticide in legal and
judicial texts. No one was being prosecuted for infanticide and
there were no laws against it until precisely 7 February 374 CE (at
around teatime) when the power-sharing Christian emperors
Valentinian, Valens and Gratian suddenly got interested and
outlawed it.

The best evidence for the notion of widespread infanticide
comes from the sweeping statements of (childless) men like
Seneca, who declared 'we extinguish portentous offspring and
drown the weak and monstrous'[22] as though he drowned a baby
every other Thursday, and Plutarch who claimed that babies
were more like plants than animals before their name day.[23] But
once you look past those flippant remarks, you find that actually
there were plenty of people with disabilities living their lives in
antiquity, so obviously 'monstrous' babies (with apologies for
Seneca's offensive language) weren't routinely drowned or 'extin-
guished'. Similarly, archaeology tells us that Romans did not
routinely murder little baby girls because they 'valued' boys
more. That myth, persistent as herpes, comes from a single letter

from Roman Egypt and a whole lot of assumption. Genetic analysis of infant burial sites that could be interpreted as 'mass graves', were one to be dramatic about it, shows that the biological sex of the skeletons (where it can be identified) is usually weighted towards male babies, or a fairly even fifty-fifty split. There is no evidence at all, from anywhere in the Roman world, of sex selective infanticide.[24] The truth is that the extreme privacy of the events of childbirth and infant death for the entirety of pre-Christian Roman history means that it is impossible to know how often people killed their babies, and that it is *completely* impossible to know what such an event meant to the Romans.

The real problem is that the birth, and death, of a baby was an intensely domestic event and, as such, is completely hidden from the spotlight of history. It is all but invisible to our beady little eyes trying to peer in on it from the future. One of the things that archaeology can tell us, for example, is that infant and baby skeletons are almost never found in cemetery settings; they are found buried in domestic settings. People whose babies died (or who killed their babies) buried them quietly, often in small pots, in their gardens and courtyards. They didn't have public funerals; everything about it was private and domestic and quiet.[25] Sometimes, over the centuries, those courtyards and gardens became accidentally full of buried babies, not because of mass slaughter but because babies are fragile and centuries are long. We can know that infanticide and neonaticide were not considered to be crimes because they were never public acts. They were family acts, and the Roman state had no right to be, or interest in, intervening in people's private lives where children or death were concerned. Murders within the family, no matter who the victim was, were primarily considered to be family business.

The intriguing gap is the lack of social response to infanticide. Even as the Empire progressed and the sanctity of the private family was gradually eroded away, to the point that emperors could stop you killing your own kids, there were never any baby-killing scandals or events; no great news stories or dramas that made the history books or even the letter collections of old men. Largely this is because old rich men were not hugely concerned with the goings on of women, which included babies. Unless the baby had the head of a pig (which was portentous), they didn't care. Even then, I couldn't promise you they'd care. They'd probably not write it down. Which leaves a yawning, aching gap in the historical record where every baby that ever died sits. Every baby that didn't survive childbirth, and every baby that died from one of the myriad things that kill tiny babies in the first hours of life, and every baby that was smothered by a weeping girl who couldn't see another way out, and every one that was deliberately and coldly killed by a man who didn't give his enslaved women permission to add to his household, and every one that was accidentally smothered when his mother rolled on him and those who were left outside in the cold because they just weren't wanted, every single child and mother and father and tear and cry and laugh is lost into that black, black hole of history. And there's nothing more that can be said about them.

The Woman of Smyrna

Women who kill their children are a completely different kettle of fish to men who kill their children. They are far less visible because of the lack of a heroic, mythical framework to hang stories on, and those we do see are often very weird. Two odd examples are found in the sole surviving work of a rich dude called Valerius

Maximus – the biggest Valerius. Valerius wrote a strange miscellany of anecdotes called *Memorable Words and Deeds* and presented it to the emperor Tiberius. It's sort of the Roman very-rich-and-educated-guy version of making a scrapbook for someone you love, but who you also think needs a good talking to. Valerius wrote nine books of memorable words and deeds split into chapters that each focus on a particular virtue, like anger, bravery, fidelity, fortitude and parental love, and which all teach a lesson that Valerius thought that Tiberius should learn. Leaving aside the gall of this random man writing a whole nine books of moralising for the literal emperor, the books contain loads of fun anecdotes. Book Eight focuses on trials, and serves to illuminate how immensely subjective and unpredictable Roman courts could be. The anecdotes are, frankly, stressful. One fairly typical one goes like this: a guy named Marcus Aemilius Scaurus was put on trial for extortion, which means threatening and stealing from the people in the province he was meant to be looking after. Scaurus' defence, says Valerius, was pathetic – totally hopeless – to the point that the prosecutor started taking the piss out of him in court. At one stage, the prosecutor said that if Scaurus could produce just 120 people from the whole province that he hadn't stolen from, he'd let Scaurus go. Scaurus was unable to do so, since he was an unrepentant crook, so it might seem to the reader that he would be found guilty. But only if that reader had not been paying attention to Valerius Maximus' previous court reporting. Naturally, Scaurus was let off because his family was old and everyone mostly liked his dad. That's the whole anecdote. The lesson, one assumes, is that you can do whatever you like if you're from a good family: go plunder all the provinces and torment all the colonial commoners you like, my friend, as long as your dad is aristocratic and nice. Plus ça change etc. On the other end of the spectrum, Valerius records the story of a man who borrowed a pal's horse to ride to Ariccia (sixteen miles out-side Rome). The man went to Ariccia, and then also went up a hill just slightly to the south of it. Then he took the horse home. When the horse's owner found out that his mate had gone slightly *past* Ariccia and up a hill, he was furious and prosecuted his mate for theft. And, despite still having the horse, which was patently un-stolen, in his possession, he won.

Book Eight is also where we find the anecdote about the brothers who killed their dad and were let off because they were found asleep. And another story about a man called Calidius of Bononia who was caught one night in a married man's bedroom, presumably by the married man who was shocked to find a nude man from Bononia chatting to his wife in his bedroom at 2 a.m. Calidius was brought to court to answer a charge of adultery, which it really does seem that he was committing. He was asked to present a defence. Maybe imagine here the praetor, in front of the jury and the crowd of onlookers and the cuckolded husband and probably everyone's dads too, demanding that Calidius answer what he was doing in someone else's marital bedroom at night. What possible reason could he have for being there? A pause. An awkward cough. The shifty look of a man about to go as low as he could to save his own life. And when Calidius finally spoke he said, 'I was there not for the woman' (name not recorded). 'I was there . . .' A pause. '. . . because I wanted to bang the slave-boy.' Valerius is great at this point. He says that Calidius was found in a suspicious place, with the wife there, in the middle of the night and that he had a reputation as a shag-ger of men's wives but, somehow, the confession of what Valerius calls 'lack of self-control' got him off the charge of adultery. These days such a bizarre event would get a name, like the Twinkie defence did.[26] This story has no relevance here. I just like it.

Anyway, in among all these little stories are two extraordinary tales of women who were neither acquitted nor convicted in their trials. Each woman is unnamed because the Romans tried to avoid naming women if they could help it – one annoying walking-uterus is much the same as another to the Romans – but each committed a murder. The first was brought before the praetor in Rome because she had beaten her own mother to death with a club. One is forced to wonder whether she tried to cover up her crime. Perhaps she tried to blame a wandering bandit or someone else. Or maybe she was found, bloodied stick in hand, bits of her mother's brain matter and offal still spattered across her tunic, proud and angry. We shall never know. The incident is unusually brutal for a Roman woman, who are very, very rarely seen to commit violence of this kind in the surviving sources. Women poison, men bludgeon. This particular woman was driven to extreme violence, however, by the actions of the mother herself. The mother had, in an act of breathtaking cruelty and heartlessness, poisoned her two grandchildren, her daughter's babies, because she was angry with her daughter (reasons unknown). When the woman learned that her children had not been taken by random illness or bad luck, but by the malice of her own mother, the ensuing grief had driven her to snatch up a stick and go ham on her mother's skull. When the jury heard this, they effectively called off the trial. They concluded that by committing the murder of her own grandchildren, the mother had forfeited her own life. Therefore, her daughter killing her was not murder, but legitimate vengeance and so the daughter couldn't be found guilty of parricide. However, the violence of the vengeance, and the fact that killing a parent was always, always wrong in Roman eyes, meant that nor could she be acquitted of parricide. She was, she admitted, guilty but equally she was morally not guilty. This is where a charge of manslaughter or second-degree murder or really any abstract concept would have come in handy, but alas the Romans weren't keen on such things. As the woman couldn't be condemned and couldn't be acquitted, the court decided to just let the whole thing go, not vote at all, and really hope the entire situation went away. Which it did. You might argue that this meant that she had, in fact, totally got away with it and you'd be right; but at least the guys on the jury didn't have to take any responsibility.

A very similar solution was found to a very similar case which occurred in Smyrna (now İzmir in Turkey) when Publius Cornelius Dolabella was proconsul in about 68 BCE. A proconsul in a Roman province had essentially unrestrained power to enact justice as he liked and a large part of his job was sorting out the problems that arose between the inhabitants of the province. You'll remember that from such stories as Pontius Pilate executing peaceful young messiahs for being annoying.[†] During Dolabella's term in the province of Asia,[27] a woman was brought to him who was accused of poisoning her husband and son. When asked about it, she said that she *had* killed them, but only because they had conspired between themselves and murdered her oldest child, her adult son from her first marriage. Dolabella was confronted with the same impossible bind with which the Roman court had wrestled. The woman had, by her own admission, killed two people in her own family. However, she had been grieving immensely and her grief was justified, and also the victims were murderers. She could not be truly found guilty, because the victims' actions had been heinous and her mind hadn't been all there. Her responsibility, as our lawyers might say, was diminished, but equally, she had killed her son. Again we lament the brutal pragmatism of the Romans. All they had was guilty and innocent and Dolabella had to come up with a solution.

---

† I know he was a Prefect but the point still stands.

Obviously, his solution was to pass the buck. He sent the poor woman to Athens to be tried again on the Areopagus. The Areopagus, for those of you who haven't been to Athens, is a very large, very pointy, very difficult to access and very uncomfortable rocky outcrop at the bottom of the Acropolis. It is where the classical Athenians tried their most important cases: murder, religious crimes, arson and the damaging of olive trees. The Athenians took olives very seriously. It's where Orestes was tried for the murder of his mother Clytemnestra in Aeschylus' tragedy *The Libation Bearers* and probably where Socrates was tried for saying there were no gods. It was a big deal back in the day. By the time of Dolabella, it didn't have quite the same power because the Romans were in charge but it still had a hefty cultural cachet, so that's where he bumped it to. The members of this jury were tied by the exact same bind, and had the added pressure of not wanting to piss off their Roman overlords who had refused to make a decision. Basically any decision they made would mean that they had disagreed with a Roman official. Simply not worth the career-limiting hassle for any self-interested local statesman. The members of the Areopagus came up with a genius idea: they postponed the trial. For a hundred years. The poor woman, presumably, returned to Smyrna to try to process the horror of losing her entire family and both her sons in a brutal whirlwind of cruelty and revenge, but at least she wasn't executed, I guess.

We can learn a lot from these horrors. First, we can see what kind of atrocity needs to occur for something to break out of the obscurity of a family *consilium* and be dealt with by the public courts. Secondly, we learn that Romans didn't think that a person could be *truly* guilty of a murder if they weren't in their right mind and this is perhaps the most interesting lesson: the Romans had an insanity defence. In Anglo-American law and practice, the insanity defence is based on the 1843 case of a guy called Daniel M'Naughten[28] who would probably today be diagnosed with a pretty hefty dose of paranoid schizophrenia but at the time was considered to be merely quite irritating by his friends and family because he would not shut up about being stalked by the Tories in Glasgow. Were he alive today, M'Naughten would have been found on niche message boards complaining about gangstalking until he was given some anti-psychotics, but in the 1840s, he was just ignored. Eventually, unsupported by his loved ones in his crusade against the local councillors he believed to be following and harassing him (council budgets were presumably bigger in the 1840s), he decided to go a bit Ender Wiggin on the situation and end the entire Tory party by killing the head Tory: the Prime Minister Robert Peel (yes, the one who started the police force, somewhat coincidentally). Sadly, M'Naughten's aim was as addled as his mental capacities and he shot Peel's private secretary Edward Drummond instead. While the wound was not fatal, Victorian medicine unfortunately was and after a few days of bleeding and leeches and god knows what else, Drummond passed away and M'Naughten was hauled up before a court to account for it.

His defence team insisted that M'Naughten had been incapable of understanding what he was doing as he literally thought that he was being stalked by Tories and was clearly insensible. And they won. He was bustled off to Bethlem Hospital (where he was described upon admission as 'imagines the Tories are his enemies, shy and retiring in his manner', which could describe so many of us) and the country got up in arms, as the British are occasionally wont to do. The resulting debate in the House of Commons concluded that 'to establish a defence on the ground of insanity it must be clearly proved that, at the time of committing the act, the party accused was labouring under such a defect of reason from disease of the mind, as not to know the nature and quality of the act he was doing, or if he did know it, that he did not know that what he was doing was wrong'.[29] This formulation went on to be the foundation of the insanity defence in English, American and Commonwealth law for a century or so and basically still is now.

The Roman version of Daniel M'Naughten was Aelius Priscus, about whom we know just one thing: he murdered his mother while mad during the time when Marcus Aurelius was co-ruling with his rubbish son Commodus. His crime is recalled in the *Digest*, bafflingly in a section which describes the duties of a provincial governor, because the governor of the province of Africa,[30] Scapula Tertullus, had written to Marcus Aurelius and Commodus to ask for help in deciding his case. On the one hand, Aelius had murdered his mother and this was a truly horrible crime that deserved the most extreme punishment (that bit is a quote). On the other, he appeared to be quite ill and have no clue what he was doing or why and so punishing him as though he were a reasonable man seemed unfair and cruel to Scapula. The emperors' reply was that Scapula must establish that Aelius was *definitely* mad and not faking it and then, should he be determined to be genuinely mentally unwell, he should be released to the custody of his remaining family because 'he is being punished enough by his very madness'.[31] This makes the Romans considerably more sympathetic to those suffering from mental illness than many in the modern world, including the four states in the USA that do not allow for an insanity defence plea or a finding of not guilty by reason of insanity, meaning that severely ill people end up stuck in prison or on death row.

A second important aside here is what happens to both Daniel M'Naughten and Aelius Priscus. As I said, M'Naughten was sent off to Bethlem Hospital. This institution is better known to you and me as Bedlam, a hospital that began housing the mentally ill in the fourteenth century where patients were considered inmates and were kept chained and naked much of the time and were provided for, in the barest minimum way, by the state. He was later moved to Broadmoor, which is still Britain's high security mental health hospital, albeit at a different location, having housed everyone from Charles Bronson to the Yorkshire Ripper to Ronnie Kray. For the rest of his life, the state took care of him. The state kept him from harming anyone else, fed him, housed him, changed his bedlinen and treated his illnesses. This approach to the murderously mentally ill is, in historical terms, unusual. In the great span of human history, the vast majority of men, women and people beyond the binary whose paranoia, delusions or broken grip on reality led them to spill the blood of innocents were sent home to their families, and their parents, siblings, spouses and children were charged with caring for them.

The Romans had a neat little twist on this, though. As well as being responsible for the care of Priscus, the Aelian (not alien) family were also made criminally responsible if he ever hurt anyone again. In fact, our pals Marcus Aurelius and Commodus continued their letter to Scapula by insisting that he find out whether Priscus' family were aware of his condition prior to the matricide incident and were 'looking after him' because 'those who have custody of the insane are not responsible only for seeing that they do not do themselves too much harm but also for seeing that they do not bring destruction on others'. Which is utterly wild to the modern eye. In our Western, individualist world, we don't even hold parents responsible for the criminal behaviour of their children. The English courts didn't prosecute the parents of Jon Venables and Robert Thompson, and they were ten when they became murderers. Admittedly, Americans are different here and do like to pursue civil suits against parents when murderers are too dead to be sued, but state prosecutors don't get involved in this weirdness, because the official stance of the state is that the person who did the killing is the only person who is criminally responsible.[32] Even if the Stockwell Strangler broke out of Broadmoor and went on another terrible rape and murder spree, no one would prosecute the Broadmoor head of security for failing in his duties, because the only person responsible for those acts would be Kenneth Erskine himself. As far as the imperial Romans of the second century CE were concerned, though, Priscus' parents, siblings and assorted relations were expected to be, literally, criminally responsible for his behaviour and be punished should Priscus somehow get away and murder someone when they should have been keeping an eye on him.

This is because the Roman family is not like the Western family. The Western family is, at least ideally, centred on a married couple. As husband and wife, mum and dad, they are the core unit around whom everyone else orbits. New family units are created when a wedding takes place. If you spend as much time on relationship advice forums as I do, firstly I'm sorry you got sucked into that too, and secondly you'll know how often Anglophone commenters tell posters that when they got married, their spouse became their primary family. This usually comes up when people are having problems with their parents disliking their spouse or when parents start needing care. Comments like 'You need to prioritise your husband over your mother' and 'You are failing as a wife to protect your husband from your mom' and 'You have your own family now and they are your priority, above all else'[33] are extremely common when conflict arises between parents and spouses. That last one, for example, is advice to a dude who is trying to care for his elderly dying mother while also supporting his pregnant wife, and the universal response to his dilemma is to put his mother in a nursing home and focus one hundred percent on his wife as his 'own family'. Such a response would not just be bizarre to a Roman, it would be repugnant. Actively offensive. It would genuinely be considered quite unnatural in a repellent kind of way. Husband and wife weren't at the core of distinct little family units for the Romans; for them (and I'm mostly talking about upper-class families here) the oldest living man formed the core of a potentially vast *familia*. Marriage did not create families for Romans. It created alliances between two *familiae*, which remained separate.

The problem with understanding this arises from the fact that English nicked the word family from *familia* so we tend to assume that *familia* describes a family when really it describes something closer to a tribe or a clan. The *familia* consists of one's whole immediate and extended family, plus people who have been enslaved, plus formerly enslaved people who have been freed who now have a limited kind of freedom but are still around and share the family name forever, plus any random men who might have been adopted in and also all the dead relatives whose death masks are on the walls and who remain a vital, living part of a *familia*'s name and reputation forever. A *familia* is a big group of people, living and dead, linked together by biology, kinship, duty, obligation, affection and the law and has little in common with the mum, dad and 2.4 kids of the modern West. The nuclear family bit of the Roman *familia* is the *domus* – the household. That's everyone who lives with you, so is much closer to the unit of mum, dad and the kids, but it also includes Polybius the ex-enslaved person, the wet nurse, and the five enslaved people who do all the work. You can kind of see (though it is stretching the point a bit) the remnants of the *familia* (this theory absolutely will not stand up to scrutiny but I'm quite committed to it) in the Sicilian capital-F Family of the *Godfather* movies. The Family is led by a boss, surrounded by advisers, and every time you think you're out with your nice non-Family wife, they drag you back in because you can't escape family, Michael. (I'm so sorry.) Seeing Roman families as tribes or clans is much more helpful than seeing them as little nuclear families in their little nuclear houses because the *familia* was something far bigger than the individual and more important than the state.[34] The *familia* underpinned the whole of Roman society and culture, especially at the very top, which is the only bit that we really have access to.

So when the emperors ask whether Aelius Priscus' family need to be held accountable for failing to prevent Priscus from going berserk on his mum, they were not asking a small group of individuals like you and me to take responsibility for their son or brother or cousin; they were asking a big structure of interconnected individuals, including those who were un-free and semi-free, to take responsibility for their failure to fulfil their duties to Roman society by keeping their problems under control and within the *familia*. As far as the state – represented by Marcus Aurelius and Commodus – was concerned, the *familia* had a duty and an obligation to protect the mentally ill person from harming himself and anyone else because he could not prevent himself.

4

Murder in Marriage

Apronia

In that context, marriage in the elite Roman world was primarily about the connection between two families. It tied the fortunes and reputations of two *familiae* together, for better and for worse. As a result, there are even fewer glimpses into what happened within a marriage than there are within single families because two families worked together to keep things quiet. We only get to see when things went wrong when the two families fell out, such as when a man from one *familia* killed a woman from another. There are two particularly high-profile cases of spouse murder from the Roman world, and they are both cases of men killing their wives. It was pretty easy for Roman men to kill their wives because the family was a unit that was mostly shielded from public scrutiny. Dealings between husband and wife rarely moved beyond the walls of their villa because women had no legal recourse outside of their families. Women were perpetual minors, unable to sign contracts or represent themselves in anything legal. They wouldn't be allowed to buy alcohol or lottery tickets in the modern world because they were viewed as being too childlike and thick to be trusted to look after themselves. They had to have male guardians to look after them and sign things for them and make sure they didn't spend all their money on shoes and eyeliner by accident. This was usually their father, sometimes their husband, sometimes just a family friend. Cicero's finest hour was dumping his wife for a young, very rich woman who was under his guardianship so he could use her money, which is super-gross. This guardianship relationship can be abusive or it can be supportive or it can be a partnership, but there is always, always a power dynamic at work and women are always the ones without power. This meant that women didn't have much in the way of recourse if something went wrong in their marriage and it turned out that their husband beat them, or worse. They could divorce, if their guardian agreed to it, or they could ask their guardian for help but they had a very limited ability to help themselves. Instead, their families had to help them and agree to enact self-service justice.

The cases of domestic murder from Rome range across the whole of Roman history and illustrate how variable the Roman notion of self-service justice could be. One of the earliest comes from the reign of Tiberius, about 24 CE, recorded by Tacitus about eighty years later, and it's an odd one. Tacitus wrote about it simply because Tiberius, for reasons unknown, got very personally involved.

Like all the best detective stories, the story opens with the body of a woman being found in Rome in the early hours of the morning. The sun was rising, the birds were singing, and a woman's crumpled body was lying on the ground. The body was that of Apronia, the wife of the praetor Plautius Silvanus, and she had fallen, somehow, from a high bedroom window and not survived the fall. This was suspicious. Apronia was the daughter of Lucius Apronius, who was a very important man in Rome. He had enjoyed a very successful military career in Germany and Dalmatia and had jointly put down a revolt in Illyricum.[1] For this act, he had been granted the right to wear Triumphal Regalia, which was a really special outfit. Being the daughter of a man who was allowed to wear the special outfit was a bit like being the daughter of Brad Pitt; everyone wanted to marry Apronia so they could hang out with her dad. Her dad had chosen Marcus Plautius Silvanus, who was a man doing well for himself. He was praetor in 24 CE, which is just below consul in terms of prestige, and the fact that he married the daughter of Apronius suggested that he was a man on the up.

Unfortunately for Silvanus, Apronia died painfully, hitting the Roman ground hard. Even more unfortunately for Silvanus, Apronius did not believe that his daughter, his good Roman daughter of excellent stock, had simply stumbled and fallen out of her bedroom window in the middle of the night by accident because that is a ludicrous thing to happen. Nor did Apronius, and please imagine here the most clichéd upstanding Roman man you can, a straight-backed, no-bullshit military man in his fine purple toga, think that his daughter had deliberately defenestrated herself, which was Silvanus' version of events. He believed that Silvanus had pushed her. He believed this strongly enough that he wanted Silvanus prosecuted for it. And he wanted this taken all the way to the emperor.

Now, you'll note that we have already diverged from what we may expect the narrative to be. In our murder mystery stories, the dead woman is found in the prologue and chapter one opens with the grizzled alcoholic detective examining the crime scene; but no police will appear to investigate Apronia's suspicious death. There was no representative of the state of Rome who would get involved in this case until Apronius took it to the emperor because, as far as the Romans were concerned, the murder of wives, children, husbands or really anyone at all was absolutely none of their business.

There's a bit in Agatha Christie's *They Do It with Mirrors* where Miss Marple advocates for locking up a man she views as a 'dangerous lunatic' for the 'good of the community'. It is, in Marple's mind, and in most of our minds, the job of the state to identify 'dangerous' people and tidy them away where they can't do any more damage. People such as murderers, of whom

Marple has known many. This is a useful demonstration of how fundamentally differently we view the role of the state to the Romans, and how we differentiate between public and private business. To most of us, it is obvious that the state has a responsibility to keep its people safe, and that it uses the apparatus of the police and the justice system to do this. When someone is murdered, the police investigate, the prosecution service prosecutes and the prison service takes the murderer away and keeps them locked up until they are judged to be safe. The relatives of the victim aren't expected to get involved because murder is a public business. The state has two broad functions here: it dispenses justice and punishes the wrongdoer, thus rebalancing the scales of justice, and it protects the people of the state by identifying a cause of harm and preventing it from causing further harm. In much the same way, the state is also now expected to make sure that rotten food isn't sold in shops and substances judged to be dangerous, like heroin, aren't freely available. We pay taxes so the state will keep us safe. On the other hand, we don't expect the state to be getting all up in our bedrooms, legalising who women can have sex with or rewarding women with public honours for having children. That's private. The Romans, however, saw things very differently. Rewarding women for babies was A-OK, making laws about how much jewellery a girl could wear was just sensible policy. But murder? That was family business. If a woman was murdered by her husband, it was her guardian's job to work that out, find a prosecutor (or act as one) and take him to court if the family wanted to or arrange a fair compensation to be paid if not. There were no police to come and gather evidence or prisons to put dangerous people into, in the same way that there wasn't a Food and Drugs Administration or Food Standards Agency to make sure that *tavernae* weren't poisoning people with old meat and that children couldn't buy knives. That sort of thing was up to the gods and the individual.

The justice system in Rome was one based purely on personal responsibility. The individual was responsible for identifying that a crime had taken place, identifying who had committed the crime, and finding a resolution. Success, however, relied on three things. First, the perpetrator had to be identified, then they had to admit that they did it, and then both parties had to agree on an appropriate level of compensation, which the perpetrator then had to actually pay. None of these was particularly easy. And we regularly see in curse tablets what happened when these steps didn't work out. Curse tablets are bits of lead on which ancient people wrote curses. They then rolled them up, nailed them shut and buried them at shrines in the hope that a generous god would smite the person who thieved their pot. We'll look at curse tablets in more detail later but, for now, trust me when I say that an awful lot of them were written by people who were super pissed off that someone stole their pig/gloves/favourite shoes and asked the gods to bring pain and death to that person. Sometimes they knew that Quintus stole their thing or killed their chicken but they couldn't prove it, so they asked Jupiter to harm Quintus specifically. The personal responsibility system was a system with flaws. It also allowed some people to have more access to justice than others. Like Apronius.

Now, Apronius could have had a sit-down chat with Silvanus himself and worked out some compensation between them but Apronius was, as previously mentioned, very important and he wanted more. He wanted public justice to be done and for everyone in Rome to know that Silvanus was a murderer and his daughter a victim. Luckily for him, he had the imperial access to make that happen. In addition, Silvanus was now acting very weirdly indeed. Apronius managed to have Silvanus pulled up in front of Tiberius for questioning very quickly, which would speak to his power and influence by itself. Emperors like Tiberius usually spent their time worrying about what entire provinces and colonised countries were doing, not what one idiot praetor did in his house. Most of the time, anyway. Tiberius was a grumpy old man, pretty much from birth, but seemed to have absolutely loved a mystery. He was a budding Miss Marple of the Roman world and something about this case caught his attention and he got really invested in it. This might have been because Silvanus' grandma was Tiberius' mother's best friend. Livia and Urgulania (Is this the worst name in history? Quite possibly yes.) were inseparable, and Livia was more than a little influential in her son's early reign. We'll come back to her later too. Or it might have been that he just really liked Apronius. First, Tiberius questioned Silvanus about what had happened to poor Apronia and Tacitus tells us that Silvanus gave an 'incoherent' answer in which he claimed that he had been fast asleep the whole time but he assumed his wife had killed herself. Unfortunately for us, it's not recorded why he thought his wife might defenestrate herself while he was sleeping. Maybe his snoring was awful. Tiberius didn't believe him. We know this because he did something really unusual: he went to look at the crime scene.

This is, I believe, the only time in recorded Roman history that an emperor decided to investigate a murder by examining the scene of the crime. These things just didn't happen in Rome because they didn't have the same ideas about evidence and crimes that we have. Their murder trials didn't involve people looking at daggers or gloves or other bits of physical evidence. They just involved people reciting really good speeches at each other, each using the same rhetorical strategies, mostly about the character of the defendant and/or victim and their general demeanour in life rather than the actual events of the case in question, until the jury or judge picked whichever person they liked best. Examining a crime scene wasn't a particularly important part of that process. Tiberius going off to have a look at the window from which Apronia fell was therefore very surprising. So surprising, in fact, that Silvanus hadn't even bothered trying to tidy up after the murder had been committed and Tiberius was able to see immediately what Tacitus calls 'traces of resistance offered and force employed'. Frustratingly, he does not elaborate on what these signs were. Maybe chairs had been flung across the room, or curtains had been torn down or there was blood on the soft furnishings. This blows my mind a little bit. Silvanus was a rich man. He had a significant household of enslaved people. And yet he apparently didn't even bother to ask them to tidy up a bit and make it look rather less like there'd been a fatal incident in the bedroom. No one took it upon themselves to have a wee whizz round with a mop while he was out with the emperor. Presumably, no one expected *the* august Tiberius to take time out of his busy day being in charge of all of Western Europe and North Africa to nip round for a look. No other emperor would have done this, even for their mum's best friend's grandson. Tiberius just loved a mystery. There are lots of nice stories of Tiberius investigating things that interested him. He pops up in Pliny the Elder's *Natural History* (basically an encyclopaedia of everything Pliny could think of) investigating some odd sea monsters who appeared due to an unusual low tide around modern Lyon (including sea-elephants and sea-rams apparently), and in the wonderfully deranged Phlegon of Tralles' collection of Greek and Roman marvels, making casts of some giant teeth and bones which had appeared in Turkey. The tooth was a foot long, says Phlegon, and Tiberius had a model of the full-sized giant measured from the tooth, making him, as

Adrienne Mayor points out, the world's first palaeontologist.[†] Tiberius was basically a wannabe Fox Mulder, wanting to investigate any weird thing that got put in front of him, and that included Silvanus' incoherent story that his wife spontaneously launched herself out of a window while he was innocently sleeping.

One Italian historian has posited another reason why Tiberius might have found this a particularly interesting case by suggesting that this Marcus Plautius Silvanus might also be the Servius Plautus recorded by St Jerome in the fourth century CE as being guilty of sexually assaulting his own son in 24 CE. If Servius Plautus and Plautius Silvanus are the same person, then he was one hell of a terrible person. He was a man who was caught somehow sexually assaulting his own son – Jerome offers only that he 'corrupted' his son so details are scarce – and then, while facing prosecution for this, killed his wife by hurling her out of a window. And let's think about the logistics of that for a second. Stop right now and really think about this. Think about trying to bundle up a grown-ass woman, who is presumably not co-operating, and getting all her limbs out of a window without her holding onto the windowsill. Imagine the very physical, very determined fight you would have to have to do that. Even assuming that he had help, this was a hard way to kill someone. It's a manner of murder that suggests both a lack of foreplanning and a serious dedication to killing the victim. And if Servius and Silvanus were the same man, perhaps that gave Tiberius (and Apronius) an idea of why he might have murdered Apronia. It's easy to imagine a wife who is deeply unhappy with her sexually abusive husband and the fight that might arise as a result. The

---

† The tooth was almost certainly a dinosaur tooth, unsurprisingly misinterpreted as that of a giant.

surprising thing is that it would happen within such a 'respectable' family home, where emotional control and maintaining face
were important cultural behaviours.

But apparently it did happen, and Tiberius found the
evidence and sent Silvanus to the Senate to be tried officially and
sentenced (he was maintaining a façade of pseudo-democracy at
the time). Silvanus was not destined to face a trial, though. His
grandmother Urgulania intervened and politely sent him a
dagger. This parcel was taken as a not-very-subtle hint from
both his family and the emperor that Silvanus should save everyone some time and money and honourably punish himself with
a quick dagger to the heart. Silvanus was not dedicated to the
idea of killing himself, probably his most relatable opinion, and
after failing to stab himself (again, relatable) he had an enslaved
man cut his wrists for him. Whether justice was served is rather
a matter of opinion. He lost his life, but there is certainly the
feeling that by being allowed to die at home by his own hand and
avoid the spectacle of a trial he rather got away with it. It feels
like history let him get away with it a bit too.

There is a whole extra level of intrigue to the murder of
Apronia that Tacitus leaves out completely, probably because he
works hard to erase female involvement in anything as much as
possible, the old misogynist. Silvanus had a sister called Plautia
Urgulanilla, who was briefly married to the future emperor
Claudius. Suetonius makes a very passing remark that Urgulanilla
was divorced by Claudius 'on suspicion of scandalous lewdness
and murder', and it is a fair belief that the murder he refers to is
the murder of Plautia Urgulanilla's sister-in-law Apronia. This
suggests that Apronia's defenestration was not a crime of passion
committed in the heat of a midnight row, but a calculated family
affair. Combined with the possibility that Silvanus was Jerome's
Servius, we get the dreadful possibility that the brother and sister

duo were both involved in some kind of horror show involving Silvanus' son and, when that was uncovered, they killed his wife together and tried, poorly, to cover it up as a suicide. Notably, all Urgulanilla lost was her husband and there is no suggestion that she was brought up before anyone by Apronius or that Tiberius was interested in her at all.

Tacitus, however, offers another motive, developed by Silvanus' friends after his forced suicide. His mates, and what great mates they were, thought that it was impossible that such a respectable man would kill his wife and concluded that he must have gone mad. Insanity was often perceived to be the result of magic or the gods, but mostly magic. We see this, for example, when Suetonius says that lots of people believed that the emperor Gaius Caligula went mad because his final wife Caesonia had given him too many love potions. Silvanus' pals came to the same conclusion about Silvanus and they hit upon his first wife Numantina as the culprit. Poor Numantina, who was presumably minding her own business and enjoying the scandal, found herself accused of witchcraft and of sending her husband insane using spells and potions. This was a very serious crime, and she was hauled in front of a jury by her accusers. Thankfully, she was found innocent – one assumes because her character was otherwise blameless. It shows, however, how very outlandish the notion of a high-ranking senatorial man killing his wife was to his friends. The most plausible explanation they could find was not that he was a bad man who killed to protect or revenge himself, but that he was suffering magically induced madness.

Regilla

That there is only one other high-profile case of wife-murder in the entire history of the Roman Empire, and that this other case doesn't appear for another century and a half suggests that either high-ranking men killing their wives was reasonably rare or people just didn't care enough when men killed their wives to bring it to public attention. That second case is that of Appia Annia Regilla Atilla Caucadia Tertulla. The Romans called her Aspasia Annia Regilla, but in English we call her simply Regilla. In 160 CE, Regilla was murdered by her husband, Herodes Atticus. You almost certainly know Herodes Atticus at least a little bit if you've ever been to Athens or seen photos of the very well-preserved, and still used, theatre built into the side of the Acropolis hill: that's Herodes Atticus' theatre. It's enormous, and it was built by a private citizen during the Roman era to honour the wife he killed: Regilla Atticus.

Herodes Atticus was the kind of man who has been effectively eliminated in the modern West, except in England. He's a figure like Boris Johnson and Jacob Rees-Mogg who can only exist in a society that has an ancient aristocracy, immense inequality and a belief that the rich are just somehow fundamentally better at things than the rest of us. He was an Athenian by birth but a Roman citizen, born in 101 CE. Extraordinarily rich, a committed patron of the arts, a vocal member of a broad group of men who claimed to celebrate intellectual virtue and were very irritating about it, he entered the Roman Senate and won at that by becoming a consul and a great pal of several emperors. He had a family that could be traced back to the classical Athenians (who were considered ancient and venerable even by the Romans) and he claimed both Achilles and Zeus as ancestors. On the Roman side, one of his many, many middle names was Claudius, giving him claim to the antiquity and prestige of a patrician and imperial Roman family. Like so many rich boys from rich parents who can do whatever they like, he was also absolutely horrible.

Short bios of Herodes, like his Wikipedia page, tend to be highly flattering and describe the books he wrote and the buildings he erected, of which there were many. Herodes was ostentatiously generous when it came to building things that would bear his name for millennia. He built games stadiums in Athens and Delphi, aqueducts in Canusium and Alexandria Troas, baths at Thermopylae (site of the legendary three hundred Spartans), a theatre in Corinth, waterworks in Troy, fountains in Olympia and on and on. He threw money at things he liked because he had an almost infinite supply of it. One of my personal favourite Herodes Atticus stories comes from a biography written by a guy named Philostratus. Philostratus claims that Herodes' third son Atticus struggled significantly with learning to read and write, which was embarrassing to the intellectual Herodes. Herodes' brilliant solution, apparently, was to bring in twenty-four boys, name them after the letters of the Greek alphabet and get the kid to learn his letters that way. Which is the kind of absurd idea only the very, very wealthy can have. To use the lives and names of twenty-four people just to teach one child a single piece of knowledge is really something and gives a little insight into how Herodes Atticus thought about other people.[†]

On top of being conspicuously extravagant in his spending, Herodes was also an angry, violent man who treated everyone beneath him and occasionally even those above him with cruelty

---

[†] Another good story about Herodes which is utterly irrelevant but great is that he once met a man whom everyone called Hercules who was eight feet tall and had a monobrow and claimed to be immortal. Herodes was so impressed by Hercules that he invited him to tea, an invitation Hercules accepted on condition that no woman touch any of his food or drink. When he arrived, he took one look at the milk, declared that a woman's filthy hands had touched it and stormed out. Herodes went investigating and discovered that a woman had milked the cow. He marvelled. That's the whole story. Its total pointlessness is part of its charm.

and contempt. One of the first things he did when his father died was scam every Athenian citizen out of the legacy that his father had left them in his will. The second thing he did was start terrorising all the enslaved people and freedmen that he inherited from his father. He spent his life getting into feuds with other rich dudes, including one extraordinary moment where he got into an argument with the emperor Antoninus Pius (don't worry, no one else remembers him either) while they were walking up a mountain together, which ended with Herodes punching the emperor in the face. Philostratus denies that an actual punch happened but concedes that Antoninus and Herodes got into a 'what-did-you-just-say-to-me' shoving match. As Antoninus Pius was the actual emperor and Herodes was merely the non-imperial governor of bits of Greece at the time, and as the general tone of approach to the imperial family was boot-licking sycophancy, for him to get into a physical fight with Antoninus is quite extraordinary and suggests that he was a real bastard.

Herodes didn't get married until he was forty, because he wanted a wife whose father was of consular rank and he was willing to wait. By the time he was forty, he had been consul and had got cosy with the imperial family as, despite the fighting, Antoninus Pius had brought him in to tutor his adopted sons and co-heirs Marcus Aurelius and Lucius Verus (again, no one else remembers Verus either, it's fine). With these connections, he was able to secure himself an ideal bride: a fourteen-year-old girl from a distant part of the imperial family.

Having become one of the richest, best-connected and most powerful men in the Empire and locked in a child bride, Herodes wasted little time in finalising his perfect life by getting himself some heirs. Regilla gave birth to her first child when she was sixteen years old and her husband forty-two. Her son died within months but she was pregnant again almost immediately. She proceeded to have two daughters when she was seventeen and eighteen, another son when she was twenty, which possibly allowed her to rest for a while, and then a final son at twenty-five. When she died, aged thirty, she was pregnant again. It's unknown whether these were her only pregnancies. Most of the reason it is unknown is that no sources cared at all about Regilla. Even modern sources on Herodes rarely bother to mention her and when they do they tend to suggest quite strongly that she was an equal partner in her marriage. Her Wikipedia page, for example, quaintly states that the first thing she did with her dowry upon marriage was buy Herodes a present of a massive villa in Rome, as if a fourteen-year-old girl made that decision *entirely* voluntarily.

There's no way of knowing what Regilla's life was like either before or after her marriage. She was immensely rich and aristocratic so she had comforts that other women never had, but she was married long before we would consider her to be a woman. It's not hard to imagine her marital life as pretty grim. She was a teenager whisked off to a middle-aged man's house and kept pregnant in Greece. Her husband was not a pleasant man. He wanted a male heir and kept her pregnant until one survived. He also filled her homes with adopted and fostered sons, whom he treated with enormous affection. Polydeuces in particular he seems to have adored in the slightly frightening manner of a much older man to whom no one can say no. Copying Hadrian (another powerful older man whose relationship with a much younger man of far inferior status is gross as hell and yet considered to be somehow adorable), Herodes erected innumerable statues of Polydeuces, more than anyone in the whole Empire erected of anyone outside the imperial family, and a whole lot of inscriptions denoting every place that Polydeuces ever stood. That's not a joke; Herodes literally put up an inscription stating that he once stood at a fork in the road with him. Such behaviour, and the fact that Polydeuces is depicted as a hottie, and the Athenian connection have led a lot of historians to suggest that Herodes was banging him. A distinct possibility. Either way, the relationship was unequal and creepy. It was made even more creepy, and probably unpleasant for Regilla, when Herodes' mum started putting up statues of Polydeuces after his death too. Because, of course, Polydeuces died young, probably while still a teenager, and under slightly mysterious circumstances. A contemporary of Herodes, Fronto, wrote that Herodes was cruel, avaricious, violent, wicked and worthless; a disloyal son, a tyrannical leader and a murderer.[2] Perhaps this man was sweet and loving to Regilla behind closed doors, but what happened to her suggests not.

Regilla died at the age of thirty while eight months into her sixth pregnancy after sixteen years of marriage to Herodes. She was beaten to death. Philostratus tells us that Herodes had her beaten for 'some small slight' and that a kick to the stomach caused her to go into labour, which killed her. She died horribly and slowly, in pain and blood and humiliation. We have no way of knowing whether this was the first time Herodes had her beaten. From what we now know about domestic abuse, it seems unlikely that this fatal event would be the first and only incident of violence in sixteen years. Speculating on the regularity of domestic violence in Roman marriages is impossible but it certainly existed and there were factions of Roman thinkers who considered beating one's wife to be basically fine. The most commonly cited example comes from Valerius Maximus who approvingly recorded a probably fictional event in which a man beat his wife to death with a wooden club for the sin of getting drunk and jeopardising her virtue. He's clearly harking back to a 'more moral' imaginary Roman past in which men were men and women were obedient rather than describing a reality, but I still wouldn't want to marry him. Nor would I shack up with Propertius, a poet who wrote love poems, one of which explicitly threatened his girlfriend Cynthia that if she slept with someone else, he would kill her and then himself: 'both our blood will drip from the same sword,' he wrote in lines which sound like a Reddit incel and literally every man who ever murdered their girlfriend.[3] More closely related to Herodes and Regilla is the emperor Nero who kicked his pregnant wife Poppea to death in a fit of rage because he was a selfish, violent little murderer. The interesting point of divergence between these cases and Regilla, however, is that Nero and this mythical clubbing man and Propertius in his imagination killed women with their own hands (or feet), while Herodes used a tool: his freedman Alcimedon. Herodes was too rich and too spoilt to even hit his own wife.

Herodes would have endured no ill-effects from murdering his wife had her brother not got involved. Regilla's brother was Bradua, as aristocratic and well connected as Herodes, also a consul and friend of the imperial family and entirely unwilling to accept that his sister had been killed in such an undignified way. Bradua publicly accused Herodes Atticus of murdering Regilla and forced the issue into court. Only someone with Bradua's immense social capital and resources could have taken Herodes to court over this; Bradua was technically the social superior as a proper Roman rather than an unscrupulous Greek newbie. However, Bradua was also an idiot, puffed up on his own pathetic ego, and he screwed it up.

In a Roman court, much like our own, the defence and the prosecution took it in turns to make their speeches and present their evidence and witnesses. When it was Bradua's turn, he stood up, in his shiny robes with the consular stripes and his special shoes with a half-moon on them that showed he was a patrician, in front of an audience of his peers at the trial of the decade and he started droning on about how good his family was. On and on he went, lavishing praise upon himself and his ancestors, tediously telling his captive audience about the ruddy bloody brilliance of everyone he had ever been related to for god knows how many generations. Eventually, he got around to making an accusation and he claimed that Herodes had ordered Alcimedon to beat Regilla, that this was an insult to his family's honour, that he couldn't prove it, no, and he didn't have any evidence but he *would* quite like Herodes convicted thank you very much. It took the expert public speaker Herodes, a man famous for being good at speeches, about four seconds to take the piss out of Bradua's obnoxious shoes, embarrassing speech and piss-poor evidence, blame Alcimedon for the murder entirely and sit down again. Herodes obviously won. He walked free forever, and spent the next year grieving for Regilla so ostentatiously and ludicrously that it screams either guilty conscience or pure attention-seeking.

Alcimedon acts as an interesting intermediary here. For Bradua, Alcimedon is not a person capable of murder, not a person worth pursuing with a conviction at least. A claim that a freedman – a man who was still considered to be fifty percent sub-human – had murdered an aristocratic Roman lady wouldn't have taken up an hour of anyone's time. Alcimedon would have been dead within a week. To Bradua, Alcimedon was not an actor capable of culpability, but a tool. He was the club and Herodes was the hand holding it. By giving the order for Regilla to be beaten (and how desperately, unbearably humiliating for Regilla to be beaten by her husband's henchman), Herodes had committed the vital act. Alcimedon would not have acted without Herodes' orders and so, to Bradua, Herodes was culpable. Herodes was the Charlie Manson, Alcimedon was just his Squeaky Fromme.

When Herodes stood up in court and stated that Alcimedon had acted by himself, had – for unknown reasons – decided to beat his enslaver's wife to death, we might expect that the court would therefore prosecute Alcimedon. After all, a woman had died at his hands. Every man involved in this, because of course no women's voices were heard, agreed that Alcimedon walked into a room and committed violence to a heavily pregnant woman until she was so injured that she died. Not even Herodes disputed that. But Rome was a self-help society. Justice required the participation of the injured family and Bradua apparently had no desire to pursue Alcimedon. He dropped it and disappeared. Nor did Herodes have any desire to punish the man who murdered his wife and unborn child, or even reduce his contact with him. Years later, Alcimedon pops up again when Herodes was taken to court for another set of suspicious deaths that occurred near him (he really attracted suspicious deaths). This time, Alcimedon's teenage twin daughters, who Herodes had taken into his personal staff (imagine me doing a look to camera here; you know what this means), died when a tower they were sleeping in was hit by lightning. For some reason, Marcus Aurelius personally held a tribunal about these deaths. Possibly because the idea that two young women had been 'hit by lightning' while asleep indoors in the care of a man who had been accused of at least two murders in the past is utterly absurd. I have no idea what happened to those two girls who were forced to spend their lives with a woman-murdering henchman as their dad and Herodes Atticus as their creepy gross patron, but I am damn sure that they weren't hit by lightning. This isn't an *X-Files* episode. Once again, Herodes blamed his freedman for everything but somehow neither he nor Alcimedon were punished. Herodes and Alcimedon were free to continue their horrid little lives.

The murders of Apronia and Regilla are two very unusual cases, because they both include an emperor. This is the only reason that we are aware of them. And they both show the same pattern of incredibly entitled men doing bad things and then punishing their wives with murderous violence for getting in their way. The closest any of them came to being punished was when Silvanus was forced to kill himself when it became clear that Tiberius was going to convict him, and that was only because Tiberius got weirdly interested in the case. These women are only visible to us because their male relatives had enough social status and money to cause an imperial level fuss. Had the social status of the men involved been even slightly lower, both of these women would have slipped into the swamp of sadness that is the majority of women's history.

We get only the slightest, most incomplete glimpses at any other cases of what modern homicide studies calls intimate partner murder in the whole ancient Roman world. One is in the form of a gravestone which dates from around the same time as Herodes Atticus and was found in Portus in Italy, Rome's main port town. The stone commemorates sixteen-year-old Prima Florentia and was put up by her parents to loudly proclaim that Prima had been murdered by her husband Orpheus, who threw or pushed her into the Tiber.[4] This is an astonishingly public way to kill one's teenage bride and I bet it was a real local scandal, but the dramas of provincial people in provincial towns don't make the history books so we only know about it because Prima's parents were willing and able to record the manner of her death and her killer in stone. Some have speculated that the fact that they did this suggests that they were unable to successfully prosecute Orpheus (perhaps he had a higher social status or better connections) or force him to pay compensation, which would require him to admit his guilt. This social shaming was maybe the only way they could get a little justice for the loss of their teenage daughter, or perhaps it assuaged their guilt over their complicity; after all, it was her parents who had arranged her marriage and her parents who had accompanied her on her wedding day to the home of the man who would kill her.

Another gravestone dates from the late Roman Empire, the fourth century CE, and was found in Lyon, so a world that it represents is far removed from the early Imperial Rome of Tiberius or the late Republican Rome of Cicero or the high Empire of Herodes. This was the deep provinces and the stone dates from a tumultuous time in the Roman world. But still, it represents the feelings of some family rich enough to carve a good long monument on expensive stone. It memorialises a woman called Julia Maiana who was murdered by her unnamed 'most cruel husband' after twenty-eight years of marriage and it was raised by her brother and one of her three sons.[5] Like Regilla, the reader is forced to question whether this fatal incident, whatever it was, was the first time this unnamed man was violent towards his wife, or whether, buried in that epithet 'most cruel', lie three decades of violence that culminated in her death. The lives and memories and experiences of Julia and every woman like her are now lost forever but for this tiny mark she left on the world which, when you think about it, was really more about her brother and son getting their own revenge on her husband than it was about her.

Gaius Calpurnius Piso

The flip side of women being beaten and thrown out of/into things by their husbands is men being killed by their wives. In the modern world, according to the UN, for every six women murdered by a partner, one man is murdered by his. Male victims of domestic violence are all but invisible in our data-saturated on-line world, and when women who kill their partners are visible, they are often victims who resorted to homicidal violence to pro-tect themselves (Dolores Claiborne in *Dolores Claiborne*, Farrah Fawcett in *The Burning Bed*) or Black Widows (Debbie Jellinsky in *Addams Family Values*, Catherine Tramell in *Basic Instinct*) The Roman world was neither data-saturated nor particularly inter-ested in the actions of women. Every example we have of men being killed by their wives comes either from the imperial family or from so far back in the mists of time, even the Romans thought they were ancient. And they all involve poison.

The Romans repeatedly told the same parable over and over about women who killed their husbands, and it is so predictable and repetitive it's a challenge to believe that it could ever have happened – but all stereotypes have their roots in something. This stereotype is that of an overbearing mother who intervenes to kill her husband so that her son can take his place. This story was told about Augustus' wife Livia to explain how the dullard Tiberius could have become emperor and it is the story told about Agrippina the Younger to explain how the dreadful narcis-sist Nero became emperor. And it was the story told about a forgotten woman named Quarta Hostilia (which is a good name for a murderer I think) who was believed to have killed her husband, Gaius Calpurnius Piso, while he was consul in 154 BCE. There are, obviously, no contemporary sources for Hostilia's alleged murder. All we have is one paragraph from Livy's *History of Rome*, which was written a very long time afterwards and which tried to contain everything important that happened between the foundation of the city in 743 BCE and the time of writing in about 27 BCE. That's a lot of history and there wasn't room for a great deal of detail so really I am grateful for what we've got with Hostilia.

Livy's story goes that Hostilia was married to Gaius Calpurnius Piso and had a large adult son named Quintus Fulvius Flaccus from a previous marriage. Calpurnius was successful and excellent and consul, while Quintus was mostly useless, at least in the eyes of his mother. In 154 BCE in Rome, a series of seemingly unrelated incidents occurred: first a praetor, Tiberius Minucius, died of a short illness. Next, both Quintus and Calpurnius ran for consul and only Calpurnius won. Finally, Calpurnius also died, apparently of the same illness that killed Tiberius. The fact that two magistrates died in the same year was initially seen as a warning from the gods, causing much rifling through holy books and cutting open of fluffy animals in the search for clues. Everyone got involved (they had to, there was a law) except Gaius Claudius who had taken Tiberius' position as praetor and felt that something was fishy. Specifically, he had a Columbo hunch that it was suspicious that Quintus had somehow managed to take his late stepfather's job as consul. Very quickly, so quickly that it is itself suspicious, some anonymous witnesses were found to describe Hostilia as being very angry at Quintus for being so rubbish at winning elections. It turned out that this had been his third attempt at running for consul and that she saw him as a total embarrassment. Like every overbearing mother with a large adult son, she berated Quintus and told him that he would be running for consul again and that this time *she* would make sure he was successful. In fact, the anonymous informants declared, she specifically stated that she would take measures to ensure that Quintus would be consul within two months. The expression, says Livy, was verified by the event. Hostilia poisoned Calpurnius. Hostilia, who was either a terrible helicopter mother willing and able to kill her husband, the most powerful man in the Roman state, for her useless son, or an innocent and confused woman who had just lost her husband, was immediately convicted on the basis of the anonymous informants and presumably executed.

These stories are infuriatingly predictable. It is impossible to tell where the tedious trope of the woman who is too interested in politics and too active in her son's life ends and where the real woman who once lived and breathed and felt and loved and maybe killed begins. The trope, the story it tells, plays so neatly into Roman ideas about the proper place of women and what happened when they got 'uppity' (i.e., good men died and it was bad) that it feels almost gullible to believe it when it appears in sources. Another woman who got too mouthy and started killing, sure, OK. Sure. But an alternative argument for the fact that we see these women, and only these women, killing men is that it is only these women who fit into a familiar Roman narrative and so only these women were recorded. In the same way that men who are beaten by their wives in the modern world and women who kill their husbands out of jealousy, rage, mental illness or a desire for control are all but invisible in the modern world because they do not fit our familiar narrative of domestic violence, while frightened beaten women who stab their violent husbands are a trope of popular soap operas. The appearance of the latter in multiple mainstream tales does not preclude either from existing in real life. The existence of multiple overbearing women who kill their husbands for their sons in Roman literature does not mean that they did not exist, nor that they were the only husband-murderers who existed. It merely means that they were the only ones the Romans were afraid of.

5

Murder in the Slave State

To start thinking about Roman slavery is to stare into an infinite abyss of deliberate human suffering. The Roman Empire is considered to be one of the genuine slave states in human history, in that, like the antebellum Southern states of America, it could not exist without slavery. Slavery was the social and economic foundation upon which the entire Roman Empire rested. But while the slave states of Louisiana and Virginia lasted 150 years before abolition, the Roman Empire stood on the backs of unimaginable numbers of enslaved men, women and children for almost a thousand years. A thousand years is thirty-four generations of people enslaved to the Romans. A thousand years before the year I wrote this, King Cnut was glaring down the sea. A thousand years is an immense amount of time. And they didn't just have domestic slaves, they had vast mines across the Empire for silver, lead, gold, iron and copper. Google the Las Médulas mines in Spain and imagine the sixty thousand enslaved people who worked there twenty-four hours a day to produce the gold the Roman Empire demanded, and then multiply that by hundreds of years and hundreds of sites and all those lives that were sent to toil for nothing and join me staring into this bottomless pit of Roman horror. Then picture the near infinite acres of land owned by the Gaius Caecilius Isidoruses and Melanias of the Roman world,[1] each maintained by chain gangs of hundreds of enslaved people. And on top of that were those enslaved in the house, the cooks and cleaners and washers and dressers, the people enslaved by the state who maintained the aqueducts and laid the roads and built all those temples and fora across the vast Empire and fought fires and carried the emperor in his litter. A general estimate (which means, of course, a total guess but a guess from someone I'd trust in a quantitative situation) is that there were between 4.8 and 8.4 million enslaved people in the Roman Empire at any time, with the city of Rome's population including anywhere from ten to twenty-five percent enslaved people.[2] Millions and millions and millions of lives, each a person with a heart full of love and hate and envy and joy and aching knees and sore eyes and dreams and thoughts and desires and hopes, all of whom were owned by another person and subject to the most extraordinary violence every day.

Pliny the Younger offers an illustrative anecdote in a letter to a pal named Acilius. The letter is two paragraphs long. The first tells a horrific story concerning a former praetor called Aulus Larcius Macedo who was murdered in the public baths (we'll come to that in a minute), and the second tries to lighten the mood with a bit of Pliny's characteristic sparkling wit. His amusing little sketch also concerns Macedo in the baths in an earlier incident, and Pliny thinks it maybe foreshadowed his eventual end. Trying to move his enslaver through the crowded baths, one of Macedo's attendants lightly touched an equestrian man on the hand to prompt him to move out of his enslaver's way, Macedo being of higher rank and entitled to the deference of the equestrian. The equestrian, however, didn't realise that the enslaved man was alerting him to Macedo's presence, so he took the touch as an insult and reacted instantly and terribly to it. He turned and threw a hard punch at the face of the enslaved man who had touched him, a blow hard enough to knock a man to the ground. The reason Pliny regales his pal with this horror story as an entertaining anecdote is not that this reaction to a slight touch is bizarre and sickening, but that the equestrian missed the enslaved man he was aiming for and his fist landed squarely in Macedo's face instead. Were Macedo not acciden-tally knocked on his arse by a presumably extremely embar-rassed businessman (for added awkwardness, please remember that everyone is naked in this scene too), no one would ever have written it down. It would have been another act of astonishing violence – for an imagined slight, enacted simply because the equestrian could – against a man who meant nothing because he was enslaved. The accidental humiliation of a dead ex-praetor was a funny story, but the extreme violent reaction to an enslaved man was not worth commenting on.

Here's another one, this time about the emperor Hadrian, told by Galen. In a fit of anger over some unknown and unre-corded issue (feel free to imagine one for yourself. I imagine that he got an annoying letter), Hadrian stabbed his enslaved atten-dant in the eye with a pen. Just straight up took up a pen and drove it into a man's eye for the crime of being nearby. When he'd calmed down a bit later, Hadrian felt bad that he had *half blinded a man* (my god!), and so he tried to buy the poor guy off. Notably, he did not offer him freedom but simply offered him the material goods of his choice to make up for the fact that he was now irreparably disabled and probably fully aware of the fragil-ity of his condition of being enslaved by this angry man. The enslaved man refused any gifts, asking simply for his eye back. The story ends there. Presumably he got nothing because he definitely didn't get what he wanted. This little nugget is quite the insight into the deified Hadrian who, as we shall see, is gener-ally remembered for his tendency to side with the enslaved over the enslaver, but apparently had a temper. It makes me think of gamers on YouTube who scream racial slurs 'in the heat of the moment' and then have to apologise for letting their terrible racist cores slip out while live-streaming PlayerUnknown's Battlegrounds. These little moments of uncontrolled rage reveal the prejudice that lies underneath their more careful persona. Some gamers on YouTube are racist in moments of rage; some Roman enslavers broke the bodies of enslaved people like Charles Foster Kane broke furniture.

That's the assumed baseline here for the experience of slavery in Rome: random violence was always at least possible if not probable on any given day. And that's just the physical violence. A super fun thing about the Romans is that they spent a lot of time writing advice to one another about how to psychologically control the people they enslaved. Men like Columella, Varro, Plutarch and Cato (a man so dreadful even the Romans barely liked him) advised their peers to keep enslaved people away from others of the same nationality and discourage them from learning one another's languages. Instead, writers encouraged enslavers to cultivate a sense of competition and discord between the people they owned to prevent them from banding together. On an individual basis, it was recommended that enslavers balance regular physical punishment such as beatings, forced nudity, confinement and starvations with the promise of future rewards, particularly the possibility of freedom one day, and small immediate rewards such as praise or the chance to build a private life. The use of enslaved families – partners and children – as rewards and punishments is particularly disturbing, and was actively encouraged. The enslaver held the power to allow a person to share a cell with their partner and children and live a family life, or to sell them, separating the family forever, and they knew how to use this power in a chillingly calculated manner to control the behaviour of the people they owned.[3]

In this world of pure domination, murder was not uncommon. The killing of enslaved people was obviously the most common and we will get to that in a while because it's a tiny bit complicated. First, we will look at something that scared the

Romans a lot: when men were killed by those they enslaved. This happens less often than you'd think. Elite free Romans made themselves exceptionally vulnerable to those they enslaved, who slept in their bedrooms, dressed them, washed them, fed them and literally carried them around. It would take just a couple of minutes to suffocate a rich wanker with their stupid toga if you were in charge of putting that toga on them, or you could whack them on the head with a particularly fancy vase, or push them into their ludicrously expensive ponds, but enslaved people almost never did these things because the punishments for enslaved-on-enslaver violence were, even for the Romans, extraordinarily horrible.

Lucius Pedanius Secundus

The most famous cases of enslaved men who killed their enslavers are remembered via the victims rather than the perpetrators. Lucius Pedanius Secundus and Aulus Larcius Macedo were both murdered by unknown groups of enslaved people, and both cases caused a stir; Macedo's because of the weirdness of the murder, and Secundus' because of the brutality of the punishment. Macedo's murder occurred in his private baths in Formiae.[4] One has to wonder a little whether he had built private baths because of the previous face-punching incident, or whether this was just a coincidence. Let's assume it was a reaction because why not. Anyway, he was nude and sweaty in his own villa's baths, relaxed and clean, when suddenly a crowd of his enslaved attendants moved with murder in their eyes. Pliny the Younger regales his correspondent with an unlikely but gleeful amount of detail about what happened. One man grabbed Macedo by the throat while others began to hit him. The first 'struck him on the forehead', which I choose to read as a headbutt, while others hit and kicked him, with a particular focus on his goolies, until he collapsed to the floor and stopped moving. The attackers then carried Macedo out of the baths and tried to pretend that he had just mysteriously and suddenly collapsed in the heat, and presumably that his bruises and marks were a result of him repeatedly falling into things that definitely were not fists before he hit the floor. His more devoted attendants put him in a cool room, at which point he came round, named his attackers and slumped back. Interestingly, he held onto life for long enough to see his attackers rounded up and executed for his murder and then died. I can only imagine that it would be both immensely satisfying and immensely surreal to be alive and with it enough to watch someone punished for murdering me. It would certainly erode my trust in the treatment I was receiving from my doctors.[5]

Pliny tells this story as a scandal in Rome: the slaves are revolting! But justice was done! He smugly points out that even kind enslavers could never feel safe because enslaved men were all natural villains. If we switch perspectives, though, and try to look at this incident through the eyes of the enslaved men, it's a pure, heart-wrenching tragedy. Pliny is pretty upfront that the attackers were driven to plan and attempt the murder because Macedo was a cruel and overbearing enslaver. Macedo's own father had been enslaved then freed and Pliny hypothesises that Macedo's painful awareness of his family's humble origins drove him to be harsh with those he himself enslaved, lest they think he was one of them. Whatever the reason, he was apparently known as a real bastard, which other enslavers saw as a fairly neutral personality trait, like having low-key middle-class alcoholism or a minor online gambling addiction. Not ideal, quite good gossip, a bit classless, but nothing to fuss too much about. For the enslaved themselves, though, it was a torment. It meant that they were exposed to physical and psychological abuse every single day; it meant that they were deprived of all the dignities and freedoms of life that even an enslaved person might be able to cling to. Everyone knows what it is like to have an overbearing micromanager boss who erodes your confidence and your self-esteem at work. Macedo was like that, but with every aspect of the lives of those he enslaved. He decided whether they ate and had clothes. He decided if they spoke or slept and what they did every minute of the day. He was utterly inescapable for them. He was so dreadful that a group of men he enslaved got together and agreed that he could not be borne any more.

He had to be killed because killing was the only escape. The decision to kill one's owner could not be taken lightly, especially a murder like this which appears to have been motivated purely by the desire to be rid of Macedo. According to Pliny, the attackers didn't run until Macedo came round and told everyone what had happened. Presumably they were planning to remain enslaved and in Macedo's heir's household should their plan have worked. All they wanted was Macedo to be gone. The best case scenario should they be caught was immediate death, almost certainly by the genuinely horrific and public act of crucifixion. The worst case scenario was torture and then death by crucifixion. If the plot had been even suspected by Macedo or any of his more devoted household, all the conspirators would have been tortured and killed horribly. The Romans, as we'll see in a minute, did not fuck about with keeping enslaved people perpetually afraid and hyper-aware of the power of the Roman state. To even hint to a fellow enslaved person that you might, maybe, consider possibly killing your enslaver was an act of immense courage and self-exposure.

The enslaved men had obviously come together as a group and formed a plot to beat their enslaver to death and pass it off as an accident (a really rubbish plot by modern standards, but they might have got away with it), which means they planned it, which means that they spent days, weeks, maybe months not only fearing Macedo but also fearing that their plot would be exposed. They had snatched meetings and whispered conversations in the minutes they could grab to themselves, and they hoped and prayed that they could trust one another. Eventually they decided on a day and time to do it, to finally be rid of their enslaver, and the tension ticked up a notch. The day of the attack, they prepared the baths, stripped themselves and Macedo and accompanied him into the hot room. The room was full of steam, and one of the slaves tended the fire in the corner which kept the pool of water hot until it reached perhaps 100 to 120°C in there and everyone dripped with sweat. Macedo was being Macedo: barking orders, snapping at the man rubbing olive oil into his back, kicking his sandal at another (I'm just making stuff up now but go with me). In the heat of the room, the tension rose with each ticking minute until one of the men gave a nod and they all rushed Macedo and knocked him down. They briefly thought they'd done it. They thought they were free of his tyranny. He lay limp and unmoving on the floor. They were exhausted and terrified and full of adrenaline. Now for the acting: they carried him out, crying that he'd collapsed, attracting wailing members of the household to take him off their hands. Maybe they allowed themselves a tiny moment of celebration before word passed out of the villa that Macedo was alive. They had failed. They had failed and they were going to die, and death was going to hurt. That moment of yawning, gaping, heart-dropping realisation is a tragedy in itself.

The whole affair was tragic and petrifying for the enslaved men because Roman law and practice took absolutely no risks when it came to those they enslaved, and the Romans' preferred method of keeping their property in line was to utterly terrify

them with consequences so harsh that they are genuinely staggering. The consequence of a person being murdered by their
own enslaved people was that every single enslaved person
living under the same roof as the murderer would be executed.
Every single man, woman and child who was legally the property of the deceased and part of the household would be taken
outside of the Esquiline Gate and would die excruciatingly. Yes,
I did say children too. Even the children.[6] This punishment
existed to make every single enslaved person constantly responsible for the wellbeing of their enslaver and for protecting their
enslaver from all threats at all times. They were held responsible
for not crying out when their enslavers were attacked and for
not preventing their enslavers from killing themselves. They
were executed for 'pretending' to help their enslavers and for
not shouting for help loud enough. They were expected to die
for their enslavers or else die because they failed to do so.[7] We
know that the Romans did this, and didn't just talk about doing
this, because one day in 61 CE, a stupidly rich man named
Lucius Pedanius Secundus was stabbed by someone he had
enslaved, and all four hundred people he owned in that household were condemned to death, a destruction of innocent
human life so staggering it caused even the Romans to pause for
a moment. Tacitus offers two possible reasons for Secundus'
death: either the unnamed enslaved man had fallen for a
catamite and wanted his owner to stop boning the boy, or
Secundus had promised to free the man and then, at the last
moment, refused the manumission. Both situations imply that
the murder was not, like Macedo's, pre-planned and premeditated, but was a crime of passion, and that blade was slipped
between Secundus' ribs hastily and impetuously. Nonetheless,
every single enslaved and formerly enslaved person in his household was, in that second, condemned to death. I wonder, as he

stood covered in Secundus' blood, what went through the anonymous murderer's mind.

The execution of enslaved people, even groups of enslaved people,
rarely caused much of a stir in Rome. By 61 CE, the law enacting
this punishment had been in effect for fifty-one years, having been
passed under Augustus' rule in 10 CE (the Senatus Consultum
Silanianum, which is super fun to say out loud) and renewed in 58
CE to include enslaved people who had been freed. Even people
who technically had their freedom were never truly free. It's
impossible to know how many entire households of enslaved
people had died under the law previously but apparently no one
protested too much because Tacitus didn't bother to record them.
When Secundus died, however, and the number of people to be
executed was revealed, the people of Rome were revolted. This is
one of those moments with Tacitus where he presents a behaviour
as stupid and laughable to his Roman aristocratic audience and
assumes they'll agree with him but which modern audiences read
entirely differently. We see it when he presents women giving fiery
speeches, thus making them look really badass to a modern reader,
and we see it now when he presents the plebs of Rome, the poor
and disenfranchised and the workers and enslaved people, marching onto the streets and demonstrating outside the Senate House
to save the innocent lives of 399 enslaved prisoners. Tacitus sneers
at the plebs for their short-sighted, un-Roman feelings and doubly
sneers at those within the Senate who attempted to stop the executions by forcing a debate on the matter, while we twenty-first-
century readers cheer on their doomed effort to save human lives.
(Let us remember, however, that the best outcome for these people
was that they remained alive, enslaved, forever.)

Tacitus doesn't record any of the opinions of those who
wanted to protect the condemned, but does present a long and

deeply pompous speech by a certain Gaius Cassius Longinus, an enormously famous jurist in his time whose opinions on matters of law were considered to be very important indeed by other people interested in Roman legal opinions. Longinus had absolutely no time for new-fangled things of any kind and Tacitus has him say that decisions made in the past were, in his view, always better and more correct, and that all revisions to the law were, without fail, wrong and bad. No matter that this law was just fifty (or, arguably, three) years old; it was old enough to be worth protecting. The conservatism of the Roman Senate and desire to see the Roman past as perfect in every way, regardless of what was actually happening at that time, is really quite extraordinary. Anyway, aside from the 'antiquity' of the law, Longinus outlined that the law was necessary in a time when rich guys like him and his mates claimed many hundreds of people as property, who were embedded into every part of their private and public lives, a vast number of whom had been born free and happy in foreign places and who had been captured and sold as war spoils by the Romans. 'The only way to control such a medley of people is through terror,' Longinus says. 'Innocent lives will be lost,' he admits with a shrug, 'but the individual injustices are outweighed by the advantages to the community.' The community, of course, being the Roman slave state and the individual lives being enslaved people.[8] The advantage he is talking about is the ability to live happily and comfortably as one free man surrounded by people who have been violently enslaved, which he says outright: 'As long as our slaves inform on one another, we can live solitary amid their numbers . . . And if we must die, we will die knowing that we will be avenged.'

As the Roman Empire grew and newly enslaved people were flooding into the city of Rome along with the necessary wealth that allowed those at the top to enslave hundreds or thousands of them, Roman enslavers suddenly became very afraid that they were outnumbered. This became an especial fear as mass slave-owning became a marker of wealth and privilege and conspicuous consumption. Romans took to owning people like modern-day social media influencers have taken to owning Hermès Birkin bags. But unlike a handbag, enslaved people could be dangerous: the more enslaved people one purchased, the more sad and pissed-off people were literally in your house to hate you. Seneca, that old Stoic, wrote about this a few times. He famously said that a (rich, slave-owning) man had as many enemies as he had slaves. He also recorded an interesting senatorial debate about whether enslaved people in Rome should be forced to wear some kind of special clothing to make their status visible and unambiguous. The proposal was voted down because the enslavers feared that if the people they enslaved could see how many of them there were in the city, they'd feel the strength of their numbers and possibly act on it. Such a reasoning is probably nonsense, not least because in a household of four hundred enslaved people everyone definitely knew that they outnumbered their one enslaver, but it's interesting that the rich experienced some anxiety about their actions. But, being Romans and being hugely wealthy men, and being very, very dedicated to the institution of slavery, the best solution the Senate could come up with was to terrorise those they enslaved into being too afraid to act against those who enslaved them.

This is why the senators shot down any motion to pardon the four hundred people owned by Lucius Pedanius Secundus, and also why the non-elite of Rome were more keen on saving them. Those who enslaved a small number of people, or none at all, or who worked alongside enslaved people, did not feel the same pressure to keep them terrified and dominated. They would never be surrounded by a group of enslaved people waking them, feeding them, dressing them and washing them twenty-four hours a day and they would never feel the need to protect both themselves and their way of life. The Senatus Consultum Silanianum protected only the interests of the mega-rich. It was for the Jeff Bezoses and Mark Zuckerbergs and Sheikh Mohammed bin Rashid Al Maktoums of the Roman world, not the people like you and me. The reasoning behind the execution of 399 innocent men, women and children made absolutely no sense to the Roman populace. It was a cruel and grotesque waste of life. This feeling had nothing to do with their feelings about slavery in general – plenty would have had enslaved people of their own – but was prompted merely by the monumental scale of the execution. The senators, on the other hand, gave no fucks about the concerns of enslaved people or the masses regarding such trifles as 'other people's lives' or 'justice'. They cared about the message they'd be sending to the hundreds of people they'd be going home to that night.

In the end, only Secundus' freedmen were let off (though a guy called Varro tried to have them all exiled for the crime of existing in the house) and the four hundred enslaved people were condemned. The execution was to be carried out almost imme-diately but the crowds of Roman people near rioted, throwing stones and threatening to set fire to stuff. They successfully prevented anyone from being nailed to a cross that day. Nero was cross enough about the whole situation to write the people of Rome a really angry letter telling them off (which strikes me as very funny but which Tacitus seems to think is quite a serious reaction). A few days later, the execution was tried again and this time the army lined the streets through which the prisoners were paraded and surrounded the site outside the Esquiline Gate where, for hours, men, women and children were tied or nailed to crosses and left for days to die for the crime of one man.

The end of Seneca's line about enslaved people being enemies is that they were not bought as enemies, but that they were made enemies by the unnecessarily cruel treatment they received from their Roman enslavers. This is Seneca wilfully overlooking the fact that a lot of enslaved people were, in fact, acquired as enemies either on the battlefield or as a result of Roman armies sacking cities, and his advocacy of kind treatment was selfishly motivated. His aim was that enslaved people would continue to be loyal and die for their enslavers if necessary. He was still an enslaver and not someone we want to root for, but he expressed a deeply felt reality for Romans. The cases of enslavers being killed by their enslaved peoples all seem to result from the enslaver meting out harsh or cruel treatment. Macedo died because he was overbearing and callous. One of the few other examples of a prominent enslaver killed by the people he enslaved is Lucius Minucius Basilus, who was one of the guys who stabbed Caesar. He was murdered because he tortured and mutilated those he enslaved, which some have read as him using castration as a punishment but might mean any kind of mutilation. Either way, his violent habits were too extreme for some of the people who were exposed to them. Only one murder can't be put in this category, and that's because the victim was so unimportant and lacking in prestige that we only know about his murder through an inscription. He was M. Terentius Iucundus, who had once been enslaved but had been manumitted and become a head shepherd for some otherwise unknown guy called M. Terentius in Mainz, Germany.[9] Iucundus was killed by his own enslaved man for unknown reasons, and the murderer then drowned himself to avoid the horrors of crucifixion. Unsurprisingly, the inscription doesn't record whether Iucundus deserved it or not, but we can perhaps assume he did, at least a bit, given the company he is in.

Panurgus

The reverse of free men being killed by those they enslave is, of course, enslaved people being killed by those who dominate them. This is, as I'm sure you'll be shocked to hear, much, much more common and, consequently, almost completely absent from the sources. A free man being killed by his property is a man bites dog situation: it is newsworthy. An enslaved man being killed by his enslaver is more along the lines of man drops $5 vase he bought from Ikea. Not really worth anyone's time or attention. We only really hear about people killing enslaved people when the laws were changed to reflect shifts in attitude towards the killing of those whom the Romans didn't think were human. There is a whole, fairly linear, history of Rome to be told in the incremental ways in which straight-up stabbing an enslaved person in the throat in a rage, or paying the local executioner to whip and crucify them, became less and less acceptable over the centuries. Or, as some might put it, the gradual erosion of a free citizen's power over his household as the centuries passed. It took hundreds of years for Roman culture to become uncomfortable with the notion of killing an enslaved person and even then the discomfort was mild. From the beginning of the Roman state, the power that an enslaver had over those he enslaved to keep them alive or kill them was pretty fundamental to the existence of the institution of slavery. What is the point of enslaving people if you can't even kill them when they annoy you, an early Roman might ask. It's not until 319 CE in the reign of Constantine, who was quite possibly influenced by Christian thought on the matter, that the deliberate killing of an enslaved person by their enslaver became a crime. It did have to be deliberate, though. Accidentally beating your enslaved people to death remained OK at all times. No second-degree murder charges here.

One murder which got a little attention was that of Panurgus in about 62 BCE. We only know about the fact that a man named Panurgus once lived and was killed because Cicero defended his owner, Roscius (a different one from his previous case), in a related property damage case. Specifically, the case focused on how much Panurgus was worth and how much Roscius was owed by the man who killed him. The short version of the case is that Panurgus had been jointly owned by Roscius and another man and they had invested a lot of money in training Panurgus to be an actor in the hope that he would make them money in the future. However, Panurgus had been murdered by Quintus Flavius before the completion of his training. Quintus agreed that he owed Roscius money for killing Panurgus, but he would only agree to pay the amount that Roscius had originally paid. Roscius argued that, as a result of the acting lessons, Panurgus had been worth more at his death than at his time of purchase and the murderer should pay his worth at the time of death. This is the same issue covered in such enormous length and bizarre detail in the Lex Aquila: who has to pay when a cow or an enslaved person dies, and how much do they have to pay? The fact that a man died, that a man was owned and sold and trained and then pointlessly killed, is completely lost in Cicero's oration. Cicero, monstrously, goes so far as to say, '[Panurgus'] body was of no value; only his skill [as an actor] was valuable.'[10] That skill was apparently worth a hundred thousand sesterces. Panurgus' body and his person were worth nothing. Had Quintus Flavius, whoever he was, paid Panurgus' owners his full value, then history, and we, would never have known that poor Panurgus ever even lived.

It took a really, really horrific event for a murdered enslaved person to become visible in the written sources. The most visible, out of a vanishingly small amount of enslaved victims recorded, are the enslaved people killed in such a gruesome and sadistic manner that it shocked even the elite Romans. These were a people who crucified anything and everything. It took a lot to upset them. But one man managed it. The man responsible was a certain Vedius Pollio. Not much is known about Pollio except that, like Macedo, his father had been enslaved, he was stupid rich and he spent his money like SoundCloud rappers do: stupidly. Also, he was inexplicably great pals with Pompey.[11] His cruelty isn't mentioned the first time he appears in the written record, which occurred when he rolled up to visit Cicero and say hi while Cicero was the reluctant proconsul of the province of Cicilia.[12] Pollio was everything that Cicero hated, especially in terms of extravagance, and so he wrote to his BFF Atticus to tell him all about how awful Pollio was. He describes Pollio turning up in two chariots, with a horse and cart, a huge retinue of enslaved attendants and, for absolutely no reason, a yellow baboon. Just a pet baboon. From sub-Saharan Africa. Riding around Turkey in a chariot with this wanker. Followed by some onagers, which are Iranian wild horses. Cicero obviously hated Pollio and proceeded to pass on to Atticus some good gossip about a third friend going through Pollio's luggage and finding five small portrait busts of women, all of whom were married to other men, which Cicero takes as Pollio keeping little trophies of his sexual conquests. Great scandal for Cicero, who loved gossip, but an even greater image for us because now we can imagine Roman shaggers asking women to hang around for a couple of post-coital hours to sit for a souvenir mini-bust.

So that's Pollio's basic level of everyday conduct and it was annoying so it's not surprising that he was a real, god-tier monster when it came to the people he enslaved. His behaviour as an enslaver was so shocking that it was recorded by four separate sources across the centuries, which is a lot. Seneca enjoyed the horror of the story so much he included it in two boring philosophical essays about different virtues, and it really does liven them up. The story goes like this: Pollio had invited the emperor Augustus over for dinner and Augustus had showed up because I guess everyone has an embarrassing mate they can't get rid of. Halfway through the evening, an enslaved man dropped a crystal goblet and broke it. Pollio, furious, ordered that the man be executed immediately. All that would be par for the course; maybe an eyebrow would be slightly raised but the incident would have been forgotten within hours had Pollio not decided to try to impress Augustus by ordering that the enslaved man be subjected to Pollio's most ingenious and terrible method of execution. Vedius Pollio, in line with his penchant for keeping exotic animals, kept a large tank of enormous sea lampreys. Lampreys were a great Roman delicacy, considered to be delicious food for rich people. They are also a fucking horror movie come to life. I don't know if you've ever seen a sea lamprey but it might be worth stopping reading this to Google them right now so you can understand the true enormity of what is happening here. Lampreys are a kind of eel which have existed in their current form for over three hundred million years. They are sixty million years older than dinosaurs and they were formed in hell to haunt our nightmares. They can be over three feet long, and they have huge, perfectly round, jawless mouths that take up basically their whole heads and which are full of dozens of sharp little teeth disappearing down, seemingly infinitely, swirling in concentric circles, into a horror throat. They feed by attaching their hellish mouths to the side of their prey and suction-cupping on, then rasping off flesh with their teeth and sharp 'piston-like' tongues while releasing a fluid that prevents the victim's blood from clotting. Death is slow, occurring from blood loss or shock, and is immensely painful. Even thinking about lampreys makes me feel quite weak. Which is exactly why Augustus was horrified when Pollio ordered that the clumsy enslaved man be thrown into his tank of sea lampreys.

The prospect of being eaten alive by lampreys was so dreadful that the enslaved man fell to Augustus' knees and begged him to order Pollio to use literally any other form of execution; such was the lot of an enslaved person in Rome that he didn't even bother trying to beg for his life. He just wanted a better death. Even crucifixion would have been preferable to being chewed on by giant eels. Pollio ignored what was happening, apparently assuming that Augustus would be as amused as he was by the novel form of 'throwing slaves to the beasts' that he'd come up with. Given Augustus' early career as an unstoppable warlord, one can't necessarily blame Pollio for his assumption, but Augustus was well into his benign politician years and also the punishment was uniquely disgusting, so instead he ordered that his own attendants break every single one of Pollio's crystal goblets and every other breakable nice thing they could find. As a result, the enslaved man was saved from execution, and could continue his life as an enslaved member of Pollio's household, which probably made him wish for death. We have no idea how many other people were fed to Pollio's lampreys, but we do know that he went down in Roman history as a bastard everyone hated. He was hated because he was considered to be unnecessarily cruel in how he ruled his household. He was a tyrant, unable to control his baser urges, acting in anger, while good men executed their enslaved people rationally and calmly.

This all happened in about 15 BCE, around the same time that Augustus and the Senate passed a law forbidding men from handing enslaved people over to be thrown to the beasts as part of public entertainments at random. This law was the first in a series that gradually eroded the free man's ability to murder enslaved people without repercussions and introduced the state into the relationship between an enslaver and an enslaved person. The Lex Petronia forced free people to bring a formal complaint against the enslaved person they wanted to hand over to get eaten by bears so that a magistrate could decide whether the enslaved person deserved the punishment.[13] It's difficult, as a twenty-first-century British person who has grown up to see the death penalty as abhorrent, to view this as an improvement on previous practice. On the one hand, enslavers could no longer randomly give enslaved people over to be killed at public expense and for public entertainment without justifying themselves. On the other hand, the Roman state implicitly decided that some of the 'complaints' that enslavers had about the people they enslaved justified their being executed at state expense and for public entertainment. We know from a brilliant story from Aulus Gellius (one that you probably already know and thought was from the Bible) about the lion with a thorn in its paw that fugitives from slavery were often condemned to the beasts,[†] and it seems a bit much that the state of Rome would consider people's

---

[†] The story is that an enslaved man called Androclus in the province of Africa ran away from his owner, the proconsul of Africa during the reign of Gaius, because of the 'undeserved and daily' floggings he received. After three years he was caught and condemned. He was put into a show with a lion that was supposed to eat him, but instead the lion licked the man's hands and nuzzled him and Androclus hugged the lion. Gaius called Androclus to him and demanded an explanation. Androclus explained that he had spent his three years of freedom hiding in a cave in the African desert and that during that time he had met this lion who was limping and bleeding from a huge thorn stuck in his foot. Androclus removed the thorn and he and the lion had lived together, sharing food and the cave, for three years until both were captured. Both Androclus and the lion were freed and spent the rest of their time living together in Rome, being showered with love and presents. Aulus Gellius claims that an eyewitness named Apion wrote this down; *Attic Nights* 5.14.

attempts to be free or to escape cruel enslavers to be a crime worthy of death but I suppose it makes sense. Romans considered freedom to be a privileged state that needed to be protected at all costs, and if some people got killed to defend it, that was a sacrifice Romans were willing to make.

An important thing to remember with this law, I think, is that those who were prevented from having enslaved people mauled by lions were not prevented from using any other form of execution. They could still crucify enslaved people or beat them to death or starve them or stab them or drown them or throw them from a cliff or, indeed, as Pollio did, feed them to their privately owned beasts. No one was going to stop them and, in fact, there were private firms which offered bespoke punishment of enslaved people and execution services for the busy enslaver who didn't have the time to do his own killings. An inscription from Puteoli (Pozzuoli) tells us that an execution could be bought pretty cheaply, just four sesterces per contractor, which included the cost of materials and disposal of the body.[14] Of course, what this mostly tells us is that the flogging and execution of enslaved people was so common a thing that other people did it for a living, day in and day out, which is probably the best insight you'll ever get into the mundane reality of a slave state like Rome and how little the lives of individuals meant to it.

The next law to try to regulate the deliberate killing of the enslaved by enslavers didn't come until the time of Hadrian, almost 150 years later, and that also simply prevented free men from executing their enslaved people without oversight from a magistrate, which is grand except we're not completely sure that Hadrian actually did this. The only source for this alleged law is a book so confusing and weird that no one is able to agree who wrote it, how many authors it had or whether it's even supposed to be a non-fiction book. It might be a novel that no one quite understands because it's certainly wrong about a lot of things. It's called the *Scriptores Historiae Augustae* and it's the only place that records Hadrian's alleged law. At the very least, this law didn't make it into the *Digest* so we can probably ignore it. In the second century CE, a jurist named Marcian wrote that 'whoever kills a man is punished without distinction as to the status of the man he killed', which some have taken to mean that enslaved people counted as people where murder was concerned by then.[15] Possibly it does, but we don't see in the sources anyone suddenly being prosecuted for killing enslaved members of their household.

Eventually, Constantine came along, a solid three centuries into the current era and just about a thousand years on from the foundation of Rome, and tried to protect the lives of enslaved peoples by outlining, graphically, all the ways they were *not* allowed to be killed any more. Roman law really likes to be specific about these things. First off, Constantine explicitly excluded the accidental killing of enslaved people during beatings or punishments. That's fine, because the only real person hurt by that was the person who lost some valuable property. However, the enslaver is made guilty of murder if they deliberately kill an enslaved person in any of the following gruesome ways: with a club or stone, with any weapon, by hanging, by being thrown from a high place, with poison, with 'the cutting of the sides with the claws of a wild beast' (grimly specific even for a Roman), by burning, or by torturing a person to death, which Constantine, with the tone of someone really enjoying himself, describes as forcing 'bodies and limbs weakening and flowing with dark blood, mingled with gore, to surrender their life in the midst of tortures'.[16] This law is titled 'The Disciplinary Correction of Slaves' and it's pretty clear that Constantine's aim is to stop execution as a form of discipline, without stopping people from beating those they enslaved to near death. That would be a ludicrous thing to suggest.

What this means is that the deliberate killing of an enslaved person, either as punishment or just for funsies, was not regulated by the state for pretty much the entirety of Western Roman history. It was simply not a crime; it was a domestic issue. That's not to say that it wasn't, shall we say, socially inappropriate to be killing enslaved people all the time. It's sort of analogous to adultery now. Adultery is not illegal in the modern West; no one gets punished by the state for schtupping someone other than their spouse. But adultery is socially punished. Infidelity is still the leading cause for divorce (where reasons are given) and people who commit adultery are subject to social punishments such as being ostracised from friendship groups or just being viciously gossiped about for ages by all the neighbours. In the twenty-first-century West between eighty-two and ninety-four percent of people consider adultery to be morally wrong, and that has social consequences for people who do it.[17] In the Roman world, people like Vedius Pollio were like modern-day adulterers. It wasn't illegal to kill enslaved people, but it also wasn't cool with everyone. Seneca wrote about Pollio, 'Who doesn't hate Vedius Pollio even more than his own slaves did?'[18] to which the answer is, actually, no one because definitely those he enslaved hated him the most, but it's nice that Seneca thought that everyone hated him. Whenever enslavers who like killing a bit too much come up in the Roman sources, it's with a distaste that suggests that slave-killing and torturing was considered to be a bit gauche, the classless behaviour of the nouveaux riches and the uncultured. Much like a gambling addiction or adultery, though, it was probably happening all the time, silently and quietly in the background of history.

Spiculus

The final area of murder in the slave state is murder in the gladiatorial arena, something that the Romans had very few moral
dilemmas about. One of the greatest ironies of the image of the
Romans as a 'civilising' force in the West is that, when the
Romans arrived in a new part of the world to civilise it, they
almost immediately introduced their new uncivilised acquaint-
ances to the good Roman pastime of murder for sport. All these
Gauls and Dacians and Mesopotamians who were living their
chill lives, drinking beer and playing board games (and who
somehow managed to survive the slaughter and enslavement
that accompanied the appearance of the Romans on the horizon), were suddenly expected to spend their afternoons hanging
around in an amphitheatre watching men try to kill each other
as a leisure activity. And drink wine. We take it very much for
granted these days that an aversion to violence is more 'civilised'
than an attraction to it. Violence for pleasure is inherently
distasteful to most of us. Even those of us who (to me, inexplicably) think that boxing is a great night out and fox hunting is a
joyful cultural activity look with abhorrence on, for example, the
Dnepropetrovsk maniacs, who killed twenty-one people in three
weeks in 2007 basically for the lols. The Romans, however,
considered watching grown men fight each other with weapons
to be the very height of sophistication, especially if those men
were enslaved or condemned and unable to refuse.

According to the Romans themselves, namely two Augustan
era writers, the first ever gladiatorial games were held in Rome
in 264 BCE by a guy named Decimus Junius Brutus who saw
some people in south central Italy doing it and liked it so much
he decided that two guys fighting was the ideal way to commemorate his father. Thus, the first ever games were held as part of
his dad's funeral in the Forum Boarum. Three pairs of

gladiators fought but no one recorded whether there were any deaths. The introduction of fighting to funerals was pretty popular – it livened things up a bit and added an element of the drama of the unexpected to an otherwise quite boring day – and very quickly the rich and desperate-for-attention in Rome took to turning their familial funerals into mini-death Olympics in order to convince loads of people to attend. Having gladiatorial fights at your uncle's funeral turned out to be a very successful way of making sure that 1) lots of people turned up and 2) everyone in the city knew your family name. It's no coincidence that this occurred at the exact time that Roman power was expanding into Italy and beyond, bringing ever increasing numbers of enslaved prisoners of war and cold hard cash into the city.

Funeral games grew rapidly. In 216 BCE, twenty-two pairs of gladiators fought at a funeral, in 200 BCE it was twenty-five, then, in 183 BCE, sixty, and on and on. Within fifty years of their introduction, gladiators were the coolest accessory in town, so special schools were set up to train the best fighters and hire them out. Then the Roman state started condemning criminals to be trained as gladiators, and those training schools became a kind of prison for strong-looking men who did bad things. But gladiatorial fights remained absolutely connected to funerals for about two hundred years from their first introduction, so a member of the family had to die before anyone could put a good games night on.

It was, of course, disruptive innovator Julius Caesar with his brilliant mind who found a way around this funeral situation and changed things forever. In 65 BCE, when JC was a low-key magistrate with a profile to match the amount of fucks he gave about tradition, but an unstoppable ambition, he held some gladiatorial games in the Forum Romanum in honour of his dad, who had died two decades previously. It was genius. Technically, it was still an occasion related to a funeral, but no members of the family actually had to die. He freed gladiatorial games from the restrictions of actual funerals. Caesar could now chuck some gladiators in a ring whenever he wanted, and he could throw as many in the ring as he could afford and call it a commemoration, because the gladiatorial games had become part of the extraordinary world of Roman conspicuous consumption. If one guy could afford to risk the lives of thirty very well-trained, very expensive men, then risking forty men was a way to show how much more money you had than that guy. And Romans loved showing off how much money they had. Once gladiatorial games became consciously uncoupled from the limits of citizen funerals, all hell broke loose. Gladiatorial games became a focus for the people of Rome to see and be seen, to court popularity and to share political opinions. They became a nightmarish mishmash of the Kentucky Derby, a Premier League football match and a political rally, with more blood. Gladiatorial games, called *munera* to distinguish them from athletic games (called *ludi*, which were things like racing and wrestling), allowed individuals to show off and, most terrifying of all, exercise the power of life and death in public.

The gladiatorial arena is a deeply weird thing to look at from where we are sitting. It is a space in which human killing and dying were sold as sport and as entertainment. They were spectacle in the way that New Year's Eve firework displays are spectacle. They acted as an astonishing show of the power of the Roman state and the power of the elite. And they were the wholesale murder of thousands and thousands of enslaved men and women – some of whom voluntarily sold themselves in order to partake – by the Roman people. Gladiators are a pure expression of how insecure and porous the line between killing and murder can be. There is an unusual little anecdote in

Suetonius' biography of the emperor Gaius Caligula in a section decrying his cruelty and capriciousness. Suetonius describes a fight between five *retiarii*, who were gladiators who used fishing gear as weapons (big net, big trident), and five *secutores* (big shield, short sword, man in the iron mask-style helmet) in which the *retiarii* surrendered too easily so the overseer ordered the *secutores* to kill them. One *retiarius* didn't like this, so, in what was undoubtedly a thrillingly transgressive day for the audience, he grabbed his trident and stabbed the five *secutores* to death before anyone could stop him. The emperor, according to Suetonius, was horrified at the 'most cruel murder' and bewailed the horror of having to witness it. He would, however, have contentedly watched the *retiarii* be stabbed by the victors. The only difference, the line between murder and sport, was the rules.

These rules are completely absent from the modern popular conception of the gladiatorial games, which is a problem because it means that everyone enters every discussion of gladiators with an image in their head of what they think gladiatorial fights looked like, and for me that image is part Monty Python's *Life of Brian* (a terrified prisoner running away from a giant faceless gladiator sent to kill him) and part Ridley Scott's *Gladiator* (Russell Crowe slicing the heads off five giant faceless gladiators who have been sent to kill him but are apparently useless while screaming, 'Are you not entertained?!'). In both of these representations, the fight is wildly mismatched: massive dudes in massive armour versus tiny dudes in loin cloths, and the point is that the audience will see a tiny dude briefly fight for his pathetic life until he dies. The outcome is predetermined. The audience, of course, is always a mass of toothless plebs dressed in sackcloth with dirt on their faces and, quite often, their tits out. These gladiatorial games are executions, which always result in death, which are put on by a benevolent but disinterested elite for a repulsive, hypersexual, undistinguished mass of poor people who get off on blood. This could not be a more fundamental misunderstanding of what the actual experience of gladiatorial combat was like.

The problem is twofold. First, we have blurred the three forms of violent entertainment put on by the Romans into one confused form. This isn't really our fault; it's mostly because Christian writers in the third and fourth centuries CE kept witnessing their mates being thrown to rampaging cows and various other animals and so rather took against the whole arena in their writings. Also, they developed this whole thing about everybody having a soul regardless of whether they were a citizen or not, which meant that they didn't love people dying for fun. They were the fun-sponges of the Roman Empire for a while there, and they, both deliberately and accidentally, presented everything that happened in the arena as a form of execution and every execution as murder. This is unsurprising, I suppose, given how many of their friends and family were being executed for monotheism. In fact – and yes, I am about to 'well, actually' the hell out of this – the games were split into three distinct parts: the morning games were animal shows, which could be either animals fighting each other, professional hunters fighting animals or, on low-key occasions, just some animals doing tricks. The lunchtime half-time show – the Roman version of Justin Timberlake I suppose – was the executions. Just as JT isn't the reason anyone shows up to the Super Bowl, the executions weren't the reason anyone rolled up at the arena but they were an entertaining diversion while the professionals were having a break and forty-five percent of the crowd went for a piss. And much as the Super Bowl half-time show has mutated from a cute show by a college marching band into an immense spectacle of international superstars doing a medley of hits, the lunchtime executions evolved from a simple stabbing by a professional executioner into massive theatrical snuff-shows to keep the audience entertained.[19] This was the capital punishment part of the day and we'll get to that later.

The second problem is that we as modern readers have been way too keen to take the opinions of a couple of extremely Stoic philosopher one-percenters and a handful of Christian theologians as being representative of reality, which is foolish. Stoics hate reality; it's too messy and emotional. Cicero and Seneca are our main Roman Stoics who wrote a lot about the games. Cicero wrote in the late Republic when the games were a free-for-all and a useful analogue for the chaos of the political world, and Seneca during the reign of Nero, which was a hellscape. Both were at the very tip-top one percent of their respective worlds politically, financially and educationally. Both were Stoics who were more interested in smugly writing about how Stoicism was greater than anything else (apart from maintaining their own money and power, obvs). Stoicism is a tedious philosophy which, to be extremely reductive about it, emphasised that knowledge and 'Reason' were the greatest goods and that life should be endured without any recourse to anything as gross as an overt emotional reaction. It is pretty well encapsulated in two lines from the third great Roman Stoic Marcus Aurelius, which are (to translate very loosely):

> If you're bothered by something outside yourself, it's not that thing which is bothering you but your reaction to it. So stop reacting to it . . . Take away your opinion and the complaint is taken away.[20]

And:

> Whatever happens to you was always going to happen
> to you; your existence and the things that happen to
> you are strands of fate woven together.[21]

Basically, Stoics hate the idea of feelings and trying to change things and they love only Reason. They're dreadful. But they had a lot of capital-T Thoughts on gladiatorial games. So, our two most vocal and evocative sources on the gladiatorial games in general had a fairly extreme perspective not shared by most of the Roman world. Imagine if every source on modern religion except for the works of Richard Dawkins and Daniel Dennett was destroyed and historians attempted to reconstruct the daily experience of American Protestantism from just their works, or if somehow only purse-lipped conservative columns about the moral degradation of *RuPaul's Drag Race* were the only piece of social commentary that survived about the Emmy Award–winning phenomenon of a TV show and you'll see what we're dealing with. But it is extremely easy to fall into believing their Stoic, elite vision of the gladiatorial games, and so many people have because they forget that the majority of the seats, and all the front rows, were given to the senators and their families and that the amorphous mass of plebs were confined to the back where the views weren't so good. Or even that Seneca and Cicero were happy spectators of the games on a regular basis.

Anyway, the real gladiatorial shows were the fights at the end of the day between pairs of gladiators or, on a rubbish day, groups of gladiators. Groups were considered to be notably inferior to the thrill of a one-on-one clash that might end in a death. This is the other major misconception in how we twenty-first-century folk see gladiatorial games: they only *sometimes* ended in death. There's a pretty big (but disappointingly civil) debate among academics over how often a gladiatorial bout would end in death and whether that was even the point of the fight. There's a not insignificant strand of scholarship which argues that the primary purpose of the fights was for the crowd to enjoy watching skilled men do fencing really well, a point of view that is undermined by quite a lot of evidence, but does add a little bit of nuance to our view of gladiators and their profession. At the very least, the primary purpose of two really well-trained, really strong and well-matched armed men attacking one another elegantly in an arena was for them to really hurt each other until one of them either died or surrendered. At the point of surrender, when the fallen gladiator held up a single finger to signal to the *editor* (the person who put on the games and paid for the gladiators) and their opponent that the match was over, the bout could end. It was up to the *editor* what happened then, as you all know from Joaquin Phoenix and his thumbs in, again, *Gladiator*.[22] He could let both gladiators walk away, one the winner, one the loser, or he could order the winner to deal a death blow to the loser. This would usually be a stab to the throat. The audience would have a say in this, of course, screaming for their favourite to be spared or for a crap fighter to be dispatched and never waste their time again.

It's this moment that is the most fascinating and horrifying to onlookers both in the Roman Empire and today. In this moment, the *editor* holds total power. He can kill or he can grant mercy. He controls not only the life of the fallen fighter but also the behaviour of the victorious one. It is the *editor* whose turned thumb transforms the victor from a trained fighter into a killer. It's that which interests me the most here. The focus of almost all scholarship on gladiators and their work tends to be on the audience or on the loser because this is what the Romans themselves were interested in. When Romans were writing about their own entertainments, they were either moralising heartily about how watching death was terribly bad for poor people (but only poor people; rich educated men were obviously immune to the degrading influence of the games and so it was fine for them to go) or were waxing lyrically and dreamily about the dying gladiator accepting death like the most Roman of all Romans. This is because they were philosophers and also rich dudes who fully participated in the structures of the Roman state, so they only looked at the things that made them feel superior or smug. The gladiator who did the killing was almost never seen and still rarely is. But this isn't a book about death or audiences; it's a book about killing, and gladiatorial games, unlike any other kind of activity, made enslaved men and athletes into killers.

We can see this in the life of the most famous gladiator whose career has survived to us: Spiculus. I know what you're thinking right now: 'But Emma, does Spiculus have a Stanley Kubrick film about his life like Spartacus does? I have never heard of this guy. Surely Spartacus is the most famous of the gladiators? You fool.' And in response I have to break it to you that, although Spartacus was sentenced to gladiator training school, he never fought in an arena and never had a career, or even part-time job, as an actual gladiator. He was a soldier who spent a couple of months in a gladiator school after being found guilty of something and immediately escaped. Spiculus, on the other hand, had an exceptional career as a *murmillo*. A *murmillo* is probably the most recognisable type of gladiator, the type usually shown in films like *Gladiator*. They were naked except for some wee pants and a big belt. They wore an immense, almost circular, helmet which entirely obscured their face (and vision) and had padding on their legs and sword arm. Their weapons were a massive rectangular shield and the simple elegant classic weapon which gave the gladiator his name, the *gladius* short sword. *Murmillones* are now the Little Black Dress of gladiators.[†]

Spiculus was around during the reign of Nero, right at the end of the first imperial dynasty. We don't know how he ended up being a gladiator, but we know that he was an enslaved man. Most gladiators were criminals who were condemned to three or five years fighting as a gladiator, or prisoners of war or enslaved men sold to gladiatorial schools. Some gladiators were free men, who pledged themselves to a gladiatorial school and gave up their freedom and civil rights in order to fight in the arena. This is a move which utterly baffles most scholars, but I suspect that the desire to go on *Love Island* or *Big Brother* or (shudder) *The Apprentice* baffles them too and plenty of people do that. Much like being the kind of reality TV celebrity who graces the MailOnline sidebar and the cover of *Heat* magazine with their cellulite circled, being a gladiator was a heavenly kind of hell. It was a life of being worshipped and adored and well looked after, and also of being reviled, despised and caged. Those who chose to become gladiators as free men always have the letter L for *libertus* (free) after their names on graffiti and show posters (painted on walls) and the commemorative glasses that were made to celebrate their victories. Spiculus did not have an L after his name. But the first person he killed did.

Spiculus burst onto the gladiatorial scene in Pompeii. He came from the elite Neronian school in Capua, which was started

---

[†] Amusingly, they were actually a reasonably late addition to the gladiator lineup. They were introduced to replace a type called the Gallus gladiators who were a kind of comedy pastiche of barbaric Gauls. After the colonisation of Gaul and the influx of Gauls into Roman life and culture, however, the Gallus became a bit uncomfortable. Like a racist sideshow. So they were quietly retired and replaced by the *murmillo*.

by Julius Caesar and was originally called the Caesarian school until Nero came along, like the little prick he was, and renamed it after himself. Early in his professional career, Spiculus was rented out to someone in Pompeii where he lucked out at being matched with the reigning champion Aptonetus. Aptonetus was a *thraex* gladiator: he had a big red plume on his helmet like you imagine Roman soldiers to have, a round shield and a curved short sword. He was a free man who had chosen to train as a gladiator and was damn good at it. He had, at the time of his fight with the newcomer Spiculus, sixteen victories. Now, the Romans didn't send rookies in with reigning champions unless the rookie had some kind of spark about him; they hated the idea of an unfair fight. It just isn't fun or sporting or particularly interesting to watch the New England Patriots play the 2017 Cleveland Browns, and when the Romans wrote about gladiatorial games, they were pretty clear on how they felt about such mismatched fights. So we can assume that Spiculus showed some promise when he was sent into this match-up, and he lived up to it. He felled the sixteen-time champion and ended his life. We know this not because anyone wrote about it, but because of a wonderful piece of graffiti. The Romans who wrote (or at least wrote the kinds of things which survived the ravages of posterity) were rich, educated politicians. They were interested in good wine, good fucking and philosophy, for the most part. They were not the people who were most interested in sports. In the same way that the members of the House of Lords are not the people analysing football tactics in the papers, the senators and imperial servants of Rome were not writing gladiator journalism. In the entire corpus of Roman literature, in Latin or Greek, a not inconsiderable number of texts, many of which talk very generally about gladiators and games, we have just one written account of a real fight, and it commemorates a deeply weird occasion when both gladiators won.[†] That's it. One. The rest of our knowledge of what actually happened in the arena comes from graffiti, drawn with a surprising amount of detail on the walls of arenas and bars and other people's houses and statues.

This piece of graffiti shows a little stick figure of Spiculus (he's labelled) with a giant helmet holding his sword and shield aggressively. His little legs and arms show a definite forward propulsion as he attacks. Aptonetus has fallen to the floor and is holding his sword arm aloft in a gesture of surrender. With a really remarkable dedication to the Roman cultural tic of portraying a fallen hero as holding himself up on one arm to demonstrate continued strength and honour (see the Dying Gaul statue, for example), the graffiti artist has drawn his tiny stick version of Aptonetus raising himself up on his tiny stick arm. It's really very impressive work for a couple of lines scratched in some plaster. It is clear from the drawing that Spiculus has won the bout and Aptonetus has surrendered. But above the drawing, the anonymous artist, who once in around 60 CE stood by a house on the Via Della Fortuna, a good half-mile away from the amphitheatre where the bout had taken place, and scratched this drawing on the plaster wall, stayed for a little longer to write an inscription containing just eight Latin words (three of which are abbreviated) and a lot of information. The inscription reads: 'Spiculus the Neronian, a beginner, defeated and killed Aptonetus, a free man with sixteen wins.'[23] Those words

---

† It's in a poem by the fourth-century poet Martial and it goes like this: 'As Priscus and Verus each drew out the contest and the struggle between the pair long stood equal, shouts loud and often sought discharge for the combatants. But Caesar obeyed his own law. What he could do, he did, often giving dishes and presents. / But an end to the even strife was found: equal they fought, equal they yielded. To both Caesar sent wooden swords and to both palms. Thus valor and skill had their reward. This has happened under no prince but you, Caesar: two fought and both won.' *Epigrams*, 31.

combined with the picture tell us all we need to know about the fight. Spiculus fought the champion hard and won. He drove Aptonetus to the ground and forced him to raise his finger in surrender. The fight stopped and the two men looked to the *editor* to decide what would happen. The crowd made their noise. Maybe we can guess from the scratched drawing that they roared for the new champion, the upstart Spiculus. Or maybe the graffiti is a memorial to the fallen hero and they cheered his valiant, quiet acceptance of his possible death. For the two men in the arena, held steady, waiting, the referee standing close by, we cannot imagine what that moment would be like. Both were trained for this moment. Gladiators were drilled like the military to behave correctly in the arena. Over and over and over in their daily exercise they would practise the right way to fall and wait for death and the right way to prepare and deliver the fatal blow. The defeated man was to be still, his neck bared, his face impassive, accepting his fate with quiet dignity. The victor was to be equally dignified and prepared to deliver a short, sharp stab to his rival's throat. The death should be simple and quick, but it's hard to imagine the moments leading up to it were, while the crowd screamed and the *editor* waited to see which way the fates blew, keeping his audience hanging on the tension before declaring his decision with a thumb (or some other way). The *editor* was not feeling merciful that day. The crowd would have a real win. Spiculus drove his sword home. He was no longer a beginner. He was a champion.

I want to be clear on what that actually would look like here. A *gladius* is a hideous weapon. I've spent more time than you really want to know about watching terrifying men on YouTube with replica *gladii* absolutely destroying all kinds of butcher's offcuts and they slide through flesh like it's soft butter. The sword pushing through a man's bared throat would not be the spectacle. The spectacle would be the pulling out. The pressure it takes your body to push thick blood up your little neck through half an inch of artery is massive. Your heart has to work against gravity that is desperately trying to drag the blood down to force it up and up into your needy squishy brain and then drain it out again. When that pressure is suddenly broken, by, for example, a blade piercing your carotid, the blood explodes out of the hole like champagne from a shaken-up bottle. In an athletic man with a strong heart, full of adrenaline and with a heart rate at its peak, the initial jet of blood could fire up to six feet in the air. The jet arcing up and over the victorious gladiator and the referee and spraying the arena would be an astonishing and genuinely spectacular sight. Even for me, sitting here now, repulsed to my core by the idea of gladiatorial death, I know that I would watch this with round eyes and an open mouth and a bit of me would think, 'Cool.' I got some doctors and combat specialists to describe this to me and they all heavily emphasised the amount of blood that would explode from Aptonetus. It's a lot of blood. A traumatic amount of blood. Spiculus and the nearby referee would be drenched. The arena floor would be soaked with puddles of it. It was not a clean kill. There's a reason that Romans loved this murder for fun so much: it looked incredible. It was less fun for the fallen man. Death from a sword to the throat wasn't always as instantaneous as the Romans thought. Unconsciousness might be instant, but there would be rattling, gurgling breaths through a crushed and shattered windpipe for up to two minutes. Breaths that no one would hear over the cheering.

There is no murder more deliberate than this. It is killing done in an arena prepped for this and only this, by men trained to kill and to die entertainingly. But who is the murderer here? Spiculus holds the sword but Spiculus is an enslaved man. He has not entered the arena freely because he cannot give or with-draw consent to be there. He cannot refuse to thrust that blade into Aptonetus' throat and become a killer. The *editor*, forever unnamed, made the decision. He put his thumb up or down or in or out or whatever and directed the murder.[†] Maybe he is the real murderer and Spiculus is his weapon. The *editor* would reject this on two counts: first, he would say that he was responding to the crowd. The crowd, he would say, had decided whether the fallen man was released to fight another day or forced to gurgle out his final breath on the sand. If pushed a little more, or if he were more introspective, the *editor* might next say that it was not him but the fates that had decided what would happen that day. The divine and inscrutable forces of the gods had made their wishes clear through signs, such as the crowd screaming for one or other of the fighters, or a bird flying overhead or even the feeling in the *editor*'s bones, and the *editor* had simply acted to carry out what was fated; he could not have acted otherwise. In this scenario, the *editor* was merely a tool of the gods, of which there were an infinite number in the Roman conception of the world, Spiculus was the weapon, and the crowd the means of conveying the gods' message. No person was responsible for the calculated death of Aptonetus because no single person made that decision. The gods had decided. They decided that Spiculus would stand over Aptonetus on the floor, begging for his life through his silent acceptance of a death which was fated as soon as they both stepped into the arena; that the *editor* would turn his thumb this way instead of that way was decided by the divine forces which permeated everything. This is also why Romans

---

† While researching this I ended up down a real rabbit hole of reading people's wild speculations about what the 'turned thumb' actually was, and let me tell you that no one knows but *boy* do people have a lot of imaginative opinions.

despised fallen gladiators who begged for their lives overtly during this pregnant pause between survival and murder. The gladiator was trained to accept the fates, was supposed to be Stoic about the situation and not react. The gladiator who wept or begged or pleaded with the *editor* and the crowd was considerably more likely to find a blade in his soft tissue than the man who acted correctly and looked worthy of being saved, because the man who was still and silent and bared his neck voluntarily looked like he was being obedient and deferential to the gods. He wasn't fighting fate and he wasn't trying to fight the divine; he was agreeing that his life was, as all lives were, in the hands of the gods. The absolute best way to beg for another day of being allowed to breathe was to look as much like you didn't care about living as possible, and that is a psychological torture all of its own.

The system is, of course, set up to morally and practically absolve everyone from the responsibility of murder. The gladiator is a weapon; the crowd is a conduit; the *editor* is merely a cog in the wheel of the divine plan of the gods. And anyway, he had to put these games on to keep the people of Pompeii happy. He had no choice. No one had any choice. Everyone was innocent and everyone was guilty. But only Spiculus got splattered, possibly covered, with Aptonetus' arterial blood and only his hands felt the resistance of the muscle and cartilage and bone. Only Spiculus and the uncountable number of his colleagues experienced the same moments of waiting and thrusting and walking away after they had become killers. The Romans knew this, which is why they covered their gladiators' faces with immense helmets that disguised them and dehumanised them to each other. That's why sometimes, maybe even most of the time, the *editor* let the fallen man go free; releasing both fighters from the burden of killing and being killed. I said earlier that it's no coincidence that gladiatorial games entered Roman culture at the exact moment that Rome started militarily expanding its power into the world outside its walls, and not just because that's when they found out what some people were doing in south central Italy. The Romans were starting an empire and gladiatorial games turned out to be an extraordinarily good way of repeatedly reinforcing the power of the state to enslave and kill people in such a way that the people would voluntarily turn up to swallow the message. A significant proportion of those who lived and died in the arena were people enslaved during Roman military action. They were taken from their homes in North Africa or Belgium or Turkey or Austria or Iraq or Croatia and enslaved and trained and sent to act out their training and die and kill for the Roman people in the centre of every Roman town. Most of the rest were criminals tried for stealing their neighbour's beehive or whatever. They were the dancing bears of the Roman state: threats neutralised, pacified and forced to perform for the loyal crowds. They were a constant, everyday reminder of what happened when you messed with the Romans. You got brought into their system and turned into a part of it. You became their propaganda.

The flip side of this is that many gladiators became stars. Spiculus became a celebrity overnight. His killing of Aptonetus transformed him from unknown rookie to prodigy. Romans adored their gladiators in the exact way we adore our reality TV stars and footballers: they simultaneously wanted to be them, fuck them and never let them marry their daughters. Spiculus kept living up to his reputation as a ruthless victor, which we know from a collection of commemorative glasses. The Roman version of a Royal Wedding mug is a glass decorated with a scene from a particularly exciting battle. People owned them to remember their favourite gladiators' wins and carried lamps and daggers with their favourite gladiators on them too. They acted exactly as people act about their favourite football stars. Little boys today get their Lionel Messi shirts or Cristiano Ronaldo boots or Mo Salah posters. Little boys in the Roman world got a Spiculus glass and a Columbus dagger. Spiculus appears on a surprisingly high number of the glasses that have survived because he was briefly the Lionel Messi of Italy in the 60s CE. He went on to defeat someone called Columbus and kill him in battle, and this was such a big deal that it is commemorated on thirteen surviving glasses. That's a lot of glasses to survive. There are only fifty-seven surviving bits of gladiator glass in existence and the Spiculus/Columbus fight is on twenty-eight percent of them, and in every single one of those representations, the result was clear: Spiculus killed Columbus. He probably killed him in battle because Columbus is never shown with his arm raised or finger extended in surrender. Instead, Spiculus is always shown coming at the fallen Columbus with his shield, suggesting that something really grim involving crushing might have taken place. We have no idea how common death during the fight was but the glass evidence suggests it wasn't super common. All the rest of the surviving glasses recount victories or losses where both men were allowed to limp, bloodied and bruised, out of the arena, possibly to die of a head injury or infection off stage. Spiculus is the only gladiator commemorated on glass as a murderous victor, killing both Columbus and another guy named Prudes.

These victories made Spiculus considerably more special than his peers. He wasn't there to fight and hope to walk away for another day like his colleagues. He wasn't hoping that his five-year sentence would pass before he got the turned thumb like the criminals, and he wasn't trying to survive to enjoy the glory and women and constant shagging like the free men.

Spiculus apparently just liked killing as many people as he could, which makes me imagine him as being a bit like Maximus Decimus Meridius just fucking shit up, except Spiculus was apparently very good at entertaining the people while he did it (and presumably didn't shout at them to make them feel bad, like a dick, Maximus). It was this which brought him to the attention of our friend Nero. This is really why Spiculus is the most famous gladiator of all time: he became Nero's pet gladiator. According to the biographer Suetonius, Nero loved Spiculus. He was his biggest, most generous fan. Nero gave Spiculus massive Roman estates in which he could live in luxury while still being enslaved, served by other enslaved people. Spiculus presumably had an endless line of groupies to shag too because gladiators sent the ladies absolutely wild.[24] Unfortunately, things didn't end well for Spiculus. When Nero's reign collapsed under the weight of its own ego, Nero was apparently (allegedly) unable to kill himself so he sent messengers to ask Spiculus to come and do it for him. Suetonius writes that Nero specifically asked for Spiculus because the gladiator was accustomed to delivering death. Spiculus was a better killer than anyone else. He refused to appear, however. Maybe he thought that killing someone he knew would be different. Maybe he was just unwilling to kill the actual emperor. Maybe he worried that this would be a real murder that might lead to prosecution and execution. Maybe he just didn't want to. Either way, he obviously saw something different in this act of killing outside of the arena that Nero did not see. Nero was an absolute tool, though. Eventually, he managed to die despite not trying very hard and a new emperor was installed, who turned the followers of Nero over to the crowds of people who despised him. According to Plutarch, a crowd occupying themselves by removing Nero's colossal statues from the Forum caught sight of Spiculus trying to flee and they rolled one of the statues over him, crushing him to death. An ignoble way to go.

Gladiatorial games have to sit at the centre of any study of Roman murder or Roman death or Roman entertainment or Roman crime and punishment or Roman almost anything because they really encapsulate how extremely different from us the Romans were. At the very core of Roman-ness sit the gladiatorial games, where enslaved men were dressed as soldiers, trained like soldiers and then sent to fight entertainingly but for real for an audience and then, sometimes, they really died. They were killed in the coldest of bloods. The Roman world considered deliberate, bloody, martial death to be brilliant entertainment. That impacts on and is drawn from how they viewed every other form of killing, which is, basically, not as seriously as we, here and now, see it. Gladiatorial fighting and killing and dying was not a perversion, no matter how hard Christians and Stoics wanted to see it as such, but spoke to something fundamental in the Roman value system. It spoke to their love of fighting and competition, to their worship of the military and their valorisation of single combat in particular. They loved to see strength and skill enacted and rewarded, whether in the courtroom or in an acrobat's leap or a singer's powerful voice or a beast-fighter's defeat of a giraffe, or in two men, armed and trained, fighting one on one. When killing and dying in battle was no longer a reality for most Roman citizens, watching two men enact their greatest values of valiant fighting and courageous killing was the next best thing.

6

Murder by Magic

The first thing you need to know about Roman magic is that there is a very, very blurry line between magic and medicine and an even blurrier one between medicine and poison. If magic and medicine are two sides of the same coin, medicine and poison are the same side seen from different angles. The Latin word for sorcerer is the same as the word for poisoner: *veneficus*. The Greek word for poisoner is the same as the word for medicine: *pharmakon*. They are, effectively, the same thing in the eyes of the ancients, but they're not to us. Love potions and aphrodisiacs were, for example, seen as being interchangeable. We would see a potion that can make someone fall in love with you as clearly magic, while a potion that could make you horny seems at least plausible. There's an article in a women's magazine once a month about aphrodisiac foods because that's *science*,[1] but rarely one about using a special little wheel to bamboozle people into loving you. For the Romans, however, the difference was negligible despite their occasional attempts at scepticism. There is a very good bit, for example, in Pliny the Elder's encyclopaedia *Natural History* where he rips the piss out of Greek magical beliefs, which he describes as clearly ludicrous, but much of the rest of the work is dedicated to chronicling ways in which plants and animal extracts can be used to affect people positively and negatively. For him, the ingestion of the Persian plant 'achæmenis' (whatever that is) was magic because it caused the person to be tormented by memories of things they felt guilty about until they were eventually compelled to confess their sins. This is, to Pliny, quite stupid. Taking the brain of a puppy which was killed at exactly seven days old and rubbing it into your eye in a very specific way, though, that's medicine. That cures glaucoma. Bodies of water which make the voice more melodious or cause forgetfulness or prevent abortion are medicine,[2] as is jamming an iron nail into the head of a person suffering an epileptic fit, as long as the nail is jabbed into precisely the right spot (where the head hit the floor).[3] Ripping a tooth from a live mole and tying it to your body to cure toothache, however, is 'remarkable proof of the frivolous nature of the magic art' and definitely not medicine.[4]

You can see this also in the sole surviving work of Marcus Porcius Cato, also known as Cato the Elder, Cato the Censor and Cato the Wise, who was an epoch-defining hard-ass. Cato's statues all show him frowning furiously, glaring in disgust and disapproval at the whole universe. He was notorious for loving austerity, asceticism and a rustic life and hating anything he considered luxurious, which was everything. He is most famous now for ending every speech he gave in the Senate, regardless of the content, with the brutal phrase 'Carthage must be destroyed' until he got his way in 146 BCE. He was a politician, a farmer and a soldier who was very good at all those things, and the very epitome of the ideal of a straightforward austere Roman gentle-man. And he believed that applying crushed-up cabbage to a dislocated arm would cure it.[5] He also thought cabbage could cure breast cancer, colic and headaches, and advocated for bathing babies in the piss of people – like himself – who ate a lot of cabbage to protect them from all illnesses. Finally, he declared that the way to basically inoculate female genitalia against all diseases was to expose them to the warmed urine of a man who eats a lot of cabbages. Specifically, he recommended cutting a hole in a chair and getting the woman to sit her nude bottom down on it. Underneath the newly created and probably quite uncomfortable commode would be placed a bowl full of his own boiling cabbage piss, the smell of which must have been ungodly. She was then covered with blankets and left for an unspecified amount of time. Until Cato decided that her lady-garden had been cystitis-proofed with piss gas, I guess. The image of Cato's grim, grim face glowering down at his poor wife as she hovers over a bowl of his stinking piss because she got thrush is almost too much to bear, to be honest.

From this distance, it's a real challenge to see the difference between magic and medicine; it all seems arcane, mystical and frankly disgusting. It is all messing about with natural ingredients and hoping that they have some kind of effect on the world, for good or for bad. Not all of it was natural either. The use of amulets to protect children was extremely common, to the extent that the *bulla* amulet was worn by, as far as we can tell, almost all elite boys. Children and generals were also protected by penises. You can go to the British Museum right now and see, hidden away at the back of the Greek and Roman galleries, a few examples of minuscule golden rings with dicks on them made for tiny infant fingers, and a coral pendant on a gold chain of a teeny willy made for a baby's neck. These are beautiful, expensive gold objects. They are not for the imaginary ignorant poor; they are magical objects wielded by the elite. It is the intent, really, which makes the distinction between magic, medicine and poisoning.

Locusta

Aside from patricides, the scariest Roman murderers were women with the almost supernatural ability to poison without detection. Women with their sneaky magical ways, mixing up mysterious powders and fluids and rubbing it into your mucous membranes until you died. Women who overturned the natural order of things by exerting their will upon the world and killing their husbands and children; women who used poison to have a power that men couldn't counter. This scared Roman men the most, and so these women were the most censured.

The most famous of all of these sneaky, witchy, powerful women was Locusta, who was only called Locusta by Tacitus. Everyone else wrote Lucusta, but Tacitus exerts a powerful influence over the modern world's view of the Romans so Locusta she is. Her fame is such that the internet's content mills produce articles about once a year in which it is claimed that she was the world's first serial killer and that she was raped to death by a giraffe, both of which are claims so astonishingly silly that it's actually quite impressive.[6] I'm forced to break it to you that people existed in the world before the Romans and therefore Locusta certainly wasn't the first person to be involved in the murders of three or more people. She wasn't even the first Roman woman in the extant sources to have killed several people.

Another thing regularly said about Locusta is that she was from Gaul. This comes from a scholiast on Juvenal. A scholiast is an ancient scholar who wrote useful notes in the margins of manuscripts to help other scholars and students understand even more ancient texts. They were the original critical editions. Unfortunately for their peers and students, however, they weren't always very good and often spent a lot of time writing helpful notes about the wrong people. But this fleeting note made in the fourth century CE by a person who didn't know their Vibius Crispus from their Passienus Crispus is all we have on Locusta's origins so we will grudgingly have to go with it. Locusta was *possibly* from Gaul, where she was, at some point in her life, arrested and found guilty of murder by poisoning. Sadly, we don't know who she allegedly poisoned but I suspect that it wasn't her doing the poisoning. I suspect that she was found guilty of supplying poisons, which in Roman law was considered to be the same as actually putting the poison in someone's wine. It's a shame that we don't know what happened with her trial because it was obviously something of a scandal at the time, and she had gathered a reputation from it as someone who was very, very good at mixing poisons. I imagine that she was an early Imperial period Madame Lafarge, with lots of public interest and gossip, particularly as her main skill was apparently the ability to brew up poisons which could mimic any symptom required and which killed as quick or slow as was needed by the actual murderer.

We know this because she comes into the spotlight of history right at the end of the reign of Claudius and Agrippina, and I mean right at the end. The story goes that Locusta's abilities with the pestle and mortar had come to the attention of the empress Agrippina, at the precise moment that Agrippina was wondering how to get rid of her ageing uncle-husband Claudius and replace him with her beloved teenage son Nero. According to Cassius Dio and Tacitus, Claudius had a torpid metabolism and a capacity for wine that was so immense it effectively protected him from traditional poisons, which is almost impressive. But it was a problem for Agrippina who needed her uncle-husband's death to seem natural. Her violent coup couldn't look like a violent coup. Locusta's talents were therefore required to mix up a poison that would kill reasonably quickly, without any overtly unnatural symptoms, and which could not be stopped by Claudius' alcohol-soaked insides. It seems that she wasn't entirely effective, as the sources tend to agree that Claudius did not die cleanly or without arousing suspicion, although they do disagree quite significantly on how the poisoning went wrong. He either got diarrhoea or vomited or had drunk so much wine that the poison was counteracted or some other combination of things and was dying very inefficiently, so a doctor gave him another dose of something fast-acting. This time it worked and Claudius limped off this mortal coil, leaving the throne to his grumpy, nineteen-year-old stepson Nero who proceeded to immediately ruin everything, as was his wont.

This could have been the end of Locusta's career, given that it didn't go great, but the initial stumble in poisoning Claudius was apparently considered to be Claudius' fault rather than Locusta's (he couldn't even get murdered properly) and she was kept on the staff by Nero. She wasn't celebrated like, for example, Spiculus was in Nero's circle. Rather she was kept hidden away in the background, brewing suspicious potions. There is very much a theatrical witchy air to the way that Locusta is presented in the ancient texts. She lurks, wielding a terrifying power, which she is coerced into using for Nero's nefarious purposes, the ultimate evil emperor. That she is coerced is pretty clear from the two sources that give detail on Nero's extremely public murder of his stepbrother Britannicus. Britannicus was Claudius' biological son, while Nero was just his adopted son, so Britannicus was a clear threat to Nero's hold on the throne. Bumping off dynastic threats is, frankly, practical policy for a monarch rather than strictly murder, but at this time in Roman history, they were still clinging a little desperately to the fiction that the Republic had been restored and that the emperor wasn't a monarch. Thus, executing members of the imperial family was still being defined as a lack of familial piety rather than strong and sensible monarchy. So Nero went about it in a sneaky way. He poisoned his stepbrother. Locusta, being a sensible woman, tried to protect her boss by producing a slow-acting poison that mimicked real illness. This was considered to be the gold standard of murderous poisoning, along with poisons that caused mental derangement, and Locusta was probably pretty pleased with herself right up to the point where she discovered that Nero was not a patient teenage emperor. He was, in fact, an irritable teenage emperor and full idiot who did not want to wait around for his fourteen-year-old stepbrother to die slowly and garner sympathy. Locusta discovered how wrong her plan had gone when Nero started beating and flogging her – with his own hands according to Suetonius – in his fury. Nero was a really bad man. After being severely beaten, Locusta, to everyone's surprise, agreed to mix up a quick poison that would kill Britannicus fast. This dose was administered at a dinner party, slipped into his drink by his own taster, and Britannicus keeled over dead within moments, to the pure horror of other guests including his step-mother and his own sister, and the joy of Nero who forced every-one to continue the party as Britannicus' body was dragged from the room.

As Nero was a teenager with teenage mood swings, he was thrilled by the effectiveness of Locusta's second dose and he gave her an official pardon for all her previous crimes, installed her in a large estate and sent her pupils to learn her ways. There he kept her, looming over his reign as a constant threat to his enemies. We perhaps see Locusta in Nero's mother Agrippina after her relationship with her son turned antagonistic. Nero attempted to poison his mother three times (according to Suetonius, but at least once according to other sources) but was each time thwarted by the fact that she took multiple antidotes every day. The poisons Nero used can only have come from Locusta and we can probably assume that the antidotes came from the same place. Eventually Nero had to resort to the sword to murder his mother but many others fell to Locusta. Nero's former tutor Burrus, a bluff old soldier with an unwavering loyalty and an even less wavering sense of old-fashioned Roman morality, obviously had to go. Nero promised to send Burrus some medicine for a sore throat and sent him a Locusta special instead. His paternal aunt Domitia, who had been a second mother to him, maybe died of old age but was maybe a victim of Locusta's arts, employed so that Nero could inherit some nice land in Ravenna. Two elderly freedmen who supported him in his early reign, Pallas and Doryphorus, dropped dead after eating food suspiciously close to Nero. Suetonius also relates the somewhat wild story that Nero once dealt with the children of a number of high-ranking condemned prisoners by poisoning them en masse at a dinner along with all their attendants. When, in 69 CE, armies rose up against him, as he was a terrible ruler, rumours spread that he planned to poison the entire Senate in a spectacular Bashar al-Assad-style scorched earth approach to winning the war.

Eventually, however, Nero stole some poison from Locusta's store and fled. Unfortunately for him, though, even his own enslaved attendants hated him and they abandoned him, taking the poison and his nice easy death with them. Again, Nero had to resort grumpily to the sword. Locusta's reputation was so strong that when Galba, Nero's successor to the throne, arrived in Rome, she was arrested, paraded through the city and publicly executed. It was a good way of ensuring that her reputation didn't die with her. Years and years later she still popped up in poems and satires as a touch-point for poisoners in the same way Ed Gein does for serial killers, despite the fact that Locusta doesn't appear to have ever given anyone any poison herself and Ed Gein wasn't a serial killer. She merely provided the means. Arguably, Locusta was as liable in the murders of all Nero's enemies as Armalite are for all the deaths that have been caused by the AR-15 semi-automatic rifle. She was less a serial killer than a weapon. But still she functioned as a usefully amusing example. She appears in Juvenal's first Satire, a satire about how generally awful the whole world was, as the prototypical poisoner, upon whose work women were constantly improving while poisoning their husbands.

Of course, Locusta was an imperial poisoner, hardly an everyday example of poisoning. The poisoner of the people was a woman called Pontia, about whom we know very little except that she was the butt of many a scandalised poem in the high Empire. She appears first in Juvenal's festival of misogyny, his sixth Satire, as an example of the very real and specific evils women could perpetrate. In Juvenal's poem, Pontia is depicted as killing both of her sons by lacing their dinner with aconite and being utterly unrepentant about it. Juvenal's Pontia laughs that had she had seven sons, she would have killed them all, leading Juvenal to compare her to Medea, who killed her children to spite her cheating husband in Greek myth and tragedy. Pontia appears again in several epigrams written by the absolute filthmerchant Marcus Valerius Martialis, aka Martial. Epigrams are short, often obscene, frequently very funny poems that usually lampooned public figures and shared entertaining gossip. They were sort of a much ruder *Daily Show* for the Romans. One of my personal favourites of Martial's epigrams is spectacularly crude and to the point. It reads:

> You love to be sodomized, Papylus,
> but afterwards you weep.
> You want the doing, Papylus,
> so why are you sorry for the deed?
> Do you regret the lewd itch?
> Or is it rather that you cry, Papylus,
> because the sodomizing is over?[7]

There's a lot about bum sex in Martial. A lot. Pontia, apparently a recent celebrity, first appears in one of Martial's epigrams sending the author ostentatious gifts of food, a lovely slice of cake or the thigh of a hare or a roasted thrush (an interesting insight there into some Roman delicacies) which Martial will not eat because of the obvious threat that they might cause horribly choking aconite-related death. The joke isn't particularly funny (lol poisoners might send poisoned food lol) but the implication that Pontia might just go around poisoning everyone for fun is interesting in the light of Juvenal's portrayal of her as totally unrepentant. Some think that this poem suggests that she was still alive at the time it was written, which would be about 86 CE. She appears in two further epigrams and Martial's audience is clearly supposed to recognise the reference just as Juvenal's was. First she is described as the worst mother that Martial can think of and later he says that he'd rather drink from Pontia's flask than call a certain Coricinus a sodomite. What he really called Coricinus was a cuntlicker, because the accusation that a man engaged in oral sex with a woman was much, much, much funnier than the accusation that he was a greedy bottom. The Romans, especially Martial, were even weirder about oral sex than they were about male homosexual sex, and they were really weird about that.

Anyway. The fourth-century CE scholiast on Juvenal attempts to explain to his readers and students who this Pontia is, and does so with a characteristic lack of accuracy. According to the scholiast, Pontia was the daughter of Publius Petronius who, after the death of her husband during the reign of Nero, murdered their two sons by throwing them a particularly good dinner party with lots of food and poisoning it, and was eventually put to death for conspiring against Nero, rather than for the murder of her children. This identification seems somewhat unlikely as Publius Petronius was a high-ranking magistrate under Gaius Caligula. He did indeed have a daughter but she happily survived the reign of Nero and was married to Lucius Vitellius who very briefly became emperor in 69 CE before he was overthrown by Vespasian. This daughter was called Petronia. As Suetonius wrote a biography of Vitellius while Tacitus wrote an entire book about the year 69 CE, I'm pretty sure that Petronia murdering her children would have come up somewhere other than in a couple of poems two decades later. So that's obviously a lie and we know nothing about her. Not that this stops it from being on Wikipedia.

As an aside, Pontia has a fascinating afterlife as the inability to identify her in the Roman sources prompted an anonymous person in fifteenth-century Spain to inexplicably invent an entire biography for her, inscribe it on a lump of stone and then pretend that it was her tombstone. For quite a long time, historians reported this tombstone as a factual account of Pontia's life, right up to the nineteenth century. Here's the Reverend Lewis Evans, whose translation of Juvenal was the go-to prose translation until about 1920, writing in 1852: 'Pontia, daughter of Titus Pontius, and wife of Drymis, poisoned her two children, and afterwards committed suicide. The fact was duly inscribed on her tomb.'[8] Her fake tombstone, which still exists, reads: 'Here I, Pontia, the daughter of Titus Pontius, am laid who, out of my wretched covetousness, having poisoned my two sons, made away with myself.'[9] The idea that a Roman man would go out of his way to buy some stone and have a big inscription hammered into it – an inscription which doesn't use a single abbreviation no less! – telling everyone that his daughter was a murderer is funny enough to me, but the dead giveaway that this is a hoax is the presentation of the suicide as bad, when we all know that the Romans idealised the suicide as brave and excellent for the most part. Pontia is also included in a fictional Roman chronicle that was written, bizarrely, by a sixteenth-century Jesuit clergyman called Jerónimo Román de la Higuera, who promoted his own work as fact leading to a manuscript ending up in the Vatican archives, which is just fun.

Martina

The final of the big three female poisoners is Martina, and she really embodies the blurry line between medicine, poison and magic in the Roman world. She also has the lowest body count as recorded in our sources because she never made it to Rome. Martina was from the Roman province of Syria[10] and was probably, though take this probably with a big pinch of salt, from the capital Antioch, as she palled around with Placina, the wife of the governor of Syria, Gnaeus Calpurnius Piso. Both were even better friends with the emperor Tiberius. Piso, Placina and Martina are remembered to history because they got caught up in the death of Tiberius' adopted son, and Rome's beloved young prince, Germanicus. Germanicus and his wife Agrippina the Elder were the young sexy adorable prince and princess of Tiberius' early reign. They were good looking, charming, incredibly fecund (they had nine children, of whom six survived) and people worshipped them. So when they took a trip to the East and then Germanicus became very sick and died in Syria, people across the Empire were distraught. In their grief, they wanted someone to blame, and their suspicious eyes turned on Piso.

Those suspicious eyes were helped along by the fact that Germanicus and Agrippina apparently believed wholeheartedly that his illness was a result of poison and magic, not any of the myriad fevers and illnesses that can infect a Western

European who'd just done a Nile cruise in a world before actual medicine. It seemed too convenient to the couple that Piso and Germanicus had fought a lot and now Germanicus was dying. Tacitus gives us some nice dramatic scenes between the ailing Germanicus and grieving Agrippina in which evidence of poison and magic are discovered in their home. Tiberius relates that spells, curse tablets, ashes and bloody body parts were found hidden in the walls of Germanicus' house, all extremely clear evidence of evil magic which will 'consign souls to the tomb'.[11] Tablets and body parts were especially ominous. Curse tablets were a part of daily life in the Roman Empire which offer a wonderful glimpse into the petty grudges and cruelties that drove ancient people just as they drive us. About one thousand five hundred curse tablets have been found all over the Empire, of which six hundred-ish are in Latin.[12] They are fairly formulaic and almost always written on lead, then rolled up and hammered closed with a nail and they contain all the bitterness, cold anger and sputtering rage you can imagine. A personal favourite of mine is this one, which demonstrates that rabid sports fans are nothing new:

> I conjure you, daemon, whoever you may be, and order you, to torture and kill, from this hour, this day, this moment, the horses of the Green and the White teams; kill and smash the charioteers Clarus, Felix, Primulus, Romanus; do not leave a breath in them. I conjure you by him who has delivered you, at the time, the god of the sea and the air: Iao, Iasdao, Oorio, Aeia.[13]

This is an unusually violent one, but you can definitely feel the sports-based fury radiating off the lead tablet. This is a person who really, really hates the Green and White charioteering teams in this moment and really wants the horses and the drivers to die. This one from Bath is equally instructive and horribly delightful:

> The person who lifted my bronze vessel is utterly accursed. I give (them) to the temple of Sulis, whether woman or man, whether slave or free, whether boy or girl, and let they who have done this spill their own blood into the vessel itself.[14]

Whoever wrote this tablet really liked that bronze jug, liked it enough to get hold of some metal, scratch in their message, roll it up, nail it shut and deposit it in the ground. And this behaviour is very common in the Roman Empire because, frankly, no one mortal was going to help the poor guy who lost his nice vase, but the gods and spirits that inhabited the world seemed like they might.

This is the kind of thing that we can imagine Germanicus found hidden in the walls of his Syrian home while he was slowly dying, alongside some human remains. To be honest, finding gore-smeared human remains hidden in my house while I was on my deathbed would absolutely freak me out too, and probably sap my will to live if I believed in the power of magic. It certainly upset Germanicus. For Roman readers of Tacitus, these passages would probably bring to mind images of wicked witches like Canidia, who was immortalised by Horace in a couple of poems as a murdering, terrifying hag. Horace was just the kind of awful guy who would swear he loved women because he liked his mum while writing jolly ditties overflowing with grotesque misogynist imagery. Canidia was his anti-muse, his most despised woman. Scholiasts in the late antique world did a little psychological work on Horace and concluded that the violence of Horace's hatred for Canidia could only be explained by her being an ex-girlfriend, specifically a perfume seller named Gratidia. I don't agree with them, but I can see how they got there because Horace's many poems about Canidia are brutal and furious.

Canidia appears in six of Horace's poems as a witch and a poisoner, where the line between those two things is blurry at best. She appears first in a letter Horace wrote to his friend Maecenas to complain about what appears to be an irritable bowel response to eating too much garlic. 'If any person at any time with an impious hand has broken his aged father's neck, let him eat garlic, more baneful than hemlock . . . what poison is this that rages in my entrails?' he wailed, and you can really feel his digestive discomfort. To illustrate his pain, he likens garlic to the magical poison used by Medea to kill her husband's mistress and questions whether Canidia had made his food for him and poisoned it. She appears again two poems later, this time doing much worse.

In her second appearance, she is murdering a child. Horace describes her wild, unbrushed hair wrapped up with venomous snakes while she gnaws on her fingernails with her horrid little teeth. She is a picture of revulsion as she and her associates, Sagana, Folia and Veia, prepare a love potion. To do this, they dig a hole and bury a young boy in it up to his neck. There they leave him to starve slowly to death. To really emphasise their wickedness, Horace has the witches place food next to the poor boy's head several times a day so that he can see it but never eat it. When the child finally dies, the witches dig him up and harvest his liver and marrow. These they mix with wild fig tree roots, cypress leaves, eggs, a squashed toad, screech owl feathers, some undefined Spanish herbs (saffron?) and some unnamed bones stolen from a stray dog to make the love potion.[15] Canidia and her friends, and indeed her love potion, are grotesque, disgusting and loathsome.

The really interesting thing here, to me, is the insinuation that love magic isn't silly tricks for silly girls, but is terrifying powerful magic. It's Gandalf magic, not Harry Potter magic, if you will. (I'm sorry.) This is re-emphasised in Canidia's next poetic appearance where she tells Horace that she will cast spells to keep him alive for as long as she can in order to torment him infinitely. (You can see how people got the idea that she was his ex.) To prove to him that she has the power to do this, she tells Horace that she can make wax dolls move, and snatch the moon from the heavens; she can raise the dead and prepare love potions that work. She doesn't make empty promises: she casts powerful spells that can reshape the world and control people's lives against their will for her own pleasure.

Horace created the character of Canidia in his first book of Satires, in a satire told from the perspective of a statue of Priapus on the Esquiline Hill, which is where the ashes of the very poor were buried. Priapus complains that the Esquiline has become infested with female sorcerers like Canidia, walking around barefoot and dishevelled, collecting herbs at night to 'turn people's minds with their incantations and drugs'.[16] Canidia and her pal Sagana are both pale and dirty, digging in the earth to create a ditch then sacrificing a little lamb by ripping it to pieces with their teeth and filling the ditch with its blood. This is fairly traditional necromancy in ancient epic literature. Odysseus does it to talk to the dead in Homer. But Odysseus did it in extreme circumstances of literally epic proportions, plus he was Greek and therefore a weird foreigner anyway. The idea of Romans doing it was vile, and this whole set-up, at night in a graveyard without tools, was repulsive in the extreme. Canidia's magic represents the total absence of civilised control and moral goodness, the opposite of the natural, scientific medicine of Pliny and Cato. This was 'Eastern' savagery.

So this is what we are thinking of when Tacitus tells us that body parts and curse tablets were found in the walls of Germanicus' house and when he tells us that an Eastern woman, Martina, was responsible for them. Tacitus is telling his readers that barbarism was afoot. He is telling them that the governor Piso and his wife Placina – and, by extension, the emperor Tiberius – had been so corrupted that they had resorted to disgusting, hidden, foreign feminine magic to get Germanicus out of the way. Germanicus died in Syria, a thirty-four-year-old father of six. Suetonius tells us, as proof that poisonous magic had been involved, that Germanicus' heart did not burn on his funeral pyre. As the rest of his body became ashes, his heart remained intact because it was so full of drugs, which just goes to show how entirely interchangeable the concepts of poison and magic were.

The death of Germanicus was traumatic for the Roman people, who adored him. It was like the death of Princess Diana. Except the Romans had some people to blame for it, and by gum they were going to get justice. Piso and Placina were formally accused in public by Fulcinius Trio and some friends of Germanicus'. Piso, Placina and Martina were recalled to Rome. The trial of the century was about to begin. Unfortunately, Martina herself did not make it to the trial. She dropped dead as soon as the ship landed in Brundisium (Brindisi). It didn't seem to be suicide, says Tacitus, but they did find a little poison concealed in a knot in her hair. Piso was widely suspected of bumping her off. Piso was the talk of the city. He couldn't blink without people gossiping about it. When his trial began, he was charged with an attempt to start a civil war and that 'with the help of poison and the black arts, [he] had destroyed the prince himself'.[17]

The speeches given by the prosecutors in Piso's trial, as recorded by Tacitus, are, to put this politely, not the best representation of Roman legal argument, The accusers claimed, with no evidence, that Piso had slipped Germanicus some poison while at a dinner party, in front of god knows how many attendees. With Germanicus presumably looking at his own plate at the time. It was a baffling accusation, which even Tacitus sniffs at, and what happened to the body parts and curse tablets? The Senate and people of Rome, however, were extremely ready to believe it because they were not able to accept that their beloved prince could succumb to something so mundane and random as a fever. The Senate were ready to prepare Piso for the death penalty, while outside the people of Rome were trying to throw his statues down the steps that led from the Capitol to the Forum Romanum. The army had to go in and stop them. The city was very ready for Piso and Placina to be punished. Piso himself was offering up all the people enslaved to him to be tortured as witnesses to his innocence, but the Senate weren't interested in evidence that might make condemning him more difficult. It became very clear to Piso and Placina that this was going badly. Placina had a trump card, though. She was good friends with the Augusta, Tiberius' mother Livia, and, as we saw with Urgulania, Tiberius tended to do what his mother wanted. The next day, Livia procured her a pardon and Placina quietly stopped turning up for her husband. After another day of a show trial in which he was subjected to more attacks while Tiberius impassively watched, Piso made a decision. He went home, closed his bedroom door, and cut his throat with his own sword. He thus saved himself from being condemned as a traitor and a murderer, and a cowardly feminine murderer at that. A murderer who used secret poisons and barbarous magic to kill, rather than the honest sword.

Rumours swirled for a long time afterwards that Piso hadn't really killed himself, but that Tiberius had sent an assassin sneaking through his window to prevent him from revealing, in a shock last-minute courtroom twist, the letter Tiberius wrote to him instructing him to kill Germanicus! What a brilliant final third of an episode of *Perry Mason* twist that would have been: Piso taking the stand, with Tiberius' cold, expressionless face watching him; Piso standing, enduring the jeers and shouts of his enemies (everyone) in stoic silence; Piso unrolling the letter and beginning to read as the crowd falls silent; Tiberius' eyes widening in horror; Piso publicly accusing the emperor of murdering his own (adopted) son and then storming from the courtroom, a righteously vindicated man, leaving uproar behind him. Were this a made-for-TV movie, this is exactly what would have happened. Sadly, this isn't a movie; it's Roman narrative history written by our queen of throwing shade, Tacitus, so all we get is the indirect insinuation that this might have possibly happened, had Piso not bled out on his bedroom floor.

This was a big drama in Roman history; it was the death of a dearly beloved prince of hearts, so it was one of the very, very few times that the accusation of magic – real magic – peeked into the spotlight of the written history of the aristocracy. But the people whose lives we see in the narrative histories are the one percent of the one percent. They are the kings and queens and dukes and viscounts. At best, the people we read about in the textual sources are the business millionaires and trust fund kids. They are the rich and the elite and those at the pinnacle of the Roman social, political and economic hierarchy. They wrote the histories because they read the histories and so the histories represent their concerns, which are not necessarily the same concerns as those of people on the street. Thankfully, though, the riff-raff like us (unless you, dear reader, happen to have a title, in which case that must be really nice) did manage to leave some scraps of their lives and concerns and feelings behind. Mostly, they did this by hammering their thoughts and feelings into stone when someone died, which means we are still only able to access the lives of those who were rich enough to afford a big bit of stone and the services of a man with a chisel, but it's better than nothing. Luckily for us, accusations that people died as a result of witchcraft and magic are not uncommon on tombstones from across the Roman Empire.

Most epitaphs claiming that the deceased died of some kind of magical interference are pretty bland, because stone is expensive, honey. They usually record the deceased's name, maybe their age and that they died of *veneficia* (poison or magic) or *malefacia* (literally 'bad deeds'), words which contain multitudes. The complexity of those words cannot really be overstated but they strongly imply a sense of wicked and mysterious wrongdoing. They imply that something unexpected and unfortunate happened, and that someone was responsible for it. For example, someone killed Attia Secunda, who lived in Salona, Dalmatia (now Salon, Croatia), as far as her relatives were concerned. She died at the age of twenty-eight, after being ill for seventeen long, difficult months.[18] What possible other explanation could there be for a twenty-eight-year-old woman wasting and dying other than a magical curse? When Abaskantos, a famous athlete at the peak of his health, returned home to the island of Andros after touring the theatres of Rome and Syria, suddenly weakened and died, there could be only one explanation: unholy curses and plants, thrown at him in jealousy of his success.[19] As the polymath Plutarch says in his *Consolation to Apollonius*, talking about the death of Euthynoos, son of Elysius of Terina, the first thing that occurred to anyone when a young person died was that magic was involved.[†]

These epitaphs express a relatable feeling: young people aren't supposed to get sick and die. It's not fair and it's not right. It hurts too much. Someone must be to blame and someone should be held accountable and it must be stopped. In our world, we want to sue the life out of a negligent doctor or raise as much money as possible for rare disease research. In the Roman world, they wanted to burn a motherfucking witch. Or at least scowl at one. The epitaph of Iunia Procula makes this really clear in the most dramatic, soap opera style. Iunia Procula became very ill and died in Rome at the age of just eight. For her father Marcus Iunius Euphrosynus, her death was the cherry on top of a terrible couple of years. First, Iunia's mother had died. After some time, Marcus felt he was ready to marry again and that he'd found just the right woman in Acte. Fortunately for Marcus, Acte was an enslaved woman whom he owned as property. Marcus offered her a deal: he would give Acte her freedom on the condition that she married him. Obviously, she took the deal. Freedom while married to Marcus was some sort of freedom, while slavery was slavery. Marcus seemed to think that he'd done a brilliant thing and that Acte should be a grateful and loving wife because Marcus was a Roman man. Acte, unsurprisingly, disagreed. The second she saw her chance, she legged it. She disappeared into the night with another freedman, presumably

---

† This story in Plutarch, *Consolation to Apollonius* 14, ends up being a ghost story. In order to find out whether his son was murdered or not, Elysius went to a temple to ask for a prophetic dream. His father and son both appear to him in his dream and hand him a piece of paper which reads: 'Verily somehow the minds of men in ignorance wander / Dead now Euthynoos lies; destiny has so decreed. / Not for himself was it good that he live, nor yet for his parents.' Which is not an answer and is, in fact, useless. The point of the story is that the soul lives on after death, but it probably won't help the living.

one she liked, and abandoned her new husband at the first available opportunity. This was a second blow to Marcus, a Roman man unused to rejection. Following his second wife ditching him, the third blow came when his beloved daughter started wasting away, slowly becoming smaller and weaker, failing to respond to the treatments he bought for her or the medicines her doctors gave her. Finally, she breathed her last. There was only one explanation in Marcus' mind: Acte had cursed Iunia. He was so convinced that Acte had murdered his daughter from afar with magic in order to hurt him that he wrote this whole interpersonal drama on the back of the altar he built for Iunia in an astonishing act of oversharing.[20] It's tough to make yourself the victim of someone else's alleged murder, but Marcus managed to do it.

Obviously what we're seeing here is people dying of any number of random chronic and long-term illnesses. They could have been dying of anything from anaemia to blood cancer to Crohn's. There's no way of knowing. What we do know is that their loved ones, and possibly they, believed that they had been murdered. Someone had to be responsible. In the 1990s, a German historian called Fritz Graf identified sixty-three epitaphs from the Roman Empire which explicitly or implicitly state that the deceased was murdered by magic, which is simultaneously a lot of imagined murders and not very many epitaphs. But if we extrapolate wildly and unethically from that sixty-three we can try to imagine all those deaths that resulted in epitaphs that were lost and families who couldn't afford a long epitaph, or even a tombstone at all, and we can imagine as many unfortunate deaths as we like. Every death from an untreated chronic illness or unexpected fever that didn't respond to treatments of cold baths and herbs likely had a shadow of witchcraft and murder hanging over it.

What this means is that, as far as the people of the Roman Empire were concerned, there were an awful lot of murders happening. If every unexplained death at a young age from what modern medicine would recognise as being a random medical accident, like cardiovascular disease or tuberculosis or lupus, is seen as a murder in the ancient world then, wow, that is a lot of murders. And it's really easy to see how something like lupus could be read as a curse: sudden rashes in butterfly shapes on the face, light sensitivity, unexplained tiredness and pains all could easily be read as inexplicable magic. The same goes for hepatitis which turns you yellow or tetanus which locks the muscles or any of the eighty million diseases spread by insects and bacteria and viruses which will kill you randomly and weirdly. So many of these unfortunate deaths were potentially read as magical murders.

Piso was either forced into suicide or assassinated by Tiberius because Germanicus got bitten by something on his holidays and caught dengue fever or something. He's really the only high-profile person we know who faced trial for using magical means to kill a rival but it's notable how very ready the entire Senate were to believe that he was guilty. Of course, Piso was a bit of a dick, and he didn't help himself at all with his reactions, but that doesn't mean he wasn't a victim. Something we will never, ever know is how many mini-Pisos there were in the Roman world, being accused of magical goings on just because they had an argument with Mamilius a week before Mamilius' daughter started coughing ominously.

One famous example of how incredibly, terrifyingly easy it was to be accused and convicted of doing magic is that of Apuleius in about 159 CE. Apuleius was born in Madaurus, a Roman-Berber city in what is now Algeria. He travelled the Empire, from North Africa, to Alexandria, to Rome and then to

Oea, now part of Tripoli in Libya. He made a reputation for himself as an orator and teacher, and wrote an absolutely wonderful novel called *Metamorphoses* or *The Golden Ass*. Not a lot of works of fiction survive from the ancient world, and most of those which do are Greek-language romance novels not dissimilar to the romance novels that make up a massive part of modern ebook sales – swoony boy meets pretty girl, girl is kidnapped by pirates, pirates sexily threaten girl's chastity, a series of misunderstandings where everyone threatens suicide, boy saves girl from pirates, boy and girl get married and live happily ever after. Apuleius' novel, however, is something else. It tells the story of Lucius, who is obsessed with magic and desperate to become a magician. In an attempt to turn into a beautiful bird, however, Lucius is accidentally turned into a donkey by an enslaved girl he is bonking. Panicked, the girl says that she can transform him back by feeding him roses, but that getting roses will have to wait until the next day. One begins to wonder whether she just wanted a night free of him. Lucius is put in the stables, which are raided overnight by thieves who steal him away.

The rest of the novel follows Lucius' adventures as a donkey travelling the Roman world trying to find a way back to his human form, with several embedded stories that he hears en route.

Metamorphoses is packed full of stories of wicked murderers and adulterers and magical happenings, and loads of shagging, so it seems right that Apuleius would eventually end up in a magical trial involving love, sex, magic and murder himself. His trial happened in around 158 CE, during the reign of the forgotten emperor Antoninus Pius. It was a time of particular peace and prosperity in the Empire and Antoninus seems to have been a thoroughly nice chap, which means that no one wrote any history books about it and it's rather a blank period of Roman history.

Apuleius was happily travelling around the Empire, possibly writing his novel, when he arrived in Oea to visit an old friend, Sicinius Pontianus. The two had been at school together in Athens. The visit went splendidly for Apuleius, who fell in love with and promptly married Aemilia Pudentilla, his school chum's mum. Pontianus was initially delighted that his mate was now his stepfather, which is a challenge for those of us who grew up on *American Pie* to wrap our brains around but the past is a foreign country. The rest of Pontianus' extended family, however, were less keen.

Two men had a specific problem: Aemilia's ex-brother-in-law (her deceased husband's brother) Sicinius Aemilianus and the father of Pontianus' wife, Herennius Rufinus. Your immediate reaction might be something like, what does it matter to you what your daughter's husband's mum does? The issue was, of course, money. They were all interested in where Aemilia's cash would go when she died and they all saw her new husband as an obstacle to her cash entering their wallets via her sons. They started to spread the rumour around town that Aemilia had sworn, on the death of her first husband, that she would never remarry and that, therefore, Apuleius, this foreigner who arrived and married their beloved Aemilia, was a wizard. They said he had seduced poor innocent Aemilia with love potions and magic and also with his really, really good hair. They managed to get Aemilia's brother Tannonius Pudens (don't snigger) and her tiny teenage son Sicinius Pudens (stop it) involved and the whole thing appeared to revolve around slanging matches at the local baths, until Pontianus suddenly dropped dead. Apuleius abruptly became the poor foreigner who came to town, magically seduced their local rich widow and then killed her son. With magic. Probably.

The whole thing would have remained at the level of local dinner-party gossip and scowls over strigils,[21] had Apuleius not lost his temper and shouted at Sicinius Aemilianus to take him to court if he really meant it. The Roman aristocratic equivalent of 'Come and have a go if you think you're hard enough.' Because these are Romans. This might be in North Africa, but our players here were Roman to their core. Roman-ness had, by the 150s CE, far outgrown the city of Rome. Anyway, Apuleius squared up to Sicinius and found, to his surprise, that Sicinius was indeed hard enough to come and have a go. Apuleius went to the nearby city of Sabratha (also now part of Tripoli) to do some business for his wife only to be hauled in front of the visiting provincial governor out of the blue to face charges of being a dangerous wizard. The specific charge of murdering Pontianus was not technically included in Sicinius' formal accusation because, as Apuleius says, Pontianus died at sea and it was a stupid accusation, but the accusation of evil magic comes under the same law, the Lex Cornelia.

Because we have Apuleius' (definitely rewritten) defence speech, we know exactly what he was accused of and what acts he had allegedly engaged in which proved his guilt, and how stupidly innocuous those acts were. These included: 1) Attempting to purchase a certain kind of fish. 2) Sending an enslaved boy into a trance using magical chants. 3) Performing a sacrifice at night. 4) Owning a mirror. 5) Commissioning an ugly statue. 6) Writing rude poems, and, most importantly, 7) Marrying a rich woman despite being a poor foreigner. All of them came together, as far as the prosecution was concerned, to prove that Apuleius was a warlock and a threat to the community. Apuleius was forced to defend himself against the accusation that he bought a suspicious type of fish, owned a mirror and had bad taste in statues; accusations that are, effectively, impossible to refute. On the upside, he did get to turn his own trial into a showcase for his rubbish poems, one of which is about toothpaste, thus fulfilling the dreams of just about every amateur poet ever born. As it turned out, the best way to defend oneself against nebulous accusations of magical evil was to be an expertly trained orator and philosopher with a surprising (and arguably suspicious) amount of knowledge about magic. Apuleius was able to take their accusations apart one by one while, in the style of Cicero, exposing the greed at the core of the whole case. We don't technically know what the governor ruled in Apuleius' case but, as he was able to polish up his speech, publish it and then publish a novel and a bunch of philosophical works, I think we can safely assume he won and got to go smugly home to his rich wife. Apuleius' accusers were unlucky, because it's easy to see from his case how little was needed to bring a formal accusation of evil magic and how hard it would be to defend oneself against such an accusation as owning a mirror. Apuleius' case ended up not being a murder case, but it shines a flickering candlelight onto what a case like Iunia's might have looked like had Acte not been out of Marcus Iunius' grasp.

Iucundus

Mysterious magical diseases aren't the only kind of magic-related murder that we can find in Roman epigraphy. We can also find the very occasional case of children who were believed to have been sacrificed by witches. Specifically, little boys.

The idea that magicians sacrificed young boys is surprisingly common in the literary sources. It is basically a terrible perversion of the very normal ancient practice of sacrificing animals then cutting them open and reading their entrails for signs from the gods and prophecies for the future. Animal sacrifice was an everyday occurrence in the Roman Empire, for priests at least, and it eventually became a spectacle in its own right as Romans got access to more and more exotic animals. The process for sacrificing an animal is only described once in the entire surviving corpus of Latin literature, by the Greek writer Dionysius of Halicarnassus, and the process was highly ritualised. The animal was forced to bow, was purified with water and was then conked on the head with a hammer and stabbed as it fell.[†] Once it bled out, the carcass was flayed open and, if necessary, the entrails would be examined for portents. Examining livers and colons for portents was a specialised job, so there was a college of haruspices specially trained in what to look for. A very famous bronze model of a liver from the second century BCE was found in Piacenza and it is covered in markings and abbreviations which, basically, show the haruspices how to interpret what they find in the animal liver. If they find a lumpy bit in the top right corner then it relates to x, while a hard bit in the middle to the left relates to y. Obviously it's all very sacred and complicated and, frankly, an obtuse and difficult way for gods to communicate with humans, but this was fairly basic Roman religion. The gods told people their intentions through lumpy bits in livers. Sure. Once you accept that, it's not too hard to leap to the idea that human livers, pure, clean, innocent child livers, might also contain information about the future. And, because accessing that information meant killing a pure, clean, innocent child, that information might be secret, and powerful and wicked.

In Roman literature the writers are only interested in those who were doing the sacrificing of these little boys, and to be honest they were not too bothered with the fact that a child had died. The problem with this behaviour for them was less the murdering and more the fact that an illicit sacrifice had taken

---

[†] Another amusing thing that the emperor Gaius allegedly did was whack one of the other priests with the hammer instead of the animal, just for laughs.

place outside the boundaries of proper religion. A religious action was being done for irreligious, selfish purposes and that was much worse than killing a kid. Take, for example, the case of Publius Vatinius, who was a Tribune in 59 BCE when everything in Rome was really terrible, senators were being murdered in the streets on the regular and the rest were all in court. Vatinius appeared in court as a witness for the prosecution of Publius Sestius, who was being prosecuted for bribing his way into office. Cicero was Sestius' defence counsel and Cicero always gave 110 percent, so he wrote and delivered an entire speech ripping Vatinius to shreds as a person in order to destroy his credibility as a witness. The speech begins with Cicero calling Vatinius unimportant and uninteresting and gets more brutal from there. It is almost ten thousand words of character assassination. It's almost as bad as YA reviewers on GoodReads. In the middle of calling Vatinius stupid, depraved, mad, shameful, the ruin of the Republic, a waste of space and a thief – and not even a famous thief at that – Cicero accused Vatinius of habitually murdering boys and reading their entrails. It sounds awful now, but his crime, in Cicero's eyes, was not the murdered boys, it was the defiling of 'the auspices under which this city was founded, by which the whole of this Republic and Empire is kept together'.[22] The killing was just part of being sacrilegious and probably wouldn't have been mentioned if Vatinius hadn't poked at the boys' livers afterwards.[†] Had he John Wayne Gacy-ed his way through life, no one would ever have mentioned it.

The same is true for pretty much all accusations of ritual murder in literature. The point was that the killer was a blasphemous and sinful bastard, not that they were a child-murderer.

---

† After all this, Vatinius and Cicero ended up being great friends in later life, probably because massive civil wars will put everything in perspective.

For some reason, these accusations appear more often in later Roman literature than in Republican or early Imperial era literature. Later emperors, ones that hardly anyone has heard of any more, get accused of being ritual murderers and wizards a lot more than early ones do. For example, Dio accuses the emperor Didius Julianus of killing boys. Julianus is a really fun emperor. He shocked the entire Roman world by literally purchasing the throne from the Praetorian Guard after they, en masse, murdered the reigning emperor Pertinax in 133 CE because he hadn't paid them. Several hundred guards stormed the palace and cut Pertinax down, then held an informal auction to sell the throne. The winner was whoever was willing and able to pay each Praetorian the highest bonus in that moment. After hours of bidding, the guards accepted Julianus' final offer of twenty-five thousand sesterces per guard (with a thousand guards, that's twenty-five million sesterces in total), opened the palace gates and declared him emperor. The Senate, being a quivering mass of useless wimps, hailed him as their glorious leader immediately. He lasted sixty-six days before Septimius Severus came along to kill him. As soon as Severus showed up, the Senate changed their minds about Julianus' glorious leadership, declared Julianus a public enemy and began to spread rumours that he was taking extreme measures to find a way to protect his life and throne: he was sacrificing little boys 'believing that he could avert some future misfortunes if he learned of them beforehand'.[23] Obviously, it didn't work.

A much later and much more suspicious source than Dio (who was at least alive and present during the reign of Julianus), the *Scriptores Historiae Augustae*, makes the same accusation about the boy emperor Elagabalus. Poor Elagabalus was really called Marcus Aurelius Antoninus Augustus but there were already a bunch of emperors with those names so, after he died, he got lumped with the name of the god of which he was priest as a child in Syria. He became emperor at fourteen years old and was about as good at ruling a military dictatorship and continent-sized bureaucratic structure as any fourteen-year-old edgelord would be. Massively lacking in charisma, uniqueness, nerve and talent, he primarily got himself some sparkly things, got himself immediately laid and, rudely, continued his Syrian religion in Rome. All these things pissed off the adult Roman senators a lot. When the anonymous author of the *SHA* came to write a life of the poor boy, he straight up said that Elagabalus had his foreign magicians kill a boy every day and then would personally examine the victims' livers and 'torture the victims after the manner of his own native rites' because the Romans were never above a little sneering at the East. To really undermine this accusation, though, the anon author claims that the emperor was not content with the boys everyone else was presumably using – that is, enslaved children – but was stealing kids from noble families around Italy because they were prettier. Leaving aside the insinuation that freedom and nobility confer good looks, this is why no one is sure whether the *SHA* is fictional or not. At least its author was slightly concerned with the murdered boys and their families.

One cannot say the same for Philostratus, who wrote a long and tedious biography of Apollonius of Tyana who was a very boring man and Neoplatonist philosopher, for the empress Julia Domna in the 210s CE, and he used the classic trick of pretending that his book was based on the diaries of Apollonius' closest enslaved friend. It's a trick used by almost every historical novelist at least once, but Philostratus did it first. Apollonius was a kind of wandering teacher who would roll up in a town, deliver some wisdom, do a miracle and then wander away, mystically. He fights a satyr, expels some demons, kicks a plague beggar, defeats a vampire. He's somewhere between Jesus, Gilderoy Lockhart and the Littlest Hobo. One place that he rolls into is Puteoli while on his way to a dramatic showdown with the emperor Domitian, who has heard about Apollonius' magical powers, which Philostratus wants you to know are good divine magic, not wizard magic. In Puteoli, Apollonius met a man named Demetrius who told him that Domitian was planning on publicly accusing him of sacrificing a boy in order to 'divine the secrets of the future which are to be learned from an inspection of youthful entrails'[24] and using those secrets to overthrow the emperor. Also, Demetrius warns, Domitian thought that Apollonius dressed badly. Apollonius, being a philosopher and a pain, refused to heed advice and made his way to Rome where he was promptly arrested and put on trial in front of Domitian himself. After some questions about Apollonius' dress sense (which Domitian really took against. Domitian did once write a book about hair care so maybe he had an especial interest in male grooming.), the emperor politely asked the Neoplatonist why he'd sacrificed a boy and to whom the boy was sacrificed. Apollonius retorted that he demanded to know whether Domitian had any witnesses to this alleged sacrifice. Apparently highly impressed by this comeback, which I can't help but feel he should have anticipated, Domitian promptly acquitted him. At which point, Apollonius said 'You couldn't have killed me anyway, because I'm not a mortal' and vanished into thin air.[25] Just like *The Littlest Hobo*. Miraculous disappearances and clear magical abilities aside, once again no one was interested in the poor boy who allegedly got cut up, presumably autopsied while still alive. They were only interested in the religion and emperor that got insulted.

So it's fascinating and heartbreaking to find the tombstone of Iucundus, set up by his parents Vitalis and Gryphus, and his enslaver Livia, which reads:

Iucundus, the slave of Livia the wife of Drusus Caesar,
son of Gryphus and Vitalis. As I grew towards my
fourth year I was seized and killed, when I had the
potential to be sweet for my mother and father. I was
snatched by a witch's hand, ever cruel so long as it
remains on the earth and does harm with its craft.
Parents, guard your children well, lest grief of this
magnitude should implant itself on your breast.[26]

It's not massively common to find tombstones for enslaved
people, and especially not ones this detailed. Iucundus was the
child of an enslaved couple, but these were enslaved members of
the imperial household at Rome and were presumably very privileged as far as the enslaved went because they were allowed to
have a recognised relationship and a child. If it weren't for the
fact they were enslaved, they'd be a charming and immediately
recognisable nuclear unit: mum, dad and baby – until little
Iucundus was snatched away. The epitaph says he was coming
up to his fourth year, which means he was three years old in
Roman counting, which is two years old in our way of counting
as the Romans counted inclusively.[27] A full blown toddler,
wobbling about, starting to speak and do things for himself until,
one day, he vanished in a tragedy that broke Gryphus and Vitalis'
hearts. Everyone involved believed that Iucundus had been
stolen by a witch to be sacrificed in a magical rite. When Dio and
Philostratus and the *SHA* and Horace and all the other literary
sources throw out the sacrifice of infants as a pithy little accusation, it is the Iucunduses of the Roman world they are talking
about. Each of these boys was someone's child, someone's baby,
snatched and sacrificed. For all that these rites apparently defiled
Roman gods, the loss of a child destroyed a tiny anonymous
family unit. Iucundus' desperately sad epitaph is open about his

parents' loss and grief and offers a warning to other parents: keep an eye on your kids, don't let them take sweets from strangers, don't end up like us. They are the humans who are so dehumanised by the literary sources' focus on the act as sacrifice rather than ritualised murder.

The reason that the literary sources are so dehumanising is that they didn't perceive killing enslaved people to be particularly wrong. It was the *purpose* of the killing which was wrong, not the death itself. It cannot be murder to the free, citizen writers of literature any more than thumping a cow with a hammer was murder, because the boys were slaves, not people. Iucundus' epitaph exposes the awfulness of that thinking. Of course, we don't know whether Iucundus was killed in a ritual manner as the epitaph says. I hope he wasn't because it wouldn't have been painless. The fact that the epitaph exhorts parents to guard their babies rather than demanding revenge from the gods as the other epitaphs do makes me wonder whether the wicked witch was known and caught and punished. Involving the imperial family in magical practice, however tangentially, doesn't seem like a particularly good idea for a witch, but of course there's no way of knowing. All we can know is that, were this cruel witch caught, she would have been charged with magical acts, not murder. In our modern conception, justice could never really be done for Iucundus.

7

Murder in the Imperial House

Livia

The rains in 23 CE were apocalyptic. They fell on Rome incessantly and relentlessly, swelling the Tiber so much it burst its banks. The rushing water swept away the bridge which connected the banks to Tiber Island and flooded part of the city. For three days, people could navigate around Rome only by boat, their homes and businesses lost. And still the rains fell. With the rains came storms, brutal winds, rumbling, roaring thunder and flashes of lightning. Sometimes the lightning hit wooden houses and they burst into flame and burnt in the midst of the rain. These were omens enough but the gods sent another. Someone caught a wolf in the city. The first seen for years. Rome was having a bad one. And not a single person had an umbrella. With the relentless rains and rising, rushing waters came chills and fevers and no one was safe. First, the emperor Augustus fell ill. There were rumours that he wouldn't make it, that he'd given his seal ring away to his right-hand man Agrippa. Tendrils of fear crept down the back of citizens' necks along with the rain. Augustus was the only man holding the illusory restored Republic together. No one wanted another civil war. No one wanted to lose any more sons of Rome. They prayed to the gods and sacrificed and made promises and their prayers were heard and their emperor recovered, cured by cold baths and peculiar potions. A little hope was allowed to blossom that the year would pass without the tragedy foretold by the wolves and weather. The omens were rarely wrong, though, especially not when they brought stagnant water full of corpses in a world without antibiotics; the people's prince, Augustus' beloved son-in-law and nephew, caught the fever and within days he had died. He was just nineteen years old.

Marcus Claudius Marcellus was the son of Gaius Claudius Marcellus and Octavia Minor. Octavia was Augustus' only sister and Marcellus was her only son. In fact, he was the only boy child that either sibling ever produced. As the closest thing that Augustus had to a biological son, everyone was absolutely gooey-eyed over him. He was the same age as Augustus' stepson Tiberius but considerably more popular due to not being a lumbering dork. As a member of the Julian family, he had the blood of the Divine Julius Caesar, descended from the goddess Venus and the Trojan Aeneas, pumping in his teenage veins. Since the age of about sixteen, nice Uncle Augustus had been grooming him to rule the Roman Empire. Augustus saw Marcellus as his great-uncle Julius Caesar had once seen him. He saw promise. Having apparently given up on sons of his own, Augustus married off the sixteen-year-old Marcellus to his thirteen-year-old biological daughter Julia, thus making his nephew his son-in-law and creating a powerful marital bond between the two men (Julia was irrelevant, because she was a girl). He then spent three years introducing Marcellus to the army, and then granting him a handful of government powers that a nineteen-year-old boy definitely shouldn't have been allowed but which Augustus had taken from the Republic with menaces so that he could now hand them to his heir. In Marcellus, Augustus was gradually building up a successor to be someone who could take on the mantle of Princeps and be the first citizen of Rome in the restored Republic, maintaining a steady hand on the tiller. Augustus trained Marcellus up to be a golden hope for the future of Augustus' Rome. And then Marcellus died in his bed in Baiae.

In any other family, this would have been a sad story. Indeed, for his biological mother, it was a sad story. She desperately mourned him, her only son, who had so much promise. But Marcellus was not a member of any other family. He was a member of the Julio-Claudians. The soon-to-be-known-as imperial family of Rome. And his death marked a distinct shift in the way that this family, especially the heads, would be seen. For Augustus and his wife Livia, the loss of Marcellus marked a significant move in Roman politics because Marcellus wasn't just a potential heir, he was the potential heir to the Empire, so his untimely death at such a young age, of a fever that so many – even his permanently sickly uncle! – had recovered from, couldn't just be a tragedy; it was a suspicious tragedy. As we learned from Germanicus, when suspicious tragedies happened in such public arenas, people began to wonder, and to talk, and to ask *'cui bono?'* and to look to the wicked stepmother. Marcellus' sudden death marked the first time that the Roman people had suffered the loss of a young prince and it was the first time they turned their eyes onto Livia and saw her as a possible murderer.

Marcellus' tragic death broke the hearts of a lot of people, and that heartbreak completed the transformation of the Julio-Claudian family from elite rich bastards with good bloodlines and swords and a lot of political power, much like any other elite rich bastard family in Rome, into the royal family of Rome. Marcellus had been presented to the Roman people as a public figure from the first day he walked out of his house in his tiny *toga virilis*. He belonged to the Senate and people of Rome as much as he belonged to his family because his family was Augustus and Augustus ruled the Senate and people of Rome. When he succumbed to whatever disease took his life, the whole of Rome felt that they had lost a son. Augustus didn't help matters. He gave Marcellus, who was technically just a nineteen-year-old with a mid-tier magistracy, an all-out public funeral that he hadn't earned and his ashes were the first to be interred in the giant Mausoleum of Augustus in the middle of the city. His name was put on a couple of buildings in memoriam. The death of Augustus' nephew was very much an occasion for the whole of Rome, unlike the death of any other nineteen-year-old magistrate. If the Republic itself died with Julius Caesar, the myth of the restored Republic died with Marcellus as it became very, very clear that Rome had a royal family.

This could have been merely an uninteresting footnote in Roman history, just another little moment of transition, but I wouldn't be writing about it unless there was something more than that. Because the other thing that Marcellus' tragic death introduced to the world was the rumour that Augustus' demure and delightful wife Livia wasn't the modest, well-behaved good little woman she presented as; she was actually a cold-hearted ambitious bitch who murdered Marcellus for being more popular than her own tedious sons. These rumours would eventually attach themselves to a number of sad and untimely deaths in the Julian family, leading to the thrilling portrayal of Livia in the ancient sources as a straight-up serial killer. If we take the Roman sources at face value, Livia is accused of killing Marcellus, her step-grandchildren Lucius Caesar and Gaius Caesar, her husband Augustus and another step-grandchild Agrippa Postumus. She is also accused of maybe plotting to kill Agrippina the Elder (yet another step-grandchild) and Agrippina's children and possibly being involved in the murder of Germanicus, her biological grandson. That's five murders, and involvement in a sixth.

Livia's alleged weapon of choice was the conveniently ambiguous *veneficas*, or, to use the words of our main historical source for the period, Tacitus, 'treachery', which serves to make *veneficas* look specific. Tacitus is a really fun source for the women of the Julio-Claudian period of Roman history because he hated women like most people hate wasps. He was, therefore, all too happy to believe and repeat any rumours about nefarious things that any woman he'd ever heard of might have done or thought about. He's very canny though, is Tacitus, and he is a genuinely brilliant prose writer so his accusations are buried under insinuation and phrases like 'the treachery of Livia', 'the secret diplomacy of the mother' and 'feminine caprice', which is as close as one can get to standing up in a crowd and screaming 'Murderer!!!' without quite doing so. No other Roman source is as mean to Livia as Tacitus, which is fun because it really exposes his swivel-eyed misogyny. For the death of Marcellus, for example, the biographer Suetonius, who is usually known for including every rumour he can think of for completeness, doesn't even mention that suspicions floated around Livia. The much later historian Cassius Dio does mention the suspicions but immediately dismisses them as unfounded. Velleius Paterculus was a contemporary historian who doesn't mention the rumours at all, but that's maybe because he was writing in the reign of Livia's son Tiberius, whom he lavishly praises at every opportunity as the greatest man who ever lived, so he absolutely cannot be trusted.[†] Tacitus, however, went for it. He paints, with exquisite subtlety and skill, an image of Livia as a creeping, cold-blooded serial murderer filled with deranged ambition for herself and her useless son Tiberius. He cements her reputation in history with a single, spectacular line, put into the anonymous mouths of other men: 'Livia, as a mother, was a curse on the Empire, as a stepmother, a curse on the house of Caesars.'[1] His Livia is a

---

† There's nothing less trustworthy than a Roman historian writing about their own emperor, except perhaps one writing ten years later.

monstrosity, a destroyer of families and of the whole Roman world. This is an image which isn't supported by any other Roman era source, but the whole world has basically bought it because Tacitus is that good.

Livia is cursed with a few problems. First, in retrospect, the deaths of six people who seemed to stand between the lumpen Tiberius and his promotion do look a bit suspicious. Once again, *cui bono?* As soon as Augustus started promoting the career of anyone on *his* side of the family by marrying them to his daughter or adopting them, they dropped dead. Marcellus got sick at the exact time that he had just thrown his first set of games to get the people to like him. So, Augustus adopted Lucius Caesar and Gaius Caesar to replace him. Lucius and Gaius were the oldest sons of Augustus' daughter Julia and his BFF Agrippa (try not to think about the fact that poor Julia had been widowed at the age of about sixteen then almost immediately married off to her dad's best friend who was in his thirties because it will make you sad for the poor girl). As his biological grandchildren, they were the closest thing Augustus had left to sons of his bloodline so as soon as they were able to hold a conversation he started training them up like he had been training Marcellus. As always, history got in the way. In 2 CE, Lucius was eighteen years old and was hanging out being the child head of the army in the city that is now called Marseille when he abruptly keeled over and dropped dead of 'sudden illness'. Were this to be filmed in the style of a classic BBC historical drama, Lucius would cough ominously into a hankie during a dramatic scene and would be dead by the end of the episode. But this wasn't too tragic at this point, because Augustus still had the older brother Gaius.

Gaius was three years older, so he was the grand old age of twenty-three when Augustus sent him off to sort some things out in Armenia. There was always something going down in

Armenia, because it was the point at which the Parthian Empire and the Roman Empire met, so one empire or the other invaded it every few years. At this time, it had a Roman-sponsored client king and the Parthians were sponsoring a rebellion in the hopes of placing a Parthian client king on the throne. It was a fairly typical proxy war, and the life of an Armenian was probably pretty stressful for approximately five centuries. Anyway, Gaius was sent to fix this latest problem but, as he was practically a child, he was a little naïve. The Parthian-backed rebel king, who I feel deserved the throne just for being named Abbaddon, sent Gaius an invite to chat in his camp. Come over to my military camp, the enemy said, let's have tea. Gaius, being apparently an idiot, pottered over, possibly bearing a gift, and was shocked – shocked! – to discover that it was a trap and there was no tea, only stabbings. He somehow escaped the camp alive but horribly wounded. He tried to get home to Italy but expired of his wounds on the way. One can't help but feel that he would not have been a brilliant emperor, but it was still a blow to Augustus' plans and, coming eighteen months after the death of Lucius, it looked bad. That was now three young, healthy, military men who had dropped dead as soon as Augustus made them his heir.

Augustus had basically no biological male relatives left, except a kid called Agrippa Postumus whom he had exiled for having bad taste and a violent temper, and the stepson no one liked. His stepson was the younger son of his wife Livia and her first husband. It was Tiberius. He was the last man standing, looking around in confusion like John Travolta in that *Pulp Fiction* GIF. With palpable reluctance, Augustus forced Julia and Tiberius to marry (which was fun because they openly despised one another) and adopted Tiberius as his heir. Then he died, at the impressive age of seventy-five, having been working hard to pretend to restore the Republic for a solid fifty-six years. He died peacefully in his bed, which was, apparently, massively suspicious. Four sources mention gossip that Livia found out something that annoyed her just before Augustus died, and two outright claim that Livia killed him by painting poison onto figs that were still hanging on the tree and getting him to pick and eat them, which is a very smart way of getting around imperial tasters. Both Tacitus and Dio give this cute story. Tacitus, Dio, Pliny the Elder and Plutarch all tell a related story, which is that, just before he died, Augustus was thinking of bringing Agrippa Postumus back to Rome to make him a proper heir to the throne and had, in fact, gone on a secret trip to Agrippa's exile island to have a tearful reunion taking just one close friend, Fulvius, with him. Fulvius, however, had told his wife what had happened on the trip and what Augustus' plans were. His wife had then told Livia about it. Now, in Pliny and Plutarch, the outcome of this is that Livia shouts at Augustus until he apologises. In Tacitus and Dio, however, this secret trip results in Livia painting poison on a fig and bumping off her beloved husband of fifty years in order to smoothly take on her true form as the power-mad mother of the emperor who hated his mother!

You can see how easy it is to make all these deaths look extremely dodgy and to set Livia up as a supervillain. With the benefit of hindsight, they look awfully convenient for Livia and Tiberius – if you believe that Tiberius and Livia wanted to be emperor and mother-of-the-emperor, that is. It is awfully fun to imagine Livia acting the puppet master in the imperial house, mixing poisons in her bedroom and sending nefarious messengers off to Armenia and France to slip some non-specific poison into the drinks of the emperor's adopted heirs, somehow, without anyone noticing or intervening. The logistics of such an undertaking are just baffling. What we actually have here, though, is the Roman equivalent of conspiracy theories about the death of Princess Diana and the accusations that Prince Philip ordered MI6 to murder her because she was pregnant by her Muslim partner Dodi Fayed. The story goes that Prince Philip was so repulsed by the idea of a non-Christian being related to the British royal family that he had Diana killed. This theory comes from Dodi's father, the billionaire Mohamed Al-Fayed, who proclaimed it multiple times in interviews and, once, in court on the witness stand. The theory has been supported by Diana's personal butler Paul Burrell and has spawned a full Metropolitan Police investigation and multiple Wikipedia pages. With those facts alone, from the perspective of a historian looking back from the future, Diana's death looks *trés* suspicious. Why were the Met investigating if there was nothing to investigate? There's no smoke without fire. Two credible witnesses close to the couple have made public statements about it. Suspicious. Except we all know that the Queen and Prince Philip did not instruct MI6 to murder Princess Diana. She died in a drunk driving accident involving parties who were not wearing seatbelts. A tragedy, not a murder. As it turns out, though, you can make any tragic young death look suspicious if you look at it from the right angle, especially if it happens in the royal family.

What we are witnessing here with Livia is the transformation of the Julio-Claudian family from ordinary private family, where gossip about their tragedies was dinner-party chat, into royal family, where gossip about their tragedies was History and therefore worthy of being written down. Livia, being a woman who appeared to benefit from the tragedies, received the full force of the gossip and suspicion because, basically, she dared to be a woman who was alive and royal and slightly visible. She had the occasional opinion and the ability to persuade her husband and son to do things, and that was basically the same as being a murderer as far as some Romans were concerned.

Livia is just the first in a litany of women in the imperial family who are painted as monstrous, murderous creatures with a lust for power that drove them to kill members of the family. The next woman in line to get this treatment was another Livia (deep sigh). This one tends to be called Livilla, which means Little Livia and is quite sweet. Livilla was the daughter of Antonia the Younger, grand-daughter of Mark Antony and Octavia, the sister of the eventual emperor Claudius and the niece of the emperor Tiberius. She was first married at the age of twelve to her second cousin Gaius Caesar (he who died in Armenia) and was widowed aged seventeen. She was then immediately married to her first cousin Drusus, who was Tiberius' eldest son. Literally in the same year as she was widowed. Everything was OK for a decade; she even had a baby called, predictably, Livia. Also her great-uncle Augustus died and her uncle/father-in-law became emperor. This meant that she was first in line to be the next emperor's wife, which was pretty nice if you like that kind of thing. Unfortunately, Livilla possessed what women weren't supposed to have, which was desires and a personality of her own. This was very bad. Especially when she started shagging around a bit. Turns out that being forcibly married to your cousin as a teenager while having absolutely no choice, agency or freedom in your life doesn't lead to happy marriages. I know; I'm shocked too. Double unfortunately, she took up with a thoroughly unsuitable man. She not only went outside of the immediate family, which was bad enough, but she didn't even shag a senator. Someone of decent and discreet standing would have at least been tolerable. No, she fell for the head of the emperor's private army, the equestrian Praetorian Prefect Lucius Aelius Sejanus. Now, if you've seen the classic 1976 TV series *I, Claudius*, you'll remember Sejanus as the absolute swine played by pre-*Star Trek* Patrick

Stewart. You'll also know why Livilla falling for him was a terrible idea.

You see, Sejanus wanted to be emperor. Or, at the very least, he wanted to be a member of the imperial family. And he had a pretty good run at it. Sejanus was Tiberius' BFF. Sejanus began life as an equestrian, became head of the Praetorian Guard and got on so well with Tiberius that, when Tibby got fed up of Rome and went to live on a tiny island instead, Sejanus was basically the only person he would talk to. Had Instagram existed in the Roman world, Sejanus would have spent his days posting selfies with Tiberius on Capri hashtagged #besties #bestiegoals #bff #bestfriendsforever and making sure everyone back in Rome saw them. Tiberius showered Sejanus with presents and honours, like letting him be consul and giving him extrajudicial powers and telling him he was great, and Sejanus loved it. But he always wanted more. First, he got his tiny infant daughter betrothed to the son of Claudius, Tiberius' nephew. This was a weak link because, at the time, everyone hated Claudius (indeed, they always did) and thought he and his offspring were useless, but it was still an entry to the Claudian family. Then Claudius' idiot son choked to death on a pear and Sejanus' baby daughter was down a husband before she even had teeth. So when Livilla and Sejanus started spending more time together it seemed very much like Sejanus was trying to make his way into the imperial family himself by marrying the emperor's niece/daughter-in-law. The existence of Livilla's husband was but a stumbling block.

The story Tacitus tells is that Sejanus persuaded Livilla to poison her husband Drusus. Or Livilla and Sejanus plotted together to poison Drusus so they could be together. The general consensus in the sources, with the exception of Dio, is that Sejanus was a criminal mastermind of Moriarty proportions.

Sejanus seduced Livilla and, having persuaded her to violate her virtue once, was able to persuade her towards darker paths by promising marriage and a share in the Empire. This accusation does seem to willingly overlook the fact that Livilla was already married to the emperor's primary heir and was a dead cert to be the next empress of Rome in her current marriage, and that killing her husband – the emperor's only biological son – and marrying his equestrian BFF would be both a massive risk and an enormous step down husband-wise. If Livilla was 'ambitious' to be an Augusta, she'd have been better off enduring her marriage to the emperor-in-waiting, rather than killing him. The only really logical explanation for why Livilla would poison Drusus is that she wanted to. She was either very into Sejanus or very much despised her husband and the lure of being empress wasn't enough to overcome either of those things.

I like to imagine that Sejanus and Livilla were really into each other and both hated Drusus. Drusus does seem to have been difficult. There's a great story in Tacitus about Drusus losing his temper with Sejanus and punching him in the face, which is a real scandal for a Roman man, who was not supposed to have rash emotions. It hints at a genuine violent animosity between the two that I enjoy. I like the image of Sejanus and Livilla as a kind of Ruth Snyder and Harry Judd Gray of their time, but more competent, because Sejanus and Livilla almost got away with it.[2] According to Tacitus, they got a doctor onside as a co-conspirator. This doctor, Eudemus, gave the poison to Drusus over a period of time and, to all onlookers, Drusus' death appeared to be the result of slow illness. Such was Drusus' lifestyle, everyone assumed that he'd died as a result of his general dissolution. Until, that was, Sejanus fell out with Tiberius and was horribly and publicly executed along with his tiny children. Sejanus himself was strangled on the day he was condemned, and his body was thrown down the Gemonian steps into the Forum Romanum for all to see. The people of Rome spent three days abusing it, apparently. His son Capito Aelianus and daughter Junilla were also strangled and their bodies disposed of, but not before the executioners raped twelve-year-old Junilla to absolve themselves of the offence of executing a virgin.[3] Their young violated bodies were also cast down the steps into the most public of Roman spaces to be further violated by the people.

In immense despair, though possibly a bit late, Sejanus' wife Apicata wrote a letter to Tiberius outlining how Livilla and Sejanus had murdered his son for their own gain, then she killed herself. Tiberius was appalled. He pulled out Sejanus' eunuch Lycurgus and Eudemus the doctor and tortured them until they confessed, which is always a sound method. With this proof, Tiberius was convinced. Sejanus was already dead, but Livilla was still around to be punished. Her fate is sort of recorded by Dio, who has a go but is unclear on precisely what happened to her. He is pretty sure she died, but either Tiberius executed her or her mother locked her in a room and starved her to death.

This story was believed to be the complete truth in the Roman world. The evidence is not excellent, though. It's a letter written by a woman whose husband and children had just been violently murdered and displayed in the streets of Rome and evidence gained by torture. I'd admit to killing Drusus right now under the lightest suggestion of torture so I'm always suspicious of that kind of evidence. But the news certainly resulted in the death of Livilla, somehow, and it was more evidence that family politics in the Julio-Claudian house was now imperial politics. It was also evidence that murder was now perceived to be a dynastic strategy.

*   *   *

It would be extremely tedious to sit and describe all the murders within the imperial family. We'd be here for a month, and anyway there's a constant air of did-they-or-didn't-they hanging over all of them, especially the women. Did, for example, Agrippina the Younger plot to kill her brother and, twenty years later, poison her husband/uncle Claudius with a mushroom so her son could be emperor? The details are strong for the latter murder, but they are also suspiciously similar in means, motive and opportunity to Livia's alleged murder of Augustus. Almost every detail is similar enough to raise the eyebrows of disbelief. Did Tiberius kill his adoptive son Germanicus because he was getting too popular? Did Claudius' other wife Messalina murder someone because she wanted to own their lovely garden? Or is it all scurrilous gossip? What matters is that the population of the Empire apparently believed that the imperial family was perpetually plotting to secretly murder one another. Surreptitious murder had very quickly come to be seen as a strategy for members of the imperial family to gain and maintain power and everyone thought that was pretty fun gossip.

The wider issue is that in every other powerful family in Rome there were similar power struggles and people trying to murder their way out of bad marriages, as we have seen, but these were private issues. No one wrote histories about them. Their household diaries weren't preserved to be pored over two hundred years later by biographers and historians looking for grand narratives or clear characters. The death of Marcellus shows us how flimsy Augustus' image of the restored Republic was, and how absolutely nobody really bought it. The Imperial era began when dinner-party gossip became historical fact, and when every death in the family became a murder.

Aulus Cremutius Cordus

The Imperial era introduced murder as a dynastic strategy to the Romans. It also introduced the exhilarating new world of entirely random executions of important people on the whim of a single person. That's right. It also brought dictatorship, with all its glorious nonsense and pointless loss of life. I shall call it Death by Emperor.

When Augustus began creating the Roman imperial system, which he cutely called the Principate, when he was still called Octavian, he did so off the back of winning two civil wars, creating his own private army, and enacting a series of proscriptions that had around two thousand people arrested and executed for crimes as minor as 'Existing as Cicero' or 'Being Really Rich' or 'Friendship ended with Marcus Favonius, now Marcus Antonius is my best friend'.[†] Thus, before the Principate even officially existed, it was bathed in the blood of the upper classes, and god knows how many working free and enslaved people died in the process. This was always remembered as a black spot on his career, but then he became Augustus, which basically means 'most holy one', and all those murders that happened were gradually forgotten. Even the fact that he basically killed Cicero. His fate was quite different to that of Sulla's followers after Sulla's retirement and death. Sulla, you'll hopefully remember, had hundreds of people killed in his proscriptions of 82 BCE, ruled as dictator for a year, retired, moved to Puteoli to live in a ménage à trois with his wife and a drag queen called Metrobius,[4] then dropped dead in 78 BCE of something disgusting.[5] All seemed well, until 64 BCE, almost two decades later, when the Republic was crumbling again and an election was coming up (the year

---

†   Favonius had 'became very selfish, Proudy, and those who shows me Attitude, I keep them under my Foot'.

Cicero won) and Julius Caesar was the quaestor in charge of the murder courts. JC decided to make a splash by prosecuting three of the men who had carried out Sulla's orders and killed proscribed men in 82 BCE for murders. He singlehandedly redefined those legal, judicial executions carried out by the one-man government as illegal murders. And he won. Two of the three, Lucius Luscius (who was a centurion) and Lucius Bellianus (who stabbed a man in the middle of the Forum), both of whom had *fantastic* names, and were very much 'just following orders', were found guilty. The third, Lucius Sergius Catilina, became better known as Cicero's arch-nemesis and Roman traitor Catiline. The fact that murder is a construct, defined by those with power, had never been made quite so clear.

Had Octavian not learned from Sulla and Caesar some lessons about giving up power but not giving up authority, there's every possibility that his proscriptions would have eventually been redefined as the bloodlust of a warlord teenager. Thankfully, he was a terrifying genius (I mean that literally; he was terrifying) and he constructed the Principate which meant that he held absolute authority until he died, but he maintained the careful, respectful illusion of senatorial democracy and functioning courts, and so his proscriptions and every execution he ordered as emperor remained legal and Not Murder. He also, to be fair to him, did try to avoid killing close friends and members of the family and senators when he wasn't proscribing them. He preferred a gentle exile. Other emperors, however, were much less smart and subtle and careful and respectful of other people. Other emperors tended to say deeply awkward things like 'Remember, I can do anything I like to anyone' or 'With a single nod, I could have your throat cut' and many of them just could not be bothered with concepts like mercy. Where Augustus got himself a reputation for rescuing enslaved men from being thrown to lampreys, some of his successors were more likely to be found cultivating man-eating lamprey ponds for funsies. And so, many of the emperors of Rome found themselves with a reputation for executing people impulsively and unjustifiably and were stamped with the label 'murderer'.

The histories and biographies of Roman emperors are bursting at the seams with grotesque tortures, impulsive executions and random punishments, but whether the acts are defined as terrible murders or perfectly reasonable capital punishment depends essentially on how much the authors like the emperor in question. So, Tiberius sending guards to execute his ex-wife (and adoptive sister) Julia the Elder and her son Agrippa Postumus on the day he became Princeps was defined as cruel, wicked and unnecessary murder driven by personal enmity. Equally, the forced suicide of Aulus Cremutius Cordus for praising Julius Caesar's assassins in a history book in 25 CE is viewed by everyone as a shocking attack on a free speech that never existed. On the other hand, for example, Hadrian had four senators executed before he'd even set foot in Rome after his accession to the throne, stabbed an enslaved man straight in the eye and forced the Greeks to deify his deceased boyfriend, but because he asked senators for advice he was their best friend. The section of his biography in the *Scriptores Historiae Augustae* dedicated to his 'innate cruelty' and the huge numbers of people he put to death and the suggestion that he poisoned his wife Sabina fills a single sentence.[6] Admittedly it's the *SHA*, but it's the best we've got. The emperor Gaius Caligula on the other hand gets one sentence on his attempt to revive the popular elections for magistrates and give them unrestricted jurisdiction without oversight, but eight lengthy paragraphs on every execution and harsh word that anyone could remember because he took no advice from anyone and thoroughly embraced being an absolute monarch. Still, Hadrian gets remembered as a good guy who fell in love with a pretty boy rather than a cruel emperor who murdered senators and abandoned his wife, while Gaius is remembered as one of the great evils of the Roman world. On the other hand, Gaius got Malcolm McDowell to play him in a big budget porn film written by Gore Vidal and Hadrian didn't, so who's winning really?

All emperors killed people, all of them, but there were certain social and cultural criteria that separated the murderers from the statesmen; the bad boys from the grown-ups. We can call this section 'So You Want to Be a Roman Tyrant?' Please read carefully. To be a wicked, murderous tyrant it was first necessary for the emperor to make all their decisions about executions by themselves. Roman men of standing had a *consilium*, a group of (primarily male) friends and family who counselled and advised and supported one another in Republican Rome. A proto-WhatsApp group chat, if you will.[7] This is because, in Roman eyes, making decisions alone was foolish at best and horrendously selfish at worst. All men's actions affected everyone in the family and social group, and as such all serious decisions should be made collectively and after much discussion. Men didn't manumit an enslaved person without talking to their friends, senators didn't make important votes without discussing their options with their *consilium* and emperors absolutely should not be executing people before they've had a serious chat with their most serious friends. Good emperors, like Marcus Aurelius and Vespasian, took daily advice from their advisers, senators and legal experts and the like, and gave the appearance at least of thinking very hard about each high-level execution and ensuring that their pals agreed with them. Admittedly, if their *consilium* was anything like my WhatsApp groups, their friends will have vehemently declared that their enemies were the scum of the earth, offered to shank them themselves in outrage, and insisted that the emperor was a perfect paragon of goodness who deserved only joy, but possibly his friends were less furiously supportive than mine. It does, at least, seem unlikely that many of them would disagree *too* strongly with the absolute monarch of the Roman Empire to whom they offered regular sacrifices and oaths of allegiance. The appearance of consensus was there, though, and that's what mattered. Bad emperors, like Gaius and Nero and Tiberius and Commodus, did not let senators have the illusion of influence in a *consilium principis*.[8] Bad emperors did what the hell they liked. Tiberius left Rome and moved to Capri and only answered letters from Sejanus because he couldn't bear to be in the same city with other senators. Gaius and Commodus laughed in the faces of senators and openly told them that they could just kill them if they wanted to. Claudius and Nero insulted the Senate even further by taking the advice of Greek freedmen and women more seriously than legal scholars and may as well have spat in their eyes. This meant that senators and the Roman elite and experts didn't feel they had any influence in a reign. The appearance of partnership wasn't there. They felt vulnerable and afraid and exposed. And then, every so often, the emperor would kill one of them.

Thus, we get stories like the ones told by Suetonius about Tiberius. Suetonius says that Tiberius put a random man to death for joking during a funeral that the deceased could tell Augustus that Tiberius had never paid his legacies. He recites these stories with the solemnly shocked tone of a man who can barely believe he's writing such horrors. Claudius executed a man because someone else had a dream that Claudius murdered them. In fact, he allegedly did this twice. Then there's that classic *Horrible Histories* story that Gaius put a man to death for offering his own life in exchange for the emperor's during a period of imperial illness.[9] Nero and Tiberius are probably the emperors who attract the most stories of bizarre and quixotic motivations for executions in Suetonius' telling. Suetonius has Nero execute men for renting some shops, having a mask of Cassius (one of JC's assassins) on their family tree, and being sullen. Tiberius' biography recounts him putting people to death for asking what books he was reading, refusing to shag him, changing clothes near a statue of Augustus, carrying a ring with his face on it into the toilet and being mean about the Greek mythical king Agamemnon in a play. Perhaps my personal favourite, though, is the accusation levied at Commodus in the *SHA* that he had planned to execute loads of men on flimsy excuses but one of his enslaved servants threw out the bit of paper he'd written their names on and he forgot who they were, so he didn't.

The problem with all of these executions is that they appear to be capricious, egotistical, somewhat random and therefore unjust. We're talking here about the executions of prominent members of the Roman community – senators and magistrates and jurists and playwrights and Praetorian Prefects; people who looked like our senatorial and equestrian authors. The seemingly random nature of these executions, which took place on the merest whim of the emperor, scared them. It rightly scared them because it restricted their freedom to do and say and write things without fear, but it also scared them because the emperors who did this kind of thing were implicitly – and sometimes pretty explicitly – interpreting themselves as the state of Rome itself, rather than a servant of the state.

The legal justification for most of the seemingly arbitrary executions which happened under 'bad' emperors was the Lex

Julia Maiestatis, which was introduced by either Julius Caesar or Augustus or both. It is usually interpreted very broadly in English as a treason law but it's more complicated than that. Treason is extreme disloyalty to the state and to be convicted of it requires you to do a lot of very active things to hurt the state. Spying for another state, or trying to kill a monarch, or joining a foreign army, for example, would all be treason and would all take a massive amount of effort. More than most people are willing to put in, to be honest. *Maiestas*, on the other hand, didn't necessarily require all that effort and activity. *Maiestas* was much closer to lèse-majesté, which broadly means affronts to the dignity of the state of Rome. Theoretically, *maiestas* laws were introduced to protect the security (*perduellio*) and majesty (*maiestas*) of Rome and its Empire but obviously security and majesty (or dignity) are highly open to interpretation. All that openness made *maiestas* a tricky little thing that was vague, abstract, uncertain and sometimes deadly. We do still see examples of lèse-majesté laws in the world today, especially in Thailand. Thailand's military dictatorship, for example, has imprisoned people such as Siraphop Kornaroot for writing poems and a woman known as Aree K. for wearing black on the king's birthday, and prosecuted MP Pannika Wanich for making a gesture at a picture of a dead king and so on and so forth.

The deal with *maiestas*/lèse-majesté in the early Imperial period of the Julio-Claudian emperors was that the emperor was a member of a divine family, the descendant of both real gods and newly made gods. The Julian family claimed descent from Venus, who was one of the Big Twelve of the Greco-Roman pantheon, which gave them divine heritage, and on top of that both Julius and Augustus were deified. It's hard to talk about Roman deification of emperors in English because we only have one word for divine and one for god, whereas the Romans had two which came to mean slightly different things. They had *deus* and *divus*. Originally, these words were interchangeable, but the deification of Julius Caesar, accompanied by a vision of his soul as a comet ascending to heaven, changed that. There was a linguistic shift which led to gods who had never been mortal being called *deus* (or *dea*) while deified mortals were called *divus*. Divus Julius Caesar, but Deus Jupiter. The distinction was slight but precise. Deified emperors were gods, but a different class of gods to Mars and Venus and Juno. Just like Billy Sharp is a professional football player (who I picked at random from the Sheffield United current line-up) but, classification-wise, he's not in the same class as Lionel Messi. Messi is Zeus to Sharp's Julius Caesar. Sharp might not be being paid $80 million a year or have a theme park dedicated to him in China or the power to allegedly enforce a no-fly zone over his enormous house, but Sharp is still getting paid to play football in the Premier League and is undoubtedly being paid thousands of pounds a week for it, and he's still in those FIFA computer games and has his name on a shirt that people bafflingly pay £50 for. He's not Zeus, but he's doing all right. And Julius Caesar, and all his descendants, still got to be sacred.

This sacredness was aligned to divinity and meant that every emperor got temples in their honour and sacrifices made to their name and their person was sacrosanct and untouchable. This was all set up by Augustus pretty deliberately in order to make his person and his position powerful and special outside of the official political system. Making both the individual emperor and the position of Princeps sacred meant that any words or acts against them, no matter how abstract or vague, could be interpreted as an attack on their dignity and majesty and sacredness. To make a joke about an emperor was a form of blasphemy against the gods and the state and therefore also a form of treason. Now, strong emperors, aka 'good emperors', who felt that their power rested on their military glory or their political acumen, did not need to worry about *maiestas*. Vespasian won a war to become emperor and crushed the Jews in Judea with a ruthlessness that still echoes today.[10] He had no anxieties about his position as emperor and knew he could kick the shit out of any opposition, so virtually no one was executed for *maiestas* under Vespasian. One guy was, though: a man named Helvidius Priscus who relentlessly refused to call the emperor by his imperial name and was just generally an insubordinate arse until Vespasian cracked and executed him, but he was really asking for it. Vespasian's second son Domitian, however, was not secure in his position. He had none of the military glory of his father and brother and had never eternally destroyed any sacred spaces. He had spent his youth being actively humiliated by his father and brother after he sort of tried to start a war in Germany at the age of fourteen. As a result he was insecure in his inherited power and his familial majesty, and he leaned into *maiestas* trials hard to maintain his rule. He came down on every slight against him because he felt that his position was fragile and could be hurt by slights. He emphasised his relationship with the gods (his father and brother were deified) by wearing golden crowns embossed with Jupiter and hammering home an imaginary old-fashioned Roman morality with the pointy end of a sword.

The same can be said for almost all the Julio-Claudian emperors after Augustus. Augustus fought his way to create the entire Principate system and exercised *maiestas* carefully to construct the concept of the sacred Princeps, but had enough confidence in his abilities as a politician and general to believe in his own majesty without needing to force it with executions. None of his successors, however, had any of that. Tiberius had some military success but had repeatedly retired from politics and knew that he was unpopular as a person, because he was dour and enigmatic without a drop of charm or charisma. Gaius didn't have a minute's experience as a politician and his only military glory was wearing the tiny uniform the German troops made for him when he was a toddler. He wandered into the Principate with nothing to support him but his name. Claudius had been actively hidden from public view and it was generally believed that Gaius only brought him into public life as a joke due to his visible disability. He was literally a laughing stock until the day he became emperor.[11] Nero's mum thrust him onto the throne at the age of seventeen and he had nothing but a terrible neck-beard and a real dedication to singing to boast about. Each of them felt the need to defend their position as both the sole possessor and the embodiment of public Roman power. Each of them chose to loudly proclaim their insecurity to the whole of Western history by prosecuting and punishing men who seemed to undermine the majesty and sanctity and specialness of the Julio-Claudian family with jokes or poems or inappropriate behaviour near a statue. The great irony of lèse-majesté charges is that the very act of asserting majesty through a prosecution only identifies ways in which the monarch feels less-than-majestic.

This is why we can see that Tiberius felt anxious about his association with the Julian family. He was reluctantly adopted by Augustus and was, by rights and for most of his life, a member of the Claudian side. He was not related to the Divus Augustus or the Divus Julius Caesar or the Dea Venus so he used *maiestas* to violently protect his adopted ancestors with the zeal of a man who clearly worried about it too much. He prosecuted men who were naked in front of statues of Augustus and who wrote histories praising Julius Caesar's assassins because his anxieties saw damage there and he felt the need to shut it down. Gaius broadcast his anxieties about himself by censuring people for forgetting his birthday (which is quite a big oversight in fairness) and executing everyone who posed even the tiniest imaginary threat to his person, having senators and magistrates flogged in the middle of the night out of fear, and dressing as a god to maximise the distance between himself and everyone else. He didn't worry about what people said about Augustus, he only worried about his own personal safety. Which made everyone terrified and, naturally, led to him being stabbed to death in a corridor. Claudius knew the fragility of his position more viscerally than any of his predecessors, having seen his nephew slaughtered and the forty-eight-hour bloodbath and tense negotiation that followed. When he finally fought his way to the throne, with the Praetorian Guard at his back, it was with the unambiguous knowledge that the Senate didn't want him and he got to stare straight into the face of several men who had been proposed as better alternatives to him. He was also immediately confronted by a bunch of people trying to kill him and an attempted military uprising. It's unsurprising then that, until Agrippina got involved, his anxieties about his safety and position were so high that he had people executed for suspicious dreams. All of them were in a hugely fragile position, which they had to fight to maintain, and all of them screwed it up by leaning on the idea of lèse-majesté and trying to create a divine sanctity that could be protected with murder.

It's important to remember, I think, that the reigns of the first twelve emperors, of which maybe three could be called good or successful, spanned only 123 years – from the day little Octavian took the names Augustus and Princeps on January 16, 27 BCE, to the day Domitian was stabbed in his own bedroom by an extortionist wearing a sling on September 18, 96 CE. One hundred and twenty-three years is just about four generations. The men who watched Domitian die had fathers who grew up under Tiberius. There are not huge spans of history between them. The best-preserved section of Roman imperial history is its infancy, when emperors were trying to work out what the hell being emperor was and meant and how to do it well while managing the deeply complex and divergent concerns of the Senate (who had their own honour and majesty to worry about), the army, the people of Rome, the family, the provinces, the bureaucracy, the priests, the border empires and, of course, the gods. And most of them were utterly terrible at it. Just really, really not capable of juggling all those balls at the same time, which seems fair enough to me because it sounds hard; but very often they resorted to murder and torture as ways of creating and maintaining their power and that is just not cool.

The final way to be a Roman imperial tyrant in the realm of murder was to think that senatorial and magistratical lives were worth as little as everyone else's lives. So-called good emperors, like Vespasian and Marcus Aurelius and Trajan, understood that lives had a hierarchy of worth in the Roman world. Emperors were at the top of the pyramid, followed by consuls and ex-consuls, followed by other magistrates (though Tribunes really lost their importance), followed by general senators, then their children, then equestrians, then other people, then *infames* and finally enslaved people and animals were seen as equally lacking in any value beyond monetary. *Infames* and enslaved people had no good name (*fama*) or reputation to make their life worth something. *Infames* usually had disreputable jobs like sex workers or actors or bar-owners. Magistrates and senators and the children of magistrates, however, had a reputation and a family name, they had *dignitas* – honour, prestige, dignity and virtue – and that made them worthy of life, which meant that taking their life was an actual issue that had to be addressed carefully. Life itself was not inherently worth anything to the Romans (we'll deal with murder from the perspective of those who lacked *fama* and *dignitas* in Chapter 9). Life itself was not protected and no person had an individual right to life. What was protected by Roman elite cultural norms was *dignitas*, which is sort of the low-key, non-sacred form of imperial majesty. *Dignitas* (and can I just say that the Swiss assisted-suicide clinic has made writing this section much trickier than it needed to be. No one ever thinks of the poor historians when they are naming things in Latin.) was earned through achievements in politics and war by men and was passed on via the family name to their sons and grandsons. It was an idealised facet of elite masculinity. Being a consul meant having the most *dignitas* and was a reputation-maker for generations. Being a praetor or a quaestor was a near bullet-proof shield of *dignitas* and *fama*, and so was being granted Triumphal Regalia for doing really well in a war or successfully winning a particularly important or sensational court case. These external achievements made a man visible, important and worthy of life. They made killing them mean more than killing anyone else.

The Roman sources, all written by elite senatorial men and members of the imperial household, get up in arms about bad emperors killing sons of consuls and quaestors and give us readers lots of detail on their executions, and then pass over little things like twenty thousand people dying in a stadium collapse in the reign of Tiberius with a single sentence.[12] Our good friend Suetonius covers the destruction of Pompeii and Herculaneum by Vesuvius in the reign of Titus in the same paragraph as a fire, a plague and some attempted informers getting flogged in public and then moves on. Those things are bad, but not quite as bad as the time Gaius had a quaestor beaten or Domitian had the governor of Britain executed for naming a lance after himself.

Bad emperors didn't care about the *dignitas* and *fama* of anyone but themselves. They didn't see the magistrates and senators as having any more worth than the people on the street who were always dying in riots and plagues. They just saw the people as trouble and beneath them, without apparently realising that no one else agreed with their conception of themselves as the only people in the Empire who had to be protected. Good emperors, on the other hand, made sure that when they had to execute a senator or magistrate for being an arsehole or revolutionary, they made a big public deal of how difficult it was. When Marcus Aurelius had to execute a guy named Avidius Cassius, who had literally proclaimed himself emperor and raised an army, he made sure that everyone knew that he was taking it very seriously and felt very bad about it actually. When Vespasian executed Helvidius Priscus, whom he had already exiled and then later decided to execute, he made a big fuss about trying to recall the men he'd sent with the swords, and then, when they apparently couldn't be reached, flopped about regretting his decision loudly. To me, this reads as annoying indecisiveness because Priscus was a prick, but to the Roman senators, it read as taking senatorial life as seriously as it should be taken.

Regulus

Roman elite men loved prosecuting one another for things. They absolutely loved it. It is impossible to overstate how much rocking up in a courtroom and shouting 'J'accuse' at one another was their favourite pastime. Cato the Elder allegedly once said about prosecution, laying out a pathway for all his spiritual descendants, 'These are the offerings we should make to our parents – not lambs or kids, but the tears of their enemies and their condemnation [in court].'[13] My absolute favourite court-based story from Rome is the story of Gaius Flavius Fimbria, whom Cicero called 'a ferocious personality' and a 'lunatic'. At the funeral of Gaius Marius (and this should give you an idea of how terribly everything was going at the time), Fimbria stabbed the Pontifex Maximus, Quintus Mucius Scaevola. Scaevola was injured but not mortally. When Fimbria heard that he had failed to murder Scaevola (at a funeral!), he lodged a charge against him instead. Baffled, a pal asked Fimbria what precisely he was prosecuting Scaevola for, as no one could work out what he was doing. Fimbria's utterly wonderful response was that he was accusing him of 'receiving [my] weapon into his body too gingerly!'[14] Isn't that just wonderful! No one ever says what the outcome of the case was, but I think it's probable that it didn't go anywhere.

Being in court was great for Roman men, especially if they were prosecuting someone really famous, because that meant they got to cling onto their fame and steal a little bit of it. Their name would be linked, at least for a little while, with the famous name and that would make their own name famous. If they won, they not only got the fame, they also got the glory of victory. Plus, in Rome, anyone was allowed to accuse anyone of, basically, anything. Imagine if you wanted to be famous and you wanted your name to be attached to, say, Taylor Swift's name. You could accuse Taylor Swift of a crime and force her to come to court and refute your accusation. The popular media would go wild for it: Taylor Swift is being accused of, I don't know, writing poison pen letters to you. Just sending you loads of abusive letters.[15] She has to come and be confronted with this ridiculous allegation because that's literally law number one of your whole civilisation. You could give interviews to *US Weekly* and *People* magazine and *The Mirror* and a sad one to *The Guardian* and a bunch of vultures from online gossip mags would camp outside the court and take pictures of everyone and an Instagram account would spring up to judge your outfits and it would suck for Taylor, who did nothing wrong, but for you, you'd have a little bit of her spotlight for a while and you'd probably be able to flip that into a stint on *Celebrity Love Island*. That is what the Romans did every single day, and eventually, in the Imperial era, they turned it into a murder weapon. From the rubble of the Republic emerged imperial informers.

Your classic Imperial era informer is, of course, Judas Iscariot. We don't tend to think of him that way because of all the Bible and religion surrounding him but that's really what he was. He went to the Roman authorities, told them that a nebulous crime was being committed and could he have some money if he told them the whos and whats and wheres, collected his reward and went on his way. It was that easy. And people did it all the time during the Imperial era. A wonderful man named Steven Rutledge (who now owns a farm called the Dancing Faun Farm, which shows you how great he is) did an unbelievable amount of work and identified 109 informers working during the early Empire, between the reigns of Tiberius and Domitian, and in doing so created a terrifying picture where anyone could denounce anyone to the emperor for just about anything and have it be called *maiestas*.[16] A whole new word was invented for people who became professional informers: *delator*, which means person who denounces. Most *delatores* denounced via a good old-fashioned traditional prosecution in a court of law. And the most famous and terrible of them all was Marcus Aquilius Regulus.

Marcus Aquilius Regulus was a real exemplar of how to make a tyrannical government work for you. For many, a despotic, capricious, semi-divine supreme leader with an ego like candy floss being washed by a racoon was a real obstacle to a happy life; but Regulus shows us that those people just weren't sufficiently unscrupulous and devoid of conscience. Regulus knew how to see things from a different angle, how to turn a lemon into lemonade, make some money and also get revenge on everyone who ever annoyed him in the process. He was a real disruptor in the reign of two of the world's most notoriously horrible emperors, and like all good disruptors, he was also a real prick.

Regulus burst onto the scene during the reign of Nero, around the late 60s CE, when he was in his early twenties and Nero was limping towards the end of his thirteen years of pissing everyone off. Regulus' father had been prosecuted for some unknown crime and exiled, leaving Regulus with his estates. He was probably comfortably off. He could have had a life that you or I would consider to be wildly luxurious and the rest of the Senate would have considered to be barely scraping by ('Only the three estates? And none in Umbria? Gosh, I don't know if I could manage.'). Regulus wasn't OK with that. He wanted fame and to restore the name of his family, and, mostly, he wanted more money. Usefully, Regulus was friends with a man named Helius, who was Nero's freedman. Nero's favourite freedman. Helius was the man who, to the utter horror of everyone in Rome, Nero put in charge of the entire city every time he pottered off to Greece to torture his subjects via the medium of song, so Helius had a lot of power and a lot of knowledge about the kind of thing that made Nero happy and prompted him to be generous.

Now, in order to understand how Regulus' career took off, you have to understand how damn weird the Roman imperial system was for the first two centuries or so. The power of the emperors rested entirely in pretending that they had no actual power at all and that they weren't tyrannical military-backed dictators. They were, in fact, just ordinary men who just happened to hold a lot of separate powers that were technically available to anyone and who everyone just happened to listen to out of respect and kindness. When emperors stepped out of the pretence, because it was stupid and annoying, like Gaius Caligula did, they got pumped full of sword holes. One of the things that was likely to get an emperor shanked by senators was executing senators without a proper trial. Part of the whole theatrical charade of the imperial system for a long time was that people who wanted to please the emperor would bring a formal accusation against a person they knew the emperor hated. That way, the informer/accuser got into the emperor's graces, the emperor looked like he was merely objectively observing a case involving two dudes that had nothing to do with him, and everyone got rid of whoever was annoying them. This is what Regulus did.

As a very young man, Regulus brought three immensely high-profile cases to court as a prosecutor. First, he dragged Servius Cornelius Salvidienus Orfitus to court. Orfitus had been consul alongside Claudius in 51 CE, making him practically Claudius' best friend and a very high-ranking, popular member of the Senate. Regulus accused him of living very close to the Forum and renting three shops. And once, being seen in those shops, with his friends no less! His insinuation, which was probably quite overt in court, was that Orfitus was somehow using his house and shops to plot against Nero's life. Orfitus, a man of consular rank and apparently unblemished record, was executed. Regulus got his stuff. Then, Regulus went after Marcus Licinius Crassus Frugi, another consul. Frugi had been chosen by Nero himself to be his consular partner just three years earlier and had done literally nothing else, except possibly prosecute Regulus' father. This was Regulus' bit of revenge; another ex-consul was bloodily dispatched and another family was ruined. Finally, in the same year, because he was an absolute whirlwind of energy – Regulus really didn't do anything unless he was going at it 150 percent – he brought an accusation against Sulpicius Camerinus, who had been a consul under Claudius in 46 CE, and his son Sulpicius Camerinus Junior. His reasoning for this one was really an insight into how an emperor's vanity could be wielded as a weapon by those smart and cruel enough to do it. The Camerinus family had been given the cognomen Pythicus many generations before for some unknown deeds of greatness. Knowing the Romans, they probably sacked a Greek city. By Nero's time, though, Pythicus was just part of the family name, probably part of the background noise of the world that no one else noticed. Except Regulus. In the name Pythicus, Regulus saw an opportunity. He took Camerinus Senior and Junior to court to try to force them to drop the name Pythicus on the basis that their having that name diminished the glory of Nero's victories in the Pythian games.

That's right. Regulus attempted to force a family to change their name on the basis that it was lèse-majesté to undermine the magnificence and majesty of the emperor's coerced wins at a singing competition in Delphi. And when the two men refused to change their names, he pressed on until they were executed. The two men, one an ex-consul, were beheaded because Regulus saw a way to make sure his name was on everyone's lips. Everyone despised him for these three prosecutions. This young man, who came out of nowhere and began accusing and informing on people for imaginary crimes and winning, was everything that good, upstanding Roman men hated. He destroyed families. Frugi had four small children who were left fatherless. Camerinus' wife lost her husband and son in a day, over their name. But Regulus didn't care. He was one of those men who didn't distinguish between infamy and fame. Like Donald Trump running

for election, Regulus didn't care if people were saying good or
bad things about him, as long as they were saying his name;
whispering and pointing as he walked through the Forum,
gossiping about him over dinner. It was all fame. Even better,
Nero was thrilled. Nero saw Regulus as a heroic protector of his
majesty and reputation and rewarded him with seven million
sesterces and a priesthood. For reference, the average salary of a
Roman worker was seven sesterces a day, or two thousand five
hundred sesterces a year. Seven million sesterces rocketed an
already rich man into the 0.1 percent. And all he had to do was
use the courts to murder four people. He didn't even get blood
on his tunic; though, as far as Tacitus was concerned, he had
drenched his soul in noble blood.

A couple of years after this, however, just as Regulus was
getting into his murdering stride, Nero was horribly overthrown,
a year-long civil war ensued, and finally the good old boy,
laconic old soldier and all-round nice guy Vespasian took the
throne. In the aftermath of Nero's downfall, a lot of his friends
and people who had got rich informing during his career had
been torn apart in the streets. Spiculus the gladiator, we already
saw, got squished by a statue. Helius was arrested and publicly
executed. Another infamous informer under Nero, Antistius
Sosianus, was exiled for the second time. Sosianus had been
exiled in 62 CE after he had been informed on by Cossutianus
Capito for reciting rude poems about Nero during dinner. After
a few years of sitting on an island, someone wrote to Sosianus
and told him that Nero was getting very generous with his
rewards for informers. So Sosianus wrote to Nero and told him
that a guy who was exiled with him, a soothsayer, was being sent
money and visitors by a man named Publius Anteius. Anteius
had been good friends with Nero's mother Agrippina, whom
Nero had already murdered, and Sosianus knew Nero's hackles

would be raised by this news. Then he sat back and waited. Before long, Anteius was dead, along with a couple of others who were in the wrong place at the wrong time, and Sosianus was on a boat back to Rome to receive a formal thumbs up from the emperor. For these murders, and a couple of other high-profile accusations after his return, Vespasian packed Sosianus back off to his island as soon as he attained the throne. Somehow, though, Regulus survived.

Regulus got really into defence cases and building nice houses for a few years, keeping his head down now that the emperor had the kind of solid self-esteem that Tony Robbins would admire. We know this because he lived at the same time as the poet Martial, who thought he was great, Tacitus, who was luke-warm about him, and Pliny the Younger, who called him the vilest thing on two legs. We also know he got really into legacy hunting during this time, when informing wasn't going to pay the bills. Pliny tells a delightful story about Regulus visiting the wife of his worst enemy while she was on her deathbed, which confused her quite a lot. He sat by her bedside and asked her when she was born, and the exact time of her birth and all kinds of questions which she, inexplicably, answered. He then fell silent and got a faraway look in his eyes and pursed his lips and started doing sums. He sat there, thinking, for quite some time while this poor woman (her name was Verania) was trapped in her bed, half-dead, watching him, politely and awkwardly wondering what the ever-loving christ he was doing. Eventually, he snapped back and told her that he had done the astrology in his head, which is definitely a thing, and that he knew that her illness was just temporary. Overjoyed at this news, and adorably lacking in guile, Verania immediately called for a wax tablet and wrote a bequest for him: when she died, he would get a little of her estate for his kindness. Then she dropped dead. Regulus got his money.† Intimidating and manipulating women kept him busy for the long decade of Vespasian's rule and the short years of Titus', until finally another weak-willed manchild took the throne and, under Domitian, Regulus could get back to his true calling. Like a bear coming out of hibernation, the weather was right again and Regulus was back: using the courts to kill.

Domitian's reign, like Nero's, was apparently a real boom time for people with no scruples. Pliny tells of an extraordinary case where two men were prosecuted – by Pliny himself with Tacitus as his co-prosecutor (please make me a movie of this) – for bribing judges, much like Cluentius did. Vitellius Honoratius was accused of paying a judge three hundred thousand sesterces to have an equestrian exiled and seven of his friends executed. That's seven deaths and an exile for 300k. His fellow defendant Flavius Marcianus was probably shocked at the deal Honoratius got because Marcianus had spent seven hundred thousand sesterces to have a separate equestrian beaten, condemned to the mines and then strangled. Just the one murder there for more than twice what Honoratius paid. Honoratius never found out about his bargain because he died before he got to court, but Marcianus was found guilty and, in a move that infuriated Pliny, all he had to do was pay seven hundred thousand sesterces to the treasury and be banished for five years. If he'd written a rude epigram about Domitian, he'd have been beheaded. No one (except Pliny) cared at all about judicial murder, which meant

---

† Another story Pliny tells about Regulus is that a nice lady called Aurelia asked him to witness her will. It was a special, and sort of sacred, occasion so Aurelia put on her nicest dress and robe. When she arrived, Regulus asked her to add a note in her will leaving the clothes she was wearing to him. Aurelia laughed, thinking it was a weird joke. It was not. Regulus pressed the issue. He really meant it. He loomed over her as she reopened her will, added what he told her to add, and resealed it. What a man.

Regulus could keep going. After bumping off a few more people, including the son of Salvidienus Orfitus (named, naturally, Salvidienus Orfitus) just at the point that he came of age and might be wanting a bit of revenge on the man who killed his dad, Regulus' own son died young and he was grief-stricken. Pliny writes that, at the funeral, Regulus sacrificed every single one of his pets – horses, dogs, nightingales and parrots were slaughtered and thrown on the pyre. Pliny paints this as weird and attention-seeking, but to me, it's quite sad. Or it would be, if Regulus hadn't been responsible for at least six judicial murders and the ruin of several families.

The interesting thing about all this is that no ancient or modern writers seem to see this behaviour as murder. To me, it is quite clear that taking someone to court on an imaginary charge, against which they almost certainly couldn't defend themselves, in front of a stab-happy emperor with tissue-paper self-esteem, is about as guaranteed to get them killed as running at them with a knife. It is very clearly using the courts as a weapon to rid oneself of enemies or gain something, usually cash. When Regulus walked into a courtroom, in front of the emperor or a panel of judges, he knew that the person he opposed would likely never go home again. He looked into their eyes and listened to their desperate attempts to defend themselves against the ludicrous accusations he had invented. He looked at the children they brought to court to inspire pity in the judges' hearts and heard them plead for their lives and, over and over again, he attacked them. He once told Pliny that his approach was to 'identify the jugular and work out how to cut it' and that's what he did. Over and over, he walked into court and used that court to murder men for no reason other than his own benefit. The 109 men listed by Steven Rutledge are 109 men who manipulated the nebulous concept of *maiestas* and the swivel-eyed, paranoiac bloodlust of a couple of emperors to get themselves very rich. I see no significant difference between this and how men like Gary Ridgeway and Willy Pickton used the transient, unregulated world of street-level sex workers to access women they could rape and murder, or Harold Shipman used the medical profession to access little old ladies to poison. Smart killers use the structures available to them to get what they need. Ridgeway wanted to hurt women, so he attacked women that no one would complain about losing; Shipman wanted money, so he forged wills and poisoned the elderly to get it. Regulus, and the men like him, wanted fame and the emperor's approval and a whole lot of cash, and they used the courts to sacrifice other men to get those things. So many were murdered this way, even under the good emperors. We tend to see the emperor as the culprit here, as the man doing the murdering, but really he was just the weapon. His temper and ego were wielded by men like Regulus to strike fear into the hearts of rivals. Cato said that the tears of his enemies and their condemnation were the offerings made to his parents in the courts, but the imperial system made that sacrifice literal.

The execution of a magistrate or senator by an emperor was, to the Roman elite eye, almost always murder, regardless of who had made the accusation or what the accusation was. The range of acceptable justifications for killing a man with *dignitas* was very narrow indeed and extended about as far as 'if the senator is running at you with a knife, then it might be OK, as long as you feel bad about it'. Most emperors did not adhere to these principles. Most emperors executed men with *dignitas* for what the other senators felt were arbitrary and unjustified reasons and didn't seem to have any regrets about it. And so those senators wrote the executions down as murders committed by unhinged blood-thirsty maniacs who had no respect for the prestige, dignity and honour of the Senate and, therefore, in their views, no respect for Rome. In the eyes of a lot of the 'bad' emperors, of course, the Senate were a bunch of irritating upstarts with no formal power but a whole lot of ego who needed to be both pandered to and controlled while it was he, the emperor, who represented, possessed and embodied Roman power and prestige. It is this clash of ideologies and perspectives which quite often led to the other type of uniquely Roman imperial murder: murdering an emperor.

Murdering an Emperor

Gaius Caligula

The first Roman emperor to be definitely assassinated was Gaius Caligula. He was the third Roman emperor proper (Julius Caesar doesn't count and I won't get into it) and he'd ruled for just about four years when his pals shanked him. There had been gossip and rumours that his predecessors, Augustus and Tiberius, had been bumped off in secret. Livia was supposed to have poisoned Augustus with a fig while Gaius himself apparently suffocated the ailing Tiberius. That Augustus and Tiberius were weak old men on their deathbeds was a mere fact in the way of a good story. Gaius, though, was unambiguously murdered. It happened around 20 January 41 CE, at the tail end of the Palatine games. The day was one of plays and dancing, rather than fights or racing, so it was slightly more relaxed than other games. The Romans hadn't built any permanent theatres yet, so they had to construct a temporary wooden theatre to hold thousands of spectators for each set of games. It's amazing what a culture can achieve with slavery. So Gaius spent the day in a slightly rickety theatre, watching a Latin farce called *Laureolus* which ended with the main character, a robber, being crucified and always involved a lot of (animal?) blood being thrown around like that school play scene in *The Addams Family*. Gaius was having a great time. He had opened the day's proceedings with a very special sacrifice: slaughtering a flamingo! I suspect this sounds cooler than it actually was. He had been delighted by the plays and had distributed fruit during the morning to spectators to keep everyone's spirits up. By midday, though, he was a bit blood-spattered and sweaty and he was persuaded by his friends to go for a wash and a wee and some food and to stretch his legs a bit. Reluctantly, but in good cheer, Gaius went for a saunter to his baths down the dark, narrow passageway leading out of the theatre, chatting happily to some dancers who were warming up for their afternoon show on the way.

As he left the dancers and began to dander down the passage-way, his Praetorian Prefect Cassius Chaerea suddenly appeared. Gaius and Chaerea didn't get on. Chaerea was a terse, gruff military man who had been a centurion in Germany under Augustus before being relocated to the leadership of the Praetorian Guard. He had a long, harsh military career which made him a hardened Roman soldier with a penchant for imag-ined Republican values. He would definitely have been a *Daily Mail* reader, puffing away about 'kids today' all the time. Gaius, on the other hand, was twenty-nine years old and would have taken to chan culture like a duck to water. Were Gaius alive today, he'd be on image boards coming up with weirdly slick social media troll campaigns to convince the gullible to micro-wave their brand new iPhones, doing 'ironic' white supremacy and having the absolute best time. He was alive in the first century CE, though, so he had to make do with IRL trolling Chaerea relentlessly. He constantly gave Chaerea rude words as the daily watchword because it made Chaerea blush to say things like Venus and Priapus. Admittedly this is a very high level of prudishness, but it was mean of Gaius. Gaius also used to wait until Chaerea was just at the point of no return when kissing his hand in greeting and then do an obscene gesture so Chaerea was forced to kiss his rude hand shape. Again, not the worst thing Gaius ever did, but apparently Chaerea was not used to young, rude emperors unrelentingly taking the piss out of his old-fashioned blushes. He was used to being respected and honoured. He did not like Gaius.

Accounts diverge somewhat on what exactly happened after Chaerea's appearance in the passage. In the Jewish historian Josephus' telling, Chaerea asked Gaius for the day's watchword and Gaius replied with something rude. In Suetonius' first version, Gaius gave the watchword Jupiter (which seems a bit obvious, but who am I to judge); in his second, neither Gaius nor Chaerea spoke at all. Tacitus' version is – unbearably – lost. All three surviving versions, however, agree that Chaerea moved like a blur and, suddenly, brutally, maintaining eye contact, drove his short sword into the hollow of Gaius' neck. He entirely ruined Gaius' nice day. The emperor stumbled. He suddenly saw a crowd of familiar faces materialise behind Chaerea, each holding a sharp blade and then, before Gaius could even fall properly, the knives rained down on him. Suetonius claims that Gaius was stabbed over thirty times. When the assassins were satisfied that their emperor was dead, they fled to find his wife and infant daughter and slaughter them before they were caught.

Much like Julius Caesar's assassins, the group of men who murdered Gaius cast themselves as saviours of the state and heroic tyrannicides. They were the new Brutuses and Cassiuses in their own minds, and it's easy to imagine a lot of dinner parties where they all talked themselves into this wildly dangerous and foolish plan by convincing themselves that they'd be hailed as heroes and liberators. Like George W. Bush in 2003, they had their 'mission accomplished' banners ready to go. Unfortunately, as always, history didn't oblige them. As had happened with Julius Caesar, it turned out that the people of Rome were actually quite keen on Gaius and were not fans of presumptuous senators and magistrates making unilateral decisions about the nature of Roman government with swords. Supreme executive power derives from a mandate from the masses, they believed, not from some farcical bloody murder. Strange men in corridors distributing stab wounds was no basis for a system of government. And to make things worse, the entire Praetorian Guard apart from Chaerea quite liked Gaius too and they had not been waiting impatiently to be liberated from his tyranny. All the conspirators ended up dead, either in the immediate chaotic aftermath, or after being declared public enemies by Gaius' successor. It was perhaps not what they were expecting.

They were, however, successful on one point: they brought the now traditional Roman practice of using murder to solve political problems into the Imperial era. They proved that emperors, even those descended from Divus Augustus, were in fact just men with squishy insides like everyone else, and so they kick-started the brand new Roman hobby of murdering emperors. And boy did the Romans take to it.

The stats on Roman imperial assassination are absolutely wild. The period known as the early Empire spans 220 years (27 BCE–193 CE) and eighteen emperors with an average reign length of 12.7 years. The late Empire period spans 283 years (193–476 CE) and a staggering fifty-nine emperors with an average reign length of six years. The average length of rule for the whole 503-year period from the naming of Augustus to the deposition of Romulus Augustulus by the Ostrogoths was 7.8 years.[1] Were the average reign of a Roman emperor a person, it would still be in primary school. According to crack quantitative historian Walter Scheidel, that's half as long as the global average for monarchs and a third as long as all other European monarchies. The longest Roman dynasty is the first, the Julio-Claudians, who managed to hold on for five emperors and ninety-five years. The global average length for a dynasty, according to Scheidel, is three hundred years.[2] And then there's causes of death. Of the

Julio-Claudians, two were brutally murdered and one was over-thrown and then killed himself. In a global perspective, that is extremely poor, but for the Romans, it's about as good as it gets. If at any stage in Roman history they got three emperors in a row who didn't get murdered, that was a winning streak. The absolute record is six in a row from Nerva to Marcus Aurelius and that's because all those emperors adopted their successors. As soon as Marcus Aurelius let his biological son get in on the ruling act, we got Commodus who ruled for fifteen years but is mainly remem-bered for being a twat and getting killed. In that whole 503-year period of Roman imperial rule in the West, forty-nine percent of emperors were murdered. And another nine percent took their own lives after being overthrown in order to avoid being murdered, which brings us to a massive fifty-eight percent of emperors having violent and unhappy ends. Nine percent died in unknown circumstances so that number might be even higher. Just 24.6 percent of all the Roman emperors managed to die in their beds.[3] Those stats are genuinely staggering to look at, but it's important to remember that the second half of the Roman Empire, from 283 CE onwards, is skewing those numbers a lot.

The later Roman Empire was a very different place to the early Empire and I am going to avoid talking about it because, although it grew organically from the early Empire and lasted longer, it has slightly different rules. It has the Third Century Crisis in it, when there were twenty-six emperors during a fifty-year period with names like Philip the Arab and Pupienus (I recommend saying this out loud because it's very fun to say) and Hostilian and Trebonianus Gallus, almost all of whom murdered their predecessor.[†] Then

† It's actually closer to twenty-four emperors in twenty-eight years if you take out the unexpectedly successful two-emperor twenty-two-year Valerian Dynasty in the middle.

there's the Tetrarchy, which is a whole thing, and it would involve a lot of explanation so let's not. We'll keep our beady eyes focused on the early and high Empire and not be distracted by things like the emperor Caracalla getting stabbed while having an outdoor piss and then trying to run away while bleeding everywhere and also presumably still pissing with his willy flopping about and then his assassin getting wanged with a javelin, because it happened in 217 CE.

Even in the more peaceful half of Roman imperial history, there's still a surprisingly large amount of emperor-murder. The early Empire has three phases: the Julio-Claudian Dynasty, which ended with a military revolt and a twelve-month civil war; the Flavian Dynasty, which ended with a murder; and the Nerva-Antonine Dynasty, which was by far the most successful period of the Empire in its entire history and ended with a murder. The Julio-Claudian period is the bloodiest of the three and the Nerva-Antonine Dynasty was the least bloody because Nerva accidentally hit on the perfect winning formula for how to do Roman emperor-ing and it was spectacular until Marcus Aurelius ruined it. Suetonius' Twelve Caesars tend to be seen as the Big Twelve. They are Julius Caesar (not an emperor), Augustus, Tiberius, Gaius, Claudius, Nero, Galba, Otho, Vitellius, Vespasian, Titus and Domitian. We shall exclude JC to leave eleven emperors, of whom seven were murdered in different circumstances and three of the remaining four were haunted by rumours that they'd been done away with. A sixty-three percent murder rate is cause for concern, and leaves you wondering just what was so alluring about being emperor.

Gaius was the first emperor to follow in JC's footsteps and be turned into a knife block and really his murder marked the first time that senators and magistrates were able to take Republican era action in the Imperial era. There had been attempts to do away with Augustus and Tiberius but nothing that came close to success. Augustus was too popular – and Rome too exhausted after centuries of civil war – for anything to catch on in his reign, and Tiberius spent too much of his reign hidden safely on the island of Capri where he could push people off the side of cliffs for anyone to get to him. Gaius, however, was the right combination of unpopular and available. He behaved in just the right kind of despotic, imperial manner – as though he were the emperor or something – to piss senators off but was always right there in Rome being annoying enough for senators to justify getting rid of him in the name of Rome. It was not, however, the murder of Gaius which marked the move from the Republic to the Empire, but the murder of his family. The brutal, cold-blooded slaughter of his wife Caesonia and his tiny baby daughter Drusilla moved this murder from a simple assassination of a tyrant into an attempt to eradicate his bloodline. Had his two surviving sisters Agrippina and Livilla not been exiled at the time, they would probably have been murdered too. His uncle Claudius was saved both by his own lack of reputation and the Praetorian Guard spiriting him away to their camp. What followed the bloodshed was two days of negotiations between Claudius and the Praetorian Guard and the Senate about what would happen next. Rex fact: Herod Agrippa, the grandson of the king of Judea Herod the Great who murdered all the babies, was the primary go-between in the negotiations, convincing the Senate to back down and agree to Claudius' rule. The Senate obviously followed his advice (as they had no available armies and Claudius very much did) and imperial rule carried on, but it was painfully clear that Chaerea and the gang hadn't planned any further than the murder. Regardless of what *Gladiator* told you, that was the last time that a Republican era murder was attempted. Its failure was the complete death of the idea of the Republic as an attainable goal.

When Claudius finally got his grubby little hands on the throne, everyone immediately tried to kill him for obvious reasons, including one guy who tried to get into his bedroom. He managed to survive many political and military attempts to murder him only to succumb at the hands of a sneaky woman. His wife Agrippina the Younger somehow managed to persuade him that he needed a better heir than his own biological son and got him both to adopt her son Nero and to follow Augustus' 'How to Train Your Successor' programme to ease him into public life as a world leader. She was really *very* good. When Claudius started to look at his own bio-son and make ridiculous statements about how maybe Britannicus could have a public life too or could be a joint successor with his adopted son, Agrippina put a stop to such talk by poisoning him with a particularly tasty-looking mushroom and had Nero acclaimed emperor before Claudius' body was cold.[4]

The interesting thing about Claudius' murder is that, in the early Empire, it is unique. There are a lot of rumours about wives and family members poisoning or suffocating emperors for their personal gain, but no other ones that are quite as convincing. On the unconvincing end of the scale we have Livia and her reputation as a deranged poison-mad witch, while Tiberius was apparently suffocated. Dio reports that Domitian killed his big brother Titus by putting him in a box full of snow while he was suffering from a fever. Even Titus, almost universally adored, was subjected to the emperor Hadrian going around telling everyone that he had poisoned his father Vespasian. No one was free of sin in the gossipy world of the Romans, who enjoyed a good conspiracy theory just as much as we do. Possibly even more. In that milieu, it would be easy to read Agrippina's poisoning of Claudius as yet another tedious accusation of secret murder with no basis in reality, except that in Claudius' case there are no other versions of his death. There is only the murder story. The telling of the story varies in its details but literally no one thinks that Claudius died of natural causes. Even Agrippina's contemporary, and eyewitness to a lot of events in her life, Pliny the Elder states outright that Claudius was poisoned. There is not even a jot of hedging in the sources. This makes Claudius exceptional in all of Roman history. Five hundred and three years, seventy-seven emperors and Claudius was the only one to be definitely poisoned by his household. Yet another reason to be incredibly impressed by Agrippina the Younger.

Forgive me for taking a sideways step here, but I find the ubiquitousness of conspiracy theories and gossip about emperors being poisoned or somehow secretly killed, regardless of how old they were or how beloved their successor was, to be fascinating. Even Marcus Aurelius, a man who is relentlessly praised for being kind, generous, humble, forgiving and actively repulsed by violence outside of warfare (he loved war, though), was accused by the *Scriptores Historiae Augustae* of poisoning his brother and co-ruler Lucius Verus. According to the *SHA*, Marcus sliced a sow's womb with a knife that was smeared with poison on one side of the blade. He then gave his brother the portion of womb which had touched the poison and, thus, killed him without arousing suspicion. Leaving aside the idea of eating a pig womb (although it is still widely eaten in Asia and is, according to the YouTube cooking video I just watched, delicious), the story is obviously a fiction. In another version, told by both the *SHA* and Dio, Verus was poisoned by his sister-in-law (and adopted sister!) Faustina in order to prevent him from killing Marcus Aurelius, and in yet another version, his mother-in-law (also called Faustina) killed him because he raped her. Just like the story that Livia killed every boy in the imperial family and then her husband, or the story that Nero deliberately started the Great 64 CE Fire of Rome, these are conspiracy theories. They are stories which offer explanations and reasons for tragic events that make more sense to the listeners than the idea that a beloved emperor can be killed by food poisoning, or that a fire could just randomly break out and rage for nine days and destroy a fifth of the city.

These conspiracies also project the concerns of a lot of the Roman people out into history via the medium of gossip. What conspiracy theories tell us is what people think is 'really' happening in their world, how their world 'really' functions. American conspiracy theorists who believe that all major death events (9/11, Sandy Hook, the assassination of John F. Kennedy, etc.) were orchestrated by the US government for nefarious purposes are broadcasting their belief – and fear – that their government is a secretive, untrustworthy organisation that would kill them as soon as look at them and is also turning the frogs gay. Romans who told these stories about their emperors being murdered secretly by members of their family were broadcasting their fears and beliefs that their world was run by an intimate family who drove history from their bedrooms and dinner tables. I know you are reading this while simultaneously rolling your eyes and thinking, 'Yeah, Emma, duh,' because we know that it was. The Roman world was a monarchy and history was being made in bedrooms. But you have to remember that we have the benefit of hindsight and for the significant proportion of Roman imperial history, they were pretending that they didn't have a monarchy. They most highly praised those emperors who pretended the hardest and put on a really good performance of letting the Senate believe that they had any impact on anything, and they most highly condemned those emperors who couldn't be bothered pretending and just acted like monarchs. The whole rhetoric and presentation of the government was that the emperor was just the First Citizen, at least until the day in 284 CE when Diocletian made everyone call him Master and transformed the Principate into the Dominate. Until then, though, the Principate insisted on telling everyone that the monarchy didn't exist. The conspiracy theories about the deaths of each emperor were the acknowledgement from the people of Rome that it did. And just as MKUltra and Operation Northwoods 'prove' to conspiracy theorists today that governments are untrustworthy and frightening, the death of Claudius proved to Roman conspiracy theorists that emperors were chosen by women and poison.[5]

Aulus Vitellius

As it turned out, though, the imperial family didn't end up constantly conspiring and bumping one another off and king-making; the Roman troops did. Claudius' successor Nero really ushered in the glorious new age of emperor-murder. He himself, impressively, was not murdered. After fourteen years of putting up with his singing, the governors of Gaul and Spain revolted against him; he was declared a public enemy, ran around like a headless chicken a bit and eventually put a dagger in his own throat with the helping hand of one of his aides, Epaphroditus. This is generally read as suicide, but it's interesting to note that, decades later, Domitian had Epaphroditus put to death for murdering Nero because his hand held the dagger. Which probably came as quite the surprise to Epaphroditus, who had been working peacefully and quietly at a very high level in the imperial house for the intervening thirty years. Such is the nebulous nature of the definition of murder, I suppose. This sequence of rebellions by a general declaring himself emperor, the Senate immediately siding with the rebels and the reigning emperor either falling or being pushed onto a sword, however, becomes very, very familiar. The next three emperors went on to really show the world how it was done by repeating the cycle very rapidly over the next twelve months.

Galba, the elderly governor of Spain who successfully overthrew Nero, turned out to be a little *too* old-fashioned and immediately pissed everyone off by being an austere fun-sponge with no sense of the joy of being a supreme ruler of an empire. Worst of all, he refused to pay the Praetorian Guard a bonus on his accession. Everyone hated him. He lasted seven months before the legions of Germany refused to swear allegiance to him, and just about instantly the Praetorians dragged him from his litter in the middle of the Forum and beheaded him. He was really unpopular. Entertainingly, Suetonius says that Galba did have some friends who ran to his aid when they heard he was being attacked in the Forum but that these friends were unfamiliar with the city and got lost so by the time they arrived it was all over. This is a film I would pay to see. The Praetorian Guard declared Otho emperor. Otho had learned from Galba that the Praetorians were key to holding power and he won them over with cash money and flattery. Otho was an unlikely emperor, being a foppish playboy pal of Nero's, right up to the point where Nero stole his wife. Then he was a grumpy divorced governor of Lusitania (now Extremadura in Spain). Then he was suddenly emperor. For three months and one day, every day of which was spent fighting the revolting German legions. It turned out that he was as good at emperor-ing in a crisis as he was at keeping wives and so he politely ended his own life to save anyone else the bother of having to murder him. Next, the general of the German legions, Aulus Vitellius, was acclaimed emperor.

Vitellius was the most successful of the three, clinging on for an impressive eight months of power, several of which were spent travelling back to Rome and almost all of the rest were dedicated to fighting off revolts from other troops. The bit in between was spent fucking, feasting and fighting and having all the fun of five reigns rolled into one. That information comes from Suetonius, though, whose dad was inexplicably in Otho's army and had many fond memories of Otho which are recounted with double fondness by Suetonius himself, so maybe take it with a pinch of salt. By the time Vitellius got to Rome, the troops in the Eastern Empire had heard that everyone in the West was declaring their general emperor and they wanted to jump on that bandwagon. It turned out that the Senate would accept literally anyone who rolled up at Rome with an army as emperor and all that semi-divine Julio-Claudian blood that everyone had been previously making a fuss about didn't matter at all. Anyone could be emperor if they had enough swords and the troops to the east of Italy wanted in on it. Moesia (now the Balkans), Pannonia (Croatia and some surrounding bits), Judea (top of Israel) and Syria (Syria) all got involved and proclaimed Vespasian emperor.

As soon as this news reached Rome, fighting broke out in the streets. At first, Vitellius held the upper hand. He forced the initial Flavian troops into the Temple of Jupiter on the Capitol and then set fire to it, which was a bold move. If anything, this spurred the Flavian contingent on to arrive in Rome faster so Vitellius barricaded himself into his palace by shoving a mattress and a sofa against the door and putting a dog on guard. When he was immediately found and his incredible siege crafts were dismantled, he then tried to lie about who he was. Who me? No, I'm just a guy in a toga hanging around in the palace. Just a doorman. Unconvinced by his acting, the soldiers put a rope around his neck, stripped him semi-nude and took him outside. They subjected Vitellius to a criminal's parade, which will seem slightly familiar to anyone who watched the fifth season of *Game of Thrones*, but more violent. Half-naked, hands bound behind his back and a noose around his neck, Vitellius was forced into the streets. One soldier walked behind him, his hand twisted in Vitellius' hair, pulling it back and forcing the ex-emperor to look forward and face the crowds who came to jeer him. Sometimes, another soldier walked alongside him, holding the point of a sword into the soft flesh under his chin, displaying his disgraced face to everyone. Along the way, crowds threw both animal and human excrement at him and made fun of his body, his scars and his belly. At the end of the walk, he was lashed, tortured and hanged. Finally, his body was pierced with hooks on the end of ropes and was dragged through the streets again to the Tiber. His brother and his son received the same treatment.

With that, there weren't any troops left to revolt so Vespasian was officially emperor. He was a glorious general and a generally nice old man (he was fifty-nine when he became emperor, which was old compared to all his predecessors) with a decent line in dad jokes and a frugality that only slightly weirded people out. He was also very good at paperwork and keeping people happy, so he ruled for a reasonably peaceful and contented decade before developing severe bowel issues rendering him unable to leave the loo, which he covered up by declaring, 'Oh dear, I think I'm becoming a god,' winking at his attendants and passing away while trying to stand up. His eldest, and overtly favourite, son Titus peacefully took his place, but only lasted two years before getting a fever and dropping dead. Intriguingly, his final words were 'I've made one mistake' but he died before mentioning what it was.[6] The conspiracy machine went haywire, of course, because the young, apparently strong and manly emperor had coughed and died very quickly at just forty-one. Regardless of what you think you know about ancient demography and ages of death, forty-one was very young to die. It was made worse by the fact that his successor, his unpopular brother Domitian, turned out to be a right dickhead who definitely seemed like he might kill his own brother.

Domitian

The key to understanding Titus and Domitian is to imagine them as stock characters in 1990s teen movies set in American high schools. Titus was the star quarterback who is dating the head cheerleader and is played by Freddie Prinze Jr. He is very successful at whatever he's doing, banging the hottest ladies and everyone loves him. He walks at the front of an entourage of football players, in slow motion. That's Titus. Walking in slow motion through the Forum, his toga hanging just right, his arm slung over Berenice, the queen of Judea, passing under the arch that bears his name and the image of him stealing a sacred menorah from the destroyed second temple, while everyone turns to gaze at him. Behind him shuffles his younger brother. Domitian is the smug school nerd who simultaneously hates himself and thinks he is better than everyone else. He talks a lot about how his brother is peaking in high school, while he'll one day be a computer millionaire. He plays a lot of first-person shooters and makes surreal memes and also cries a lot. In a real nineties film, this character would have been played by Clea DuVall with dyed black hair; in the eighties, Ally Sheedy with a fringe. The angry nerds sit by themselves at lunch and tell anyone who smiles at them to go fuck themselves. They vocally despise the high school hierarchy, but also desperately want to win at it. They loathe the star quarterback, but also want to be him (or bang him). They only get to walk in slow motion in comedy scenes which end with a record scratch and the nerd falling into a bin. That's Domitian. He was the rubbish brother, who tried so hard to be good at being a firm, moral, military emperor but was weird and rude and harsh and a bit creepy and spent a lot of time alone and just freaked people out a bit. And he did the classic nerd power fantasy thing of taking revenge on everyone who had previously rejected him by hurting them with brutal moral codes. Also he called sex 'bed-wrestling'. So they killed him.

The stories that were told about Domitian's murder are very funny because they are laden with cute little details, while omitting any of the substantial facts. They are told like lies a kid might tell about how they lost their homework which contain a great many details about the colour and breed of the dog that ate it, all in an attempt to obscure the fact that said homework never existed. In Domitian's case, the main narrative comes from Suetonius who was writing under the emperor Hadrian. Hadrian was an adoptive descendant of Nerva, the man who took Domitian's throne, and so Suetonius tended not to implicate his employer's adoptive grandfather in treasonous murder plots. In Suetonius' telling, the whole plot was created and enacted by two freedmen and a gladiator and Nerva simply tripped into the throne like a nerd in a nineties film might trip into a bin. In his version, the plot was led by Domitian's *cubicularius* Parthienus. A *cubicularius* is a bit like the head butler, also known as a chamberlain. He ran the household, made sure everything was done right, tucked the master of the house in at night, that kind of thing.[†] For some reason, unrecorded because it didn't exist, Parthienus decided to murder his boss and gathered a group of like-minded individuals from the imperial house to join him. One of Parthienus' freedmen, Stephanus, volunteered to actually do the deed because he was under investigation for embezzling imperial house funds and he felt that murder was the best way to handle that misfortune. A classic mistake.

It all went down, in the traditional narratives, on 18 September 98 CE when Domitian had finished in court for the morning and had wandered back to his bedroom to freshen up after a hard few hours of listening to senators whinge. He was stopped by Parthienus and Stephanus who told him, quietly, that Stephanus had something urgent to tell him. Something about a conspiracy they had uncovered. Stephanus had prepared for this moment by spending the few days leading up to the 18th wearing a fake bandage and sling on his arm, and in his other hand he clutched some tablets. Domitian, as with all emperors, loved hearing about plots against his life. He invited Stephanus, this apparently injured freedman, into his bedroom to talk in private. In the bedroom, they were alone except for the small enslaved boy whose job was perpetually attending the tiny shrine to Domitian's household gods there. He watched with wide eyes as Stephanus explained that his tablets outlined the plot he had uncovered, and thrust them into Domitian's hands. Domitian took the tablets eagerly and began to read but, as soon as the emperor bowed his head, Stephanus whipped a dagger out of his fake sling and drove the blade hard and fast into Domitian's

---

† The current Lord Chamberlain of the United Kingdom of Great Britain and Northern Ireland, which is now a purely ceremonial position, is David George Philip Cholmondeley, 7th Marquess of Cholmondeley, should you ever wish to wonder at what the UK looks like from the outside. If you want to repeat this fact in pub quizzes, remember that Cholmondeley is pronounced Chumley.

groin. Straight for the dick and balls. Domitian hit the ground instantly but he was absolutely not going to give up life easily. He fought hard, holding Stephanus back, and shouted for the unnamed boy to bring him the knife he kept under his pillow. The boy, miraculously not stupefied with terror, ran to help his emperor only to find that Parthienus had already removed it. Even worse, the screaming and yelling had brought Parthienus and a couple of other plotters – some more freedmen, a gladiator, some dude from the army – running in, also armed. They were greeted with the sight of the emperor, son and brother of deified men, bleeding profusely from the dick region, trying to claw Stephanus' eyes out with hands shredded by what homicide investigators would call 'defensive wounds'. They leapt in to help Stephanus and showered their boss with stabs. That noise brought even more people running and, in the chaos, Stephanus was also killed. The rest managed to get away. Here the narrative ends. The later story of Dio's, writing under Severus Alexander, is about two sentences but tells broadly the same tale. It's not until a Gallic-Roman historian in the fourth century CE, a guy named Eutropius who wrote under the reign of Julian the Apostate, that the Praetorian Prefect was implicated in Eutropius' one-sentence summary of the event.[7] All of them, however, then skip straight to later that same day when Nerva was being hailed emperor, against the wishes of most of the army and the people of Rome, but with the full and unexplained support of the allegedly surprised Senate and Praetorian Guard.

Now, the idea that a bunch of freedmen and gladiators took it upon themselves to straight up murder the emperor and that, when the Senate and Guard found out about this, after the emperor was dead in a pool of his own congealing blood on his bedroom floor, they shrugged and picked the next guy peacefully and unanimously within a matter of hours is laughable. If nothing else, the murder of a head of household by members of his household would be a gross and terrifying violation of the rules of the hierarchy that would warrant mass panic among the super-rich. If *cubicularii* can just go around stabbing their enslavers willy-nilly without severe consequences, there may as well be anarchy in Rome. The whole story that is told by Suetonius and Dio is just a giant cover-up for an obviously high-level conspiracy, with Nerva and the Praetorian Prefects at the centre of it. The Praetorian Guard themselves were not thrilled by the murder and tried to insist that Domitian be deified. When the Senate instead decided to enact a *damnatio memoriae* and tried to eradicate Domitian from the historical record, the Praetorian Guard compromised by forcing them to execute Parthienus and chums, which the Senate were notably reluctant to do.

With the death of Domitian and the ascension of Nerva, the early Empire really ended. Nerva was sixty-six with no children when he became emperor and dropped dead fifteen months later, leaving the Empire to the definitely-not-involved-in-any-plots-at-all general of the Rhine troops, Trajan. The next phases of imperial succession almost ended the fiction that the imperial seat could be inherited through the family line because the Senate and people and armies of Rome would respect a son – or nephew or grandson or uncle – because of their bloodline. Instead, it became more and more accepted that the Principate was primarily a military position, to be passed via adoption or execution to the next military dictator. There were exceptions of course, each of which ended in disaster. Marcus Aurelius destroyed the glory of the Six Good Emperors by making his rubbish son Commodus emperor instead of adopting a good one. Less than twenty years later, Septimius Severus made the same dumb mistake by handing his throne to his useless idiot son Caracalla (to be honest, names beginning with a *C* were a very bad sign for emperors: Caligula,[8] Claudius, Commodus, Caracalla, Cordianus I, II and III were all murdered. Claudius Gothicus breaks the curse in 270 CE by dying of the Plague of Cyprian), and then his weird teenage grandnephews, who creeped everyone out by not being Roman enough, and after that the idea of familial succession really died because it was clearly wildly stupid and every single one of them ended up getting murdered. With the death of Domitian, though, we enter the 'high Empire', which is a glorious century where almost no one got murdered.

The high Empire was an exception, though. For the most part, the imperial system at Rome was staggeringly blood-soaked from top to bottom. No one who wanted to be part of the imperial system, whether in the court or the Senate or the magistracies, was safe from the threat of murder from all quarters. Those who were born into the system were perhaps the most dangerous and endangered of all. And these are the murders about which we know by far the most, because they involve the people who mattered the most to those who wrote histories in the Roman world. They were the friends and family and ancestors and colleagues of the men who wrote the books we now hold in our hands and try to interpret Roman history from, so they seem the most important to them and, by proxy, to historians. It's important, as often as possible, to remember that they weren't.

Judicial Murder

The imperial system didn't just grind up those who worked within it; it also worked its way through an immense number of invisible lives lived outside of it. These lives are usually the least imagined. They are the lives of those who were executed by the state every day on every corner, and those sacrificed by the state to a higher power. These deaths were innumerable, a choking sea of human suffering that went, for the most part, unremarked, because the deaths were legal and reasonable and didn't matter at all.

Pasiphae

There is an extremely good, by which I mean horribly graphic, mosaic from the Sollertiana villa in El Djem, Tunisia, which shows a man being eaten by leopards. He is tied by the hands and being held up by a prison guard of some kind and, somehow, even though he is made out of tiny little chips of stone, he manages to radiate an air of extreme distress while a leopard is literally eating his face. There is a lot of blood splashing on the ground. It's a very impressive piece of mosaic work; you can really *feel* the pain and horror in the scene. I have absolutely no idea why anyone would want it on the floor of their house. I feel the same about another mosaic, this time from Silin in Libya, which depicts a prisoner being pushed on his knees by a guard towards an enormous angry-looking bull while acrobats walk on their hands behind him. Romans were maniacs.

Killing criminals and offenders is way easier and more cost-effective than imprisoning or rehabilitating them, so most human

cultures have had capital punishment. Plus, the threat of death
is usually seen, at a kind of common-sense level, as being an
effective deterrent to crime. It's not, but it feels like it should be.
Mostly, it's retribution on behalf of the state. There are no
second chances with capital punishment: you screw up, you die.
No rehabilitation or serving your time and then getting another
go at being a good citizen. In the modern West, only America
has held on to the death penalty, and they have resisted pressure
from the rest of the Western world to abolish it because they
think, fundamentally, that some crimes are so bad that the perpetrators forfeit their right to life. Implicit in this, though, is the
idea that everyone has a right to life. Romans, as a culture, would
not agree with that notion. They were pretty clear that only
people with *fama* and *dignitas* had a right to life, and that was only
really to protect their prestige and dignity. A dude called Aulus
Gellius straight up wrote that the only purpose of punishment
was to maintain the dignity of the victim, which implies that
those without prestige and dignity didn't require protecting.

The Roman version of the American surrendering the right
to life was the citizen who became classed as *infames*. Obviously
the English word infamous comes from this, but *infamia* (they've
all got it infam . . . no, it doesn't work in Latin . . .) was a legal
condition in Rome. *Infames* were citizens who had done things
that 'mainstream' Roman society considered to be so gross that
they had surrendered their right to participation in the Roman
state. Some people were considered to be *infames* because of their
job: sex workers, sex workers' pimps, actors, gladiators, gladiator
trainers and bar-owners. Others, however, became *infames*
because they had committed a crime. Sometimes, for things like
adultery, being *infamia* was the punishment in and of itself. For
others, however, becoming *infames* was the first step to becoming
horribly and publicly dead. Enslaved people were, obviously,

always *infames*. They were basically dead anyway.[1] The concept of *infamia* is fascinating to modern readers of Rome because the idea of telling a person to their face in a court of law that they literally don't matter as far as the state is concerned seems utterly wild. *Infamia* meant that a person was excluded from the legal system, unable to prosecute harms against them and unable even to make a legal will. If you were *infames* and someone tried to kill you, tough titties. The law won't help you. In fact, the law is quite cross that you're wasting its time. Maybe this seems barbaric to you, but really it is just an admirable honesty.

Romans would also find quite weird the Western idea that, if one absolutely *must* murder a person for the good of the state, then it should be done quickly and cleanly. Why on earth, they might wonder, would you want death to be easy for the criminal? They caused suffering, so they should suffer. Romans wanted people to suffer a lot and suffer publicly. They wanted everyone – everyone – to know that the only rewards of crime were abject humiliation, excruciating pain and, eventually, death. This was important because death wasn't considered to be that much of a punishment in the Roman world view. Enslaved people and *infames* were already socially dead; literal death was a formality. The suffering was the important part. And boy oh boy, were the Romans good at finding ways to make people suffer.

That's pretty damn clear in the main kind of execution that people generally associate with Romans: crucifixion. Crucifixion was a torture and an execution in one and it was specifically designed to be humiliating, agonising and extremely public. The Romans, therefore, loved it. They didn't invent it, though. The Greeks occasionally crucified a person, but they hated it. Alexander the Great, in the 300s BCE, would sometimes go on a crucifixion spree when he was very cross indeed, such as when a city failed to surrender to him. The Carthaginians and Persians were quite into it as well. But we don't associate crucifixion with them; we associate it with Romans because no one did it with quite the same industrial zeal.

Crucifixion in the Roman world was (mostly) a punishment reserved for the very lowest of the low. Enslaved people and foreigners and the like. People who were already worth nothing. It was a spit in the eye as well as a punishment for the victim, and a terrifying, very loud, warning for other people who might be tempted to commit really bad crimes, like banditry or practising Christianity. As an aside, an interesting development in Roman history is that, as the Empire aged, from the second century CE onwards, more people became eligible for crucifixion because the population became split into two broad castes: the *honestores* and the *humiliores* – the honourable and the lowly. The *honestores* were the landowners and the politicians who had dignity. The *humiliores* were those who lacked dignity or prestige; they were the tenants, and they broadly became permanent *infames*, which meant they could be crucified even if they were Roman citizens with a reasonable job, like a baker. So that's nice.

The general process for a Roman crucifixion is slightly obscure. Even for the Romans, crucifixion was a really gruesome thing, truly the worst thing they could wish upon a person. Unlike execution in the arena, which we'll get to, there was no fun spectacle and spurty blood to enjoy. Just agony and a long slow death. Because it was so icky, Romans didn't tend to write descriptions of what a crucifixion actually looked like very often. As a general rule, the victim would be stripped naked and whipped and beaten until they bled. We have a nice line from our Stoic chum Seneca on the 'ugly weals on the shoulders and chest' of the crucified from the whip. The only purpose of this was to make the victim bleed a lot and be in pain and really exacerbate their suffering in the next stage. The suffering was really *very* important. The next stage was being attached to a cross with either rope or nails. There's quite a lot of argument over whether nails were commonly used in Roman crucifixion or only on special occasions. You know, when you really want a crucifixion to hurt. Like when you're executing Jesus. If that were the case, the use of nails would almost be a compliment. You'd have to really piss off the Romans to get a nail (please imagine me saying this in the voice of Michael Palin in *Life of Brian*). The main argument against the use of nails is that there are hardly any in the archaeological record, not anywhere near as many as you'd expect to find given the sheer number of crucifixions the Romans did all the time, every week, for hundreds of years. It's believed that the main reason they're missing is that Roman people saw crucifixion nails as immensely powerful amulets and healing charms so they nicked them and kept them in special places and that makes them unrecognisable to archaeologists. There's also some dreadfully tedious medical arguments about the use of nails and different types of foot bone that are incomprehensible to me and therefore seem very convincing indeed, so I'm working here on the basis that people were mostly being nailed to crosses because that's more fun.[2]

In practice, Roman soldiers, who were probably nice young men who were good to their mums and had lovely wives and a few kids and maybe some had a dog and enjoyed a nice game of dice in the evening, would routinely hold a wriggling, bleeding beaten person down, a person probably begging for mercy, and line a nail up against the heel of their foot. Unlike most representations of Christ on the cross, the feet weren't nailed crossed over at the front and through the ankle. That wouldn't last. They were almost certainly positioned either side of the vertical beam and the nail would go through the calcaneum, which is the sticky-out heel bit of your foot. We know this because we have one single ankle bone from Giv'at Ha-Mivtar in Jerusalem which still has the nail through it. The ankle belonged to a man named Jehohanan. Try not to think about it or whatever your heel is touching right now. The soldiers would line the nail up so it went through the bone rather than the tendon above so it couldn't rip out, and then they'd hammer that nail home. It would take a while, I imagine, to force the nail through the flesh and the bone and then into the hard wood. But it would have to be done twice, and the second time the screaming might be even worse. And this is just the beginning. Next come the hands. They are stretched across the cross beam, and again the soldier, perhaps by now indifferent to the screams, lines up the nail to the sinewy middle of the wrist, avoiding those pesky messy arteries, and hammers it home through the delicate little bones and into the wood behind. None of this is necessary. It would be perfectly possible to just tie the victim to the cross and leave them there to die, in pain, of exhaustion and dehydration. The nailing just added to the agony and humiliation, which is all it needed to do.

The cross was then raised up in a public part of town to make sure that everyone saw the victim's suffering. As the jurist Quintilian says, people were crucified in the busiest places because the penalty was aimed not so much at the offender themselves but at setting an example for others.[3] Crucifixion was potentially days of physical suffering for the victim and psychological suffering for everyone they were dying near.

There's actually not much agreement on what would eventually kill a crucifixion victim as they could die of about ten different crucifixion-related things. Some will have asphyxiated as the weight of their own body dragged the shoulders from the sockets and pushed their chest up and made breathing very difficult indeed. Some will have developed acidosis as a result of not being able to exhale properly, causing a massive build-up of carbon dioxide in their blood which would then become acidic, leading to heart failure. Some will have died from exhaustion and dehydration as the agony of alternating between trying to hold their weight on the nails in their shattered ankle bones and their paralysed wrists caused massive fluid loss leading to hypovolaemic shock and organ shut-down. There are plenty more alternatives because, as it turns out, being nailed into a stress position in the Mediterranean heat shortly after being whipped and losing a whole lot of blood and having no way to support your own body weight creates a whole host of physical problems that will kill you slowly and painfully. Who knew? The victims would be guarded by soldiers, who had to listen to the screams and wails and moans and keep away onlookers and families for hours. Sometimes, people took too long to die on a cross or were too loud, so the soldiers would break their legs. This prevented them from being able to support themselves on anything other than their weak broken wrists, leading to a swift but terrible suffocation. That's how Romans interpreted the concept of mercy.

The problem with crucifixion, though, was that it wasn't very fun for anyone. It went on for a long time and there probably wasn't even that much screaming after a while, given how hard it was to breathe. You couldn't even tell when the criminal had died if they fell into unconsciousness first. It was a rubbish show; it had no theatre at all. And the Romans loved theatre. Virtually everything in Roman life and culture had a theatrical, performative aspect to it, from the varying costumes of different social castes to the blowing of trumpets at every vaguely religious occasion to hide 'inauspicious sounds'. They were a people who loved everything to be public, performed and ideally dressed-up fancy. So obviously they had other forms of execution that were more spectacular, of which the most spectacular was being fed to the beasts. Equally obviously, over time, as the Empire got richer and the Romans became more cynical, executions involving beasts became more and more theatrical as every politician tried to put on an execution that no one had ever seen before. That lives were being lost in this theatre was beside the point. And anyway, they deserved it.

The Tunisian mosaic described at the start of this chapter shows the most boring and bog-standard form of animal-based execution. The animal is a big cat and it's eating the face of a bound victim. It's utterly dreadful to look at in still life, but watching it from the middle of the stands in the midday heat, it was probably vaguely interesting at best. So, just as they competed with each other over everything, politicians across the Empire competed with each other to come up with the most entertaining way to kill people who were defined as criminals and the enslaved. Strabo, a geographer from the late Republican period who came to Rome from Turkey, describes a particularly impressive one that he saw first-hand somewhere between 44 and 29 BCE. He watched the execution of a bandit gang-leader named Selurus who had been terrorising the Mount Etna area of Italy for a long time. As a sign of how much he had pissed off the government, he was sent to Rome when they caught him, for punishment in front of the largest number of people possible. He was sentenced to the beasts in the Forum Romanum, and whoever put on the show got creative with how to ratchet up the narrative tension that was otherwise missing from a good execution. They built a large structure in the centre of the temporary arena, tall and high, which apparently reminded Strabo of Mount Etna itself. The executioners perched Selurus on the top of this structure, which I have to assume was made of wood. Underneath him, hungry beasts paced in fragile wooden cages, waiting. Disappointingly, Strabo doesn't identify the beasts, but it could have been anything from big cats to angry cows. For a little while, nothing happened; it was clear that somehow Selurus was going to end up with the beasts, but no one knew how or when. The tension was delicious. This notorious bandit and criminal sat on display for all Rome to see and his fate waited impatiently below him. Suddenly, somehow, the contraption collapsed, and Selurus fell into the cages of the beasts, which were, in turn, broken open as he fell on them. The beasts were thus released and able to tear at the delicious meat that had been flung to them. Selurus was torn apart and suitably punished. The crowd went wild.

This is told by Strabo as an interesting aside in the middle of an otherwise tedious description of the geography of the Etna area because the form of the execution was unusual. Even in Rome, you didn't get tension like that in the arena every day and, in a world that was sorely lacking in multi-part television dramas with a will-they-won't-they subplot, or indeed any satisfying fictional drama (their plays were universally dreadful), a little suspense over when and how this person would die was brilliant entertainment. You can easily imagine the Republican crowd watching the set-up, a little hushed at first as they waited to see what would happen, then gradually getting louder, almost certainly upsetting the animals. When I imagine the crowds at events like this in Rome, I think of those who turned up at the prison in Florida where Ted Bundy was sent to the electric chair in 1989. Hundreds and hundreds hung around in a car park outside Florida State Prison all day singing a bizarre version of 'American Pie' with Ted Bundy-themed lyrics and letting off fireworks while wearing 'Burn Bundy Burn' t-shirts. You can see the footage on YouTube of them cheering and drinking and celebrating and genuinely screaming for joy when the guard announced that Bundy was dead. Even today, in a culture that protects the individual right to life more than any other in history, people can be found who will party in a car park, wearing celebratory t-shirts and burning effigies because some guy from the news is being electrocuted in a nearby building. Imagine how much more excited they'd have been if they'd got to see it. Or if Bundy had been trampled to death by elephants, like the Roman deserters in 167 BCE, or tied to a stake and burnt alive, or amusingly dropped into a pit of angry cows. They'd have loved it. The Roman audiences loved it.

The electric chair was, as a method of execution, mostly reaching the end of its life in the 1980s but it was invented in the 1880s as a kinder, more humane alternative to hanging. People were constantly refining hanging to make it faster and reduce suffering. The long drop was developed to break the neck even more quickly than the standard drop method, which was itself hoped to be quicker and better than the short drop strangulation method. The electric chair was gradually replaced by the lethal injection in the USA, where a combination of drugs is given to anaesthetise and paralyse the prisoner and then stop their heart. The aim of all these developments in the USA has been to reduce the suffering of the person being killed, to make their death as painless and unspectacular and dignified as possible. The killings take place in private rooms, with only very tiny numbers of people allowed to watch, so the privacy of the executed is protected. The prisoner is given a final meal, final words, a final chance to exert their agency and individuality and then, after death, their bodies are disposed of according to their wills. In modern, Western (American) executions, the state acts bizarrely and paradoxically as both the murderer and the protector of the victim. Although the crowds outside the prison might scream and cheer and dance, the prisoner is at all times protected from harm and suffering right up until the point that they are killed by the very same structure and people. It is really odd.

The Romans would laugh their tits off to look at American executions. The Romans had no such paradoxes, no confusion or anxiety over the right to life or privacy or dignity. Dignity was a privilege afforded to the very, very few. Life was something you earned, mostly by being rich, useful and a citizen who followed the rules. Those who didn't manage those things deserved everything they got. A Roman would ask what the point of the state murdering someone was if no one got to see it. An execution can't be a proper example or deterrent, they'd argue, if it's a secret. Nail them up and put them at the crossroads. Strip them nude and parade them through the streets and into the arena when half the city is watching and really show the citizens what happens when you mess with the Romans. Torture them, torment them, make them bleed and scream, make them listen to the jeers and shouts of the crowd that despises them and hear the Roman people cheering their pain. Make them endure unimaginable humiliation, tear their limbs from their bodies and burn them alive and crush them and cut them and display every minute of it for the people to learn from and enjoy. Then throw their torn bodies into a pit and move onto the next lot. That's a deterrent and an example. That's a punishment. That's true vengeance. That's what happens when you mess with the Romans.

There is, of course, a problem with this. For the Romans, that is. There are about eight million problems for us as modern Western readers with an ingrained sense of individual self and inalienable personal human rights. The problem for the Romans was simpler: once you've seen *one* guy get stabbed or hung or burnt or eaten by a leopard, you've basically seen them all. One stabbing is the same as the next. Burnings are barely distinguishable from one another.† Animals are a bit unpredictable, but eventually they're gonna eat the guy's face and, you know, I already saw that on a mosaic the other day at my mate's house. And it's lunchtime so I might nip out and get some bread because, between forty elephants getting killed this morning and the fifty pairs of gladiators later, yet another dude getting his face eaten is a bit old hat. There's an Italian inscription which commemorates a low-key, provincial four-day festival of games in some small town – absolutely not the top end of games here, very low- to mid-tier – which ended with an entire day of executions. A whole day of people being executed, over and over and over.⁴ Of course that got dull. People get bored easily, and people need innovation in their entertainments and the men who populated the Roman state were very, very, very rich and very good at coming up with new ways to kill and make it fun and sexy. And as an added bonus – like the world's most terrifying drama club – they loved dressing up.

The first person to begin to merge the cultural delights of theatre and the civic necessity of public executions of increasingly large numbers of non-citizens was Julius Caesar. JC was nothing if not an absolutely relentless innovator. He also had an awful lot of captured prisoners of war and enemy soldiers that he didn't know what to do with. He appears to have resolved the dual problems of too many prisoners and the possibility of tedious executions by forcing the prisoners to re-enact battles in the arena for the entertainment of the crowd, thus forcing them all to kill one another. This is the kind of genius that gets a month named after them. Mock battles were different from gladiatorial

---

† Except one time in Domitian's reign when a guy was being burnt but a massive rain storm put the flames out. His bonds were burnt through and he fell to the ground, leaving him possibly feeling reprieved, right up to the point where a pack of dogs ran up and tore his delicious barbecued body apart. That one was probably quite a fun watch for the crowd.

battles. While gladiators were trained to fight elegantly and according to the rules of engagement and, ideally, not go into a berserker mode and randomly kill one another, mock battles were far uglier and less constrained. They were a form of execution so the suspense and tension lay not in the question of whether anyone would die or in enjoying the skill of the fighters, but in watching desperate men fight to be allowed to live literally another minute longer. As part of his triumphal return to Rome in 46 BCE, to celebrate his military destruction of all the Romans who opposed his monarchical rule, Caesar threw a couple of thousand men into the arena, three hundred of them on horseback, and sat back to watch them kill one another. You'd think that after all the wars and genocides and invasions Caesar had led, he'd have had enough of watching men fight for their lives but apparently you'd be very wrong about that.

His greatest innovation in the arena, though, was mock naval battles. He dug out a pit in the Campus Martius, where the horse races were held, filled it with water and threw another six thousand prisoners of war out on boats to try to kill each other while pretending to be Tyrians and Egyptians. According to Suetonius, people were so thrilled by this new form of entertainment that they camped in tents for days beforehand and, in the crush to get a good look at everything, several people were killed. There's a strange sort of irony to spectators dying as a result of their impatience to see people executed. And this was just the beginning. Augustus staged an even bigger naval battle, creating an entire artificial lake and making thirty triremes' worth of men re-enact the battle of Salamis. Then, in 52 CE, Claudius made everyone traipse all the way to an actual natural lake, the Fucine Lake in central Italy, where he made nineteen thousand criminals fight on floating wooden barges, and probably what most people saw was drownings. He had to use criminals because he was rubbish at war, so he didn't have any POWs to kill. His adopted son Nero was less keen on leaving Rome and more keen on building big things, so he built a wooden amphitheatre, again on the Campus Martius, filled it with water and marine creatures (some poor dolphins and tuna had an absolutely terrible day) and covered it with an awning painted with stars, then reenacted a battle between Athenians and Persians. Why? Because he could.

You'll note that between Augustus and Nero these spectacular displays of death became less about dealing with an oversupply of prisoners and more about putting on a spectacular display and finding the requisite bodies to fill it. This is a trend. Once one emperor had done something immensely spectacular and amazing that would have children asking their parents 'where were you the day the Divine Augustus built his own lake and held a battle on it?', there was pressure on the next emperor to do something similar. The same goes for provincial governors and local elites and every guy who wants to make his mark in his little backwater town in Belgium. If you want to be remembered, you have to do something people will talk about, even when it comes to executions.

The most theatrical of all emperors, who really pioneered a new approach to judicial murder for fun, was Nero. Nero loved dressing up almost as much as he loved murdering the women in his family, which he loved almost as much as he loved getting his own way. He introduced costume to public executions by dressing a thief called Meniscus up as Hercules and then burning him alive during the lunchtime executions. In comparison to a massive naval battle, this doesn't sound like much but you have to remember that a massive mock battle was a once-in-a-lifetime sight. People getting burnt alive for slights like stealing from the emperor's gardens was a much more everyday occurrence. All it took to dress someone up like Hercules was a lion skin but this was apparently enough to really liven up proceedings. Enough that someone called Lucilius wrote a whole epigram about it. In Greek. Describing it as a very famous spectacle. Evidently executions had got really boring. Thankfully for urbane audiences in the city of Rome, the Flavians were about to build the world's biggest amphitheatre and show the entire universe how killing for fun should be done.

The Flavian Amphitheatre is now universally known by its colloquial name the Colosseum. These days, it's such an embedded part of Rome's architecture and the idea of Roman-ness that it is very hard for people to imagine an ancient Rome without it, but it wasn't started until 72 CE and not completed until 80 CE. None of your favourite Julio-Claudians even imagined such a thing, I'm afraid. The emperor Titus opened the Colosseum with an orgy of human and animal bloodshed that made the spectators' eyes stand out on stalks. Historians both ancient and modern have tended to focus on the five thousand to nine thousand animals that were slaughtered and the innumerable gladiators who participated in the immense mock naval and infantry battles, the female beast hunters who killed lions and the elephants that were pitched against one another in a fight that is truly horrible to imagine but probably breathtaking to witness. The one eyewitness we have, though, was equally interested in the spectacular executions which took place as part of the inauguration. The poet Martial wrote a series of epigrams celebrating and commemorating what he saw in the Colosseum, and the miraculous scale of the building itself. He has six epigrams which describe, in awed tones, staged executions of anonymous criminals which used up so many sophisticated resources and were so carefully orchestrated that it sends a chill down the spine to think about it.

His first epigram describes something so astonishingly awful that the mind kind of veers away from it. It reads, in polite translation:

> Believe that Pasiphae was united with the Dictaean
> bull; we have seen it, the old legend has won credence.
> And let not hoary antiquity plume itself, Caesar: what-
> ever Fame sings of, the arena affords you.[5]

To translate from that, Martial is describing a re-enactment in the Colosseum of the myth of Pasiphae, the daughter of the sun god Helios and the wife of Minos of Crete. Poseidon lent Minos a pure white bull which Minos was supposed to return via sacrifice but, because it was so beautiful, he didn't. Poseidon was not a particularly forgiving god, so he punished Minos by cursing Pasiphae with a powerful and insatiable sexual attraction to the bull. Unable to control herself, Pasiphae persuaded master-inventor Daedalus to build her a hollow wooden cow with which to trick the bull. Pasiphae lay inside the wooden cow, waited until the bull came to mount it and then presented herself to the bull's penis. Thus, she kinda raped a bull. The offspring of their union was Asterion, better known as the Minotaur. This is apparently what was performed in the arena in between lions being hunted and gladiators beating each other up: a woman placed in a wooden cow and forcibly penetrated by a bull in a live bestiality rape show which ideally ended in her death. If it didn't, her throat was presumably cut off stage. It is beyond comprehension.

There is a great desire to think of this epigram as fiction but historians often use Roman fiction to support it as fact. You may remember Apuleius' *Metamorphoses*, the novel we talked about in Chapter 6. In *Metamorphoses*, there is a notorious section where the protagonist, Lucius, who is having adventures in the form of a donkey, is forced to be the bestial partner in the rape of a female poisoner. The idea in the novel is that a wild beast will appear while the woman is being penetrated by a donkey in front of the arena audience and will eat them both. A fun day out for the whole family. Lucius, though, being the donkey, doesn't want to be eaten so he waits until no one is looking and runs away. I will never forget reading this section as an undergraduate in room 4D of the University of Birmingham library and transforming into pure silent 'what the fuck' energy for a while. And then finding as many friends as possible and making them read it. It is mindbogglingly nasty but apparently it is a thing the Romans did.

All of the dramatic executions described in Martial's epigrams involve huge sets and dramatic, mythological back-stories like this. In the next, a new and alarming level of realism was brought to the play *Laureolus*. You may remember this as the play being performed right before the emperor Gaius was assassinated in 41 CE. In the Colosseum, however, Titus decided that actors acting being fake crucified wasn't good enough. He wanted the real thing. So a real criminal, then a man with a family and a life and a mum, now anonymous and dehumanised, was tied to a cross in the arena then ripped to shreds by a bear. Martial leaves little to the imagination:

> As Prometheus, bound on a Scythian crag, fed the tireless bird with his too abundant breast, so did Laureolus, hanging on no sham cross, give his naked flesh to a Caledonian bear. His lacerated limbs lived on, dripping gore, and in all his body, body there was none.[6]

In epigram seven, a man dressed as the inventor Daedalus, the father of Icarus and creator of the trick wooden cow, is ripped apart by a bear and Martial jokes that he bet the man wishes he had wings to fly away with now. There's no great myth or play about Daedalus' death so this one was just made up. In another epigram, the stage is set like the lush grove of the Hesperides, the three Greek nymphs of the evening. The grove contains trees which grow golden apples and every kind of peaceful wildlife. Martial describes tame animals filling the stage, and the air heaving with birds of every kind. In the centre of this scene of mythic tranquillity, a man dressed as the poet Orpheus reclined, waiting, with painful tension as the crowd ooh-d and ahhh-d at the little animals, until, suddenly, a trap door in the floor of the arena opened and a bear appeared, which leapt for Orpheus' throat and tore it out. 'This thing alone was done contrary to the legend,' says Martial. The crowd went wild.

There are plenty more examples of executions like this in Rome. Executions which were theatre: suspenseful, dramatic, full of ironic tension and mise-en-scène. Executions which were performed according to a script and involved a great deal of sophisticated planning and stage-management; which left their audience goggling in awe at the cleverness and elegance, their interpretation of myth, their uniqueness. Each one was a staggering display of the richness and power and innovation of Rome and the Romans. Each one was a glorious, expensive celebration of the joy of punishing those who had been deemed non-Roman, but each was a living breathing human who felt and blinked and farted and once stubbed their toe and then died. Michel Foucault once wrote that 'there is no glory in punishing', but the Romans would not agree.[7] There could be a lot of glory in punishing if you made it spectacular enough.

The process of these dramatic executions, which were always an outlier, never the norm, displayed state killing as something which could be a great deal of fun. It displayed death as something which could be planned and staged and the person at the centre of it – the criminal being executed and their crime – could be the least important part. In Martial's epigram about the real crucifixion and execution of 'Laureolus', he doesn't even know who the criminal is or what he did. He murdered an enslaver or his father or robbed a temple or something. Whatever. Whoever he is, he deserved it, is all Martial knows. The state had taken its vengeance on whoever this poor man was; it revelled in his suffering and erased his name from history.

Roman sources only show public executions as being either very boring or very spectacular. They were either mundane, everyday crucifixions and beheadings or wildly exhilarating theatrical displays praised for their stagecraft. What a modern reader never sees is any writer wrestling with the extraordinarily cavalier approach to human life. When the white supremacist terrorist Timothy McVeigh asked to have his execution by lethal injection televised, he was refused 'in deference to the penal system' and because there was a real concern that actually watching someone die might turn the American people against the idea of capital punishment, or at least open up a discussion about it that no one in the political, judicial or penal systems wanted to have.[8] Academics were also concerned that the televising of executions would, paradoxically, normalise state violence to the point where they stopped being spectacle and became background noise, which is what they became for the Romans.[9] Until an execution reached truly remarkable heights of stagecraft and became a pageant in itself, it wasn't worth even noting. Unless it was to include in your home decoration.

Cornelia, Vestalis Maxima

In 91 CE, the inhabitants of Rome witnessed a sight they had hoped never to see. It was an appalling sight, which cast a gloom over the whole city. A funeral procession marched through Rome like funerals did every week, friends and family loudly lamenting their loss and wailing their grief into the air; but this one carried a unique horror. On the bier, instead of a body, lay a living woman, tied and gagged and blinking at the sky. The funeral procession passed through the city, past the *subura* and along the long, straight road to the Colline Gate in the ancient walls of the city. This was the way to the camp of the Praetorian Guard, but that's not where the procession was going. Outside the gate, the procession stopped by a small ridge, which contained an opening. A couple of hastily hewn steps led down into a small, dark cubby-hole dug out of the earth. If you walked down the steps and peeked inside, you'd see a small cot, and a few little jars on the floor beside a lump of bread. The jars contained oil, milk and water. It was here that the restrained woman was being brought. The woman was Cornelia and she had been, up to this moment, the head priestess of the Vestal Virgins. She was about to be buried alive.

The Vestal Virgins stood at the centre of Roman religious life; six women and girls, ranging in age from ten to fifty, drawn from powerful families, they dedicated thirty years of their life to chaste religious work. Their primary role was to care for Rome's hearth, the sacred fire at the centre of the city which burnt perpetually, and its associated household gods. Every wife and mother in the Roman home tended the hearth and cared for the gods of the household, represented by small statues. The Vestals cared for the wellbeing of the state. The hearth was the beating heart of Rome, the core of its life force. The gods the Vestals tended were those brought to Italy by Aeneas as he escaped the burning of Troy and the hearth they cared for protected Rome and its interests. They also produced and stored the special secret blend of salt and grains (the *mola salsa*) used in every official sacrifice inside and outside Rome.[10] For their work, they were expected to remain virgins until they retired. In return for their childhood promise never to touch a boy, they were given privileges, like good seats at the theatre and the ability to grant asylum and being inviolate in the same way a Tribune was. The downside was that if they got caught touching a boy, they could be subjected to this ritual murder. They were escorted inside a tiny cubby-hole outside the Colline Gate, in which the bare necessities for a week or so of life were placed, and they were sealed inside and left to die.

This is what happened to Cornelia in 91 CE. She was sent there by the emperor Domitian after someone accused her of having sex with a man named Valerius Licinianus. Licinianus confessed to his crime and so Domitian exiled him (he later became a teacher in Sicily, which Pliny the Younger called 'pitiably sad' suggesting that Pliny had a bizarrely misplaced sense of what was sad). He was just a dude, though. Some random orator. Cornelia was the Vestalis Maxima, the head Vestal, the woman on whose shoulders rested the security and safety of the entire Empire and everything that bore the name of Rome, and Domitian was on a conservative crusade to Bring Back Traditional Roman Values. Much like a Conservative politician will suggest the idea of national service in the UK every few years so that kids today can learn imaginary traditional British values like the stiff upper lip and enduring cold showers, Domitian thought that there was a need to return to imaginary traditional Roman values like stoicism, asceticism and extreme harshness. The Romans idealised an early Republic where Romans were believed to be uncompromising, unemotional and unadorned, in much the same way that a certain subset of British people idealise the 'Blitz Spirit', and Domitian was one of them. So, he became the first person since the consuls of 113 BCE to send a woman to the Colline Gate. And Cornelia, who had been a priestess since she was a small child, sat on her tiny bed as the small opening through which she had been forced was filled in and sealed. And she sat in the dark, with her bread and milk, and waited for death to come. Maybe she eked out her hunk of bread and her liquids for weeks. How long could you make a couple of pints of milk and water last? Maybe she destroyed it all in a furious rage and later wept and screamed as she starved and clawed at the walls. Maybe she lay and refused to eat and let herself stoically and peacefully die. The unrelenting helplessness of being trapped in a pitch-dark hole, knowing that no one will ever come and save you and you cannot try to save yourself, inspires a yawning horror.

Every other Vestal Virgin who was condemned to this slow, cruel death existed in the legendary Roman past. The more common practice in the historical period was to politely behead them. In 82 CE, Domitian had kindly allowed two Vestal Virgins to choose their own method of execution, which wasn't necessarily nice but was certainly more normal (for Romans) than Cornelia's death. The reason that Domitian was one of the only people in the Imperial era to execute a Vestal Virgin in this solemn, ritualised way which both ensured the death of the woman and simultaneously distanced the state from it, was that it edged just a little too close to the feeling of sacrificing a person. The Romans were repulsed by human sacrifice. They considered it too wicked and disgusting for words. Which is why they had only done it three times.

Two Greeks and Two Gauls

In 228 BCE, 216 BCE and 114/3 BCE, the Romans found four people, a Greek man and woman and a Gallic man and woman, probably enslaved people, and buried them alive in the Forum Boarum. Three times they ritually executed four innocent people in an overtly religious rite. They did this each time because they were facing military defeat and so they consulted the Sibylline Books to ask them what to do. Conveniently, the books are not in the kind of vague verse that you might expect from a prophecy or horoscope. The bits of book which have survived (which are dubious to be honest, but we work with what we have) and the historical evidence we have for what the Romans did when they consulted them are remarkably clear. Suffering a plague in 293 BCE? Best import the cult of Aesculapius and build a temple to him. The Latins are revolting? Nip off to the narrowest part of the Tiber and sacrifice some pregnant pigs. All very specific directions, which the Romans appreciated. Sometimes, they were facing something scary, like the Gauls gathering on the horizon in 228 BCE or a horrific defeat at Cannae in 216 BCE, and they consulted the books and the books said, 'This is really bad, guys. Best ritually murder some humans.' You can imagine the awkward silence in the room when the priest read that one out. The absolute heart sink as they realised what they had to do.

Thankfully for them, the books didn't ask them to slaughter the human victims in the way that they slaughtered cows and goats, with all that bashing and cutting. Rather, they asked for a bloodless burial where the Roman priests and magistrates could brick some poor people up and walk away and try hard not to think about it. Which is good, because the Romans were deeply, deeply uncomfortable with the fact that they had got involved in human sacrifice. All the sources we have about these three events come from the Imperial period, one to two centuries after they occurred, when all that was left of them was some 'mysterious and secret ceremonies' performed in the Forum Boarum every November to somehow commemorate the victims.[11] The Romans who were writing about these events were the same Romans who were always smugly congratulating themselves for eradicating Gallic and British druidism, which they strongly believed practised human sacrifice. Especially in Anglesey. Obviously, they had eradicated druidism by slaughtering all the druids but Pliny the Elder, for example, considered wiping out overt human sacrifice to be the greatest gift the Romans gave the world.[12] So when these writers wrote about what their forefathers had done, they did so in tones of great discomfort, highlighting that the books made them do it, or that it was 'wholly alien to the Roman spirit'.[13] It was tough for them to reconcile the strong Roman belief that everything the Republic did was perfect with the fact of human sacrifice so they mostly tiptoed around it.

An odd thing about the Imperial era Romans is that they would crucify enslaved people in their thousands every year, and go to the games regularly to watch criminals be tortured and eaten and they'd walk past the scourged, bloody bodies of the executed on a daily basis and not even blink. They were surrounded by state-sponsored death virtually every day, in a city, then an empire, built on slavery and suffering, but once the idea was raised of killing someone in a solemn, ritual setting, they were sick on their shoes. That was too damn far. Offer a human life to the gods, or add any element of religion to the murder of unwilling humans, and suddenly everything had to be bloodless and clean and distant. Human sacrifice was barbaric and ritual murder was icky at best; feeding a person to a bear, though, that was a family day out. There's no real answer for why this is. My best theory, which would be more correctly termed a guess, is that they simply didn't see executing and crucifying enslaved people and people deemed to be criminals as real killing. Those people were, in their hearts and minds, already effectively dead. They meant nothing – literally nothing – to the kind of men who wrote histories and poems and satires and lived lives of luxurious leisure. They were slaves killed by slaves. It was all irrelevant to the life of a Roman senator. You may as well have asked them to think about the ants they stepped on. The sacrifice of Gauls and Greeks, and the ritualised execution of Vestals, though? That implicated them. That involved them. That was something they could empathise with. That Vestal Virgin was their friend's daughter or sister or niece. She mattered. She had a name and a lineage. The consuls and priests who had to brick up the Gauls mattered. They were truly alive to our source writers. The Roman state, especially as a Republic, was truly alive too, and infinitely more important than these criminals bleeding out at the entrance to the *subura*.

My best evidence for this, which is not good evidence admittedly, is that when the ritual murders involved enslaved people, Roman writers became far less squeamish about it. Suddenly, they thought it was a fascinating lark, to be written about all the time. Mainly, I'm thinking of the priesthood of the goddess Diana known as the Rex Nemorensis. Rex Nemorensis translates roughly as the King of the Grove and it was a priesthood based at a small sanctuary to Diana in a lush wooded grove inside the crater of an extinct volcano, containing a small lake, at Aricia, about eleven miles outside Rome. It was isolated and fairly wild and in it there was a sacred tree. All of this was a bit unusual, but what made it really weird was that the Rex was always a fugitive from slavery, and the only way to become the Rex Nemorensis was to kill your predecessor in single combat. And the only way to challenge the reigning Rex was to sneak into the grove and cut a golden bough from the sacred tree. The priesthood of Diana was always a potential beacon of hope for enslaved men in Italy, a legitimate way out of slavery if they could overcome all the immense obstacles in their way. If they could escape their bonds, and reach the Appian Way – the busiest road in Italy – and climb the long road without being caught, and enter the grove, and identify the right tree, and snap off a branch before they were seen and start the ritual and still be strong enough to fight and kill the priest, they could be free. Once a man reached the summit and murdered the reigning Rex and took on the position, they were, like Mad-Eye Moody, doomed to a life of constant vigilance. Constantly listening to the sounds of the wood, wondering if that noise meant that a desperate fugitive was coming to attack, constantly looking over their shoulder waiting for the day a wild-eyed escapee burst from the trees and came to confront them, constantly prepared for the moment that they had to be confronted once again with a battle to the death, waiting to kill or be killed. If they were really unlucky, they could hold the position for decades, fighting off everyone who came to challenge them, and then be stuck with Gaius as an emperor getting jealous of their longevity and hiring a young, strong enslaved man to kill them.[†] There was no peace for the Rex Nemorensis, and the Roman writers absolutely loved it.

The ritual of the Rex Nemorensis appears, with a kind of gleeful fascination, in Roman authors ranging from Ovid to Statius to Suetonius to Plutarch to Pausanius to Strabo. Geographers, poets, biographers and historians were all

---

† In my imagination, Gaius' hired man is Jason Statham and the priest is a doddery old man, which is terrible for the battle, but then allows me to imagine Jason Statham being a priest for the rest of his days in the woods, which, for absolutely no reason, I find very funny.

fascinated by the Rex, who presented them with a story too good not to share. Ovid loved it so much he wrote about the ritual three times, including in his epic poem on how to pick up ladies (*Ars Amatoria*) where he includes it as one of the many, many, many places where women can be found and therefore hit on. He therefore suggests that going to look at the jumpy killer-slave-priest was a tourist attraction. It even plays a small but significant role in the *Aeneid*, when Aeneas has to grab the golden bough in order to make his way to the underworld to chat to his dad. The battle between the two fugitives from slavery, the desperation and fear that ooze out of the whole set-up for the empathetic outside observer, was nothing more than an amusing day out for the Roman writers, and an odd little Roman quirk for the Greeks. It was a curious human interest piece at best, and a place to try to look up girls' skirts for Ovid. They gave not a single fuck for the men who actually engaged in the process of being the priest or who fought to become it. The reality of a priesthood which forced men to murder one another was entirely lost on them, because these were not men to the Roman writers; they were slaves.

None of these forms of ritual murder were central to Roman life. They were very much in the margins and footnotes of Roman life, culture and religion. But they were always there, as little blemishes, yet more legal ways to take a person's life and to rationalise doing so. Yet more ways for murder to be a part of the Roman experience and for life to mean a tiny bit less.

A Fatal Thing Happened on the
Way to the Forum: The End

Life, for the Roman state and Roman culture, didn't mean breathing and heartbeats and feeling and loving and higher brain activity, or even the presence of a soul implanted by God. Life was a social creation. Life that was worth protecting, worth policing, was a life that had dignity, majesty and social recognition. What the Roman state protected when it protected anything (which was rarely) was not its inhabitants, not the people who baked bread and soled shoes and wove cloaks and imported wine and called themselves Roman – rather it was itself and its own structures.

The wrongness of a homicide is a dynamic concept, which is why I have interpreted it so broadly here. Infinite variables make up whether a homicide is a murder. It is murder when a *retiarius* kills four *secutores* against the rules, but a game when one *secutor* severs the artery of a *retiarius* with his hand raised in surrender. It is punishment when a man nails another to a cross to suffer for days, but murder when a man tries to feed another to a lamprey. It is murder when a husband throws his wife from a window, but family business when a father strangles his daughter for having sex outside of marriage.

This is not to say that the Roman people individually did not care and cry and wail when their friends and family died, whether old or young. Just that every single inhabitant of the city lived surrounded by people they had enslaved, walked past a crucifixion once a week, sat through criminals being burnt on the streets and eaten in the arena, stepped over the bodies of the executed being dragged to the Tiber, cheered when their favourite gladiator cut the throat of their opponent, and not one of them ever thought to do a thing about it. And that's before we even get to what was happening inside people's homes. Homicide – the deliberate, wilful killing of another person – was embedded so deeply into Roman daily life that it is suffocating if you think about it too hard.

The study of Roman murder tells us more than just that, though. It shows us the Roman world underneath the marble columns and fancy mosaics and cool buildings and so-called civilisation. The Ciceros and Senecas and Plinys who are still hailed as brilliant men and models of wisdom (I'm looking at you, *Ancient Wisdom for Modern Readers*) were enslavers who, for all their moralising, sat in the front row at the games. The temples and columns that form the basis for half the government buildings in the Western world were built by enslaved men, and outside them men, women and children (and sometimes dogs) were nailed to crosses. Inside the gorgeous villas that dot the European landscape to this day, sparkling with lush frescos, men threw their wives out of windows and women beat their enslaved attendants to death and babies were buried in little anonymous pots. Looking at murder in the Roman world allows us to see the Empire's grim underbelly, its brutal barbarism so often obscured by neoclassicism and an imagined dream of 'Rome'. It lets us imagine the world of the Romans from the perspective of the underdogs and the victims and losers, and not just the winners. Murder offers us a glimpse at both how like and unlike us they were. Because, although gladiators and slavery and crucifixion and socks with sandals went out of fashion, murder never has.

Glossary

Augustus: the first emperor of Rome and the founder of the Principate. Born Gaius Octavius, he was Julius Caesar's nephew. He was posthumously adopted by Caesar at the age of nineteen and went on to avenge Caesar's assassination via the medium of civil war. Over a fifteen-year period he defeated every other powerful man in Rome, including Cicero whom he proscribed, and then claimed to restore the Republic. He took the title of Princeps, meaning first citizen, and the name Augustus, meaning most sacred, to cement his unofficial position of emperor. The name later became a title granted to emperors when they ascended to the throne.

consilium: a Roman advisory council consulted by individuals when making important decisions. The domestic *consilium* was associated with the earliest eras of Roman history and idealised by later writers. It would contain family members and, often, family friends. The *consilium principis* was a semi-official but revered group of advisers to the emperor.

consuls: the chief magistrates, basically the prime ministers of Rome. Two were elected each year. The position was designed to have all the powers of the king spread across two people for a limited amount of time. During their term, the consuls held almost unlimited power but they could also veto one another. Being elected consul during the Republic was a demonstration of immense personal popularity and prestige. During the Principate, consuls became largely ornamental. They were chosen by the emperor, who usually held the position himself, and had little formal power but the position continued to confer significant prestige upon its holders.

damnatio memoriae: the official posthumous erasure of those marked as enemies of the state. Usually, statues were destroyed, names were erased from inscriptions (and sometimes coins, in the case of emperors), and a man's *praenomen* (first name) was banned within his family.

dignitas: worth, excellence, dignity and esteem. One's formal standing in society.

early Roman Republic: the period between 509 BCE and about 133 BCE when Rome was ruled by the Senate, characterised by multiple wars of expansion into Italy and around the Mediterranean.

equestrian: the upper middle or business class of Rome. The term derives from the idea that they were initially the Roman cavalry. They emerged as a specific class around 129 BCE when senators were specifically excluded from the equestrian order. To be counted as an equestrian, men had to be of free birth and hold property worth at least four hundred thousand sesterces. They were mostly self-made men, men from the provinces and businessmen, a plutocracy who dominated the economic life of the Empire rather than politics. As a class they had significant economic power and status but less prestige and authority than the senatorial class and none of the specific status markers.

fama: a reputation, or, fairly literally, 'what is said' or thought about a person. One's informal standing in society.

familia: generally refers to those under the power of the *pater-familias*, which included biological and adopted family members, enslaved people within the household, and formerly enslaved people who remained under the power of the *paterfamilias*. It could also refer to a lineage or family name (such as the Julian *familia*) and as such was much broader than the term family.

fasces: a bundle of rods approximately five feet long bound together with a single-headed axe by red leather thongs. They were carried by lictors and were a constant, visible sign of the legitimacy of the magistrate/state and their right to execute citizens. The emperor's *fasces* also had laurels on top.

Forum Boarum: Rome's cattle market and an important area for traffic and meeting in the centre of the city. It sat at the northern end of the Circus Maximus at the base of the Capitoline Hill. It housed a number of temples of moderate importance and was a space where early gladiatorial fights and entertainments were held.

Forum Romanum: the major Roman Forum and the centre of civic activity. It housed the temples of Saturn and Vesta. After Julius Caesar, it also held the Senate House (the *curia*). The *rostra* was there, from which politicians gave speeches, and it was the end point for Triumphs. It gradually became cluttered with government offices, small temples and statues.

infamia: a legal term referring to a number of formal, social disabilities. Those who are marked as *infames* have no *fama* or *dignitas* and as such are not allowed to represent themselves in legal situations.

imperium: from which English gets the words imperial, Empire and emperor. *Imperium* means the ability, right or authority to command, i.e. to command armies and senators, to create and interpret the law, to have one's will be made reality. It is a supreme and unchallengeable power over others.

late Republic: the period beginning about 133 BCE until 31 BCE. Rome was technically still run by the oligarchic Senate but this period is characterised by intense competition within the Senate, which erupted into a number of violent clashes and, eventually, civil wars.

lictors: attendants who accompanied magistrates at all times carrying *fasces*. They walked in single file before the magistrate and cleared all people from his path. Consuls had twelve lictors; emperors also had twelve inside Rome, and twenty-four outside the city.

magistrates: these were the formal jobs in the Roman government to which people were elected (although they were not paid positions). The highest office was consul and the lowest was quaestor. Magistracies were held in a sequential order by politically ambitious men, as each had a minimum age requirement. Each had different powers in the domestic and military spheres.

optimates: a name taken by Roman politicians who opposed the *populares* and enacted their power through and for the Senate. It translates to 'the best men', a meaning they took both morally and socially. They were conservative and generally opposed to social reform. Sulla, Pompey, Titus Annius Milo and Cicero were *optimates*.

patrician: the most privileged class in Rome. Patricians were the elite of the elite families and dominated Republican politics. The name probably derived from *patres*, meaning fathers, and they were perceived to be the descendants of the first men chosen by Romulus to advise him or to be the descendants of Trojan families. Thus, patrician status was hereditary. By the late Republic, patrician dominance over the magistracies and priesthoods had declined but the intangible authority and prestige of being part of a patrician family never waned. Both the Julian and Claudian families were patrician. Patricians wore a specific kind of shoe adorned with a crescent moon to distinguish them from everyone else.

plebeian: the mass of Roman citizens, which initially meant anyone who was not a member of the patrician families. In the early Republic, plebeians were legally prevented from holding government and religious offices and from marrying patricians. The often violent process by which plebeians were able to win the right to representation and some political equality with patricians is known as the Conflict of the Orders and it was central to the development of Roman political culture throughout the Republic. After the institution of the Principate, plebeian came to refer to the mass of Roman people who were not members of the senatorial or equestrian order and were therefore disenfranchised from government entirely.

populares: a name adopted by Roman politicians after Tiberius and Gaius Gracchus which meant 'on the side of the people'. It denoted that they drew their power from and enacted power through the people via referenda and tribunician powers rather than through the Senate. They usually presented themselves as working in the interests of the people of Rome and focused on issues which affected the plebeian populations, such as land reform. The Gracchi brothers, Gaius Marius, Clodius Pulcher and Julius Caesar were all *populares*.

praetor: the second highest magistracy available to Roman men. When the Republic was instituted, there were two praetors but this was increased over the years until Caesar's dictatorship, when he increased the number to sixteen. They oversaw the administration of law within the city of Rome, oversaw (and financed) the games and held *imperium*.

Praetorian Guard: an elite military force of either one thousand or five hundred soldiers who acted as a personal guard for the emperor. They were instituted as a permanent fixture of Roman life by Augustus.

Praetorian Prefect: the commander(s) of the Praetorian Guard, of equestrian rank. Augustus originally instituted two Praetorian Prefects, but at various times in imperial history this was reduced to one. They were the only officials allowed to wear a sword in the presence of the emperor and had huge personal influence that exceeded their formal social status as equestrians.

Princeps: an abbreviation of *princeps senatus*, a title meaning First Citizen of the Senate. This was the honorary title invented by Augustus to denote his unofficial power rather than a formal magistracy or dictatorship. It held Republican associations, while clearly highlighting his status as the leader of the Senate.

Principate: the period beginning in 31 BCE which saw Rome ruled by a single emperor. It is generally considered to have ended in about 284 CE when Diocletian initiated the Dominate.

rostra: the speaker's platform in the Forum Romanum, so named because it was originally decorated with the prows (*rostra*) of ships captured in battle. Later it was adorned with statues and a sundial; Julius Caesar added a hemicycle structure making it a significant piece of architecture, and moved it to his Forum.

Senate: an oligarchic governmental institution of approximately three hundred aristocratic men. Many were holders or ex-holders of one of the magistracies, but many were not. Members were initially appointed by the kings, and then by consuls during the Republic. During the Principate, the emperor chose members. Membership was for life but members had to meet property ownership requirements which increased over time. The Senate formally existed to advise kings, then magistrates, then the emperor, on matters of domestic and foreign affairs. They debated and voted on legislative proposals and held enormous power as a body, but never held any military power.

senators: a specific class in Rome, granted particular clothing rights to mark them out from regular citizens. They wore the *toga praetexta* (a toga with a purple border) at formal occasions, and a tunic with a broad stripe to mark their status. They were the only men allowed to wear a gold seal ring. They were banned from engaging in any kind of mercantile activity or business as they had to own a huge amount of property in order to be eligible for senatorial status and thus all of them were men of independent income from land.

subura: the 'dangerous' area of Rome. Rome's Soho. It lay in the valley between the Viminal and Esquiline hills and was notorious for its noise, dirt, business, dodgy wooden high-rise apartment buildings and as the place to go to hire a sex worker.

Tribunes of the Plebs: officers of the government first created in around 500 BCE to represent the plebeians and give them a voice in the government of the patricians. Ten were elected by the plebeian assembly and their role was to defend the property, persons and interests of the plebeians. Their person was sacrosanct within Rome and they held the power to call a meeting of the Senate and to veto any decision made by any other magistrate and the Senate. This gave them immense power during the Republic.

Bibliographical Note

I read a lot of books and articles for this book, and compiling them all would be boring for both me and you. Mostly me. Here are the important bits.

All the texts and translations consulted are the Loeb Classical Library editions, which you can access online if you have (or have a friend with) institutional access. A lot are also available on either Bill Thayer's amazing LacusCurtius site (http://penelope. uchicago.edu/Thayer/E/home.html) or the Tufts University Perseus Digital Library Project at perseus.tufts.edu, both of which are invaluable. Sometimes I fiddled with the translations, just to make them less stodgy. I owe particular debts to the work of Daniel Ogden, J. D. Cloud, Judy E. Gaughan, Mark Cooney, O. F. Robinson, Thomas Weidemann and Matthew W. Dickie, who all shaped my thinking at various points. I am particularly indebted to P. Gabrielle Foreman and her community-sourced guidance on writing about slavery without reproducing the dehumanising language of domination and (white) supremacy. Specific books are all referenced below.

These are the books I cite or quote in the text:

Audollent, A. M. H. 1904. *Defixionum Tabellae*. Paris: Fontemoing

Carroll, M. 2018. 'Archaeological and epigraphic evidence for infancy in the Roman world.' In Crawford, S., Hadley, D. and Shepherd, G. (eds). *The Oxford Handbook of the Archaeology of Childhood*. Oxford: Oxford University Press

Crook, J. A. 1955. *Consilium Principis: Imperial Councils and Counsellors from Augustus to Diocletian*. Cambridge: Cambridge University Press

Evans, L. and Gifford, W. 1881. *The Satires of Juvenal, Persius, Sulpica and Lucilius with Notes, Chronological Tables, Arguments &c.* New York: Harper & Brothers

Faerman, M., Kahila, G., Smith, P., Greenblatt, C., Stager, L., Filon, D. and Oppenheim, A. 1997. 'DNA analysis reveals sex of infanticide victims.' *Nature*, 385, pp. 212–13

Fife, S. T. 2016. 'Adultery, Cultural Views of.' In *The Wiley Blackwell Encyclopedia of Gender and Sexuality Studies*, 1–3. DOI: 10.1002/9781118663219.wbegss499

Foucault, M. 1977. *Discipline and Punish: The Birth of the Prison.* New York: Pantheon

Gager, J. G. 1992. *Curse Tablets and Binding Spells from the Ancient World.* Oxford: Oxford University Press

Hassan, N. A.-M., Brown, K. A., Eyers, J., Brown, T. A. and Mays, S. 2014. 'Ancient DNA study of the remains of putative infanticide victims from the Yewden Roman villa site at Hambleden, England.' *Journal of Archaeological Science*, 43, pp. 192–7

Luck, G. 2006. *Arcana Mundi: Magic and the Occult in the Greek and Roman Worlds*, 2nd ed. Baltimore, MA: Johns Hopkins University Press

Lynch, T. 2001. 'We should witness the death of McVeigh.' *New York Times*. 20 February 2001, section A, p. 21

Moore, A. 2009. 'Hearth and home: the burial of infants within Romano-British domestic contexts.' *Childhood in the Past*, 2, pp. 33–54

Retief, R. P. and Cilliers, L. 2005. 'Causes of death among the Caesars (27 BCE–476 CE).' *Acta Summa Theologica Supplementum* 7, pp. 89–106

Rutledge, S. H. 2001. *Imperial Inquisitions: Prosecutors and Informants from Tiberius to Domitian.* London: Routledge

Sarat, A. 2001. *When the State Kills: Capital Punishment and the American Condition.* Princeton, NJ: Princeton University Press

Scheidel, W. 2011. 'The Roman slave supply.' In Bradley, K. and
Cartledge, P. (eds). *The Cambridge World History of Slavery Vol. 1.
The Ancient Mediterranean World.* Cambridge: Cambridge
University Press
—— 2015. 'The Lives of the Twelve Hundred Caesars: Roman
emperors, global comparisons' as the First Annual
Distinguished Lecture in Ancient History, California State
University Los Angeles, May 5, 2015
Syme, R. 1961. 'Who Was Vedius Pollio?' *The Journal of Roman
Studies,* 51, pp. 23–30
Tatum, W. J. 2014. *The Patrician Tribune: Publius Clodius Pulcher.*
Chapel Hill, NC: The University of North Carolina Press
Veyne, P. 1999. 'La vie privée dans l'Empire romain.' In Ariès, P.
and Duby, G. *Histoire de la vie privée. 1: De l'Empire romain à l'an
mil.* Paris: Seuil
Zias, J. 2012. 'Crucifixion.' In *The Encyclopedia of Ancient History.*
DOI: 10.1002/9781444338386.wbeah10027

An incomplete list of other books I reference is as follows:
Alston, R. 2015. *Rome's Revolution: Death of the Republic and the Birth
of the Empire.* Oxford: Oxford University Press
Amato, E., Citti, F. and Huelsenbeck, B. 2015. *Law and Ethics in
Greek and Roman Declamation.* Berlin: De Gruyter Saur
Baldwin, B. 1974. 'Herodes Atticus: Philanthropist or Rat?'
Echos du Monde Classique, 18(2), pp. 33–6
Bauman, R. A. 2000. *Human Rights in Ancient Rome.* London: Routledge
—— 2004. *Crime and Punishment in Ancient Rome.* New York, NY:
Routledge
Black, D. 1993. *The Social Structure of Right and Wrong.* San Diego,
CA: Academic Press, Inc.
Bodel, J. and Scheidel, W. 2017. *On Human Bondage: After Slavery
and Social Death.* Malden, MA: John Wiley

Bohm, R. A. 2007. *Deathquest 3: An Introduction to the Theory and Practice of Capital Punishment in the United States*. Newark, NJ: Mathew Bender & Company

Bradley, K.1988. 'Roman Slavery and Roman Law.' *Historical Reflections/Reflexions Historiques*, 15(3), pp. 477–95

—— 2015. 'The Bitter Chain of Slavery.' *Dialogues d'histoire ancienne*, 41/1(1), pp. 149–76

Breij, B. 2006. 'Vitae Necisque Potestas in Roman Declamation.' *Advances in the History of Rhetoric*, 9(1), pp. 55–79

Brookman, F. 2005. *Understanding Homicide*. Thousand Oaks, CA: Sage

Brookman, F., Maguire, E. R. and Maguire, M. 2017. *The Handbook of Homicide*. Malden, MA: John Wiley

Calhoon, C. G. 1994. *Livia the Poisoner: Genesis of an Historical Myth*. University of California, Irvine

Cantarella, E. 2003. 'Fathers and Sons in Rome.' *The Classical World*, 96(3), pp. 281–98

Cassibry, K. 2018. 'Spectacular Translucence: The Games in Glass.' *Theoretical Roman Archaeology Journal*, 1(1), p.5. DOI: http://doi.org/10.16995/traj.359

Carter, M. J. 2007. 'Gladiatorial Combat: The Rules of Engagement.' *The Classical Journal*, 102(2), pp. 97–114

—— 2009. 'Gladiators and Monomachoi: Greek Attitudes to a Roman "Cultural Performance".' *The International Journal of the History of Sport*, 26(2), pp. 298–322

Cartmill, M. 1996. *A View to a Death in the Morning: Hunting and Nature Through History*. Cambridge, MA: Harvard University Press

Cilliers, L. 2019. 'Cherchez la Femme: Three Infamous Poisoners of Ancient Rome.' In Wexler, P. (ed.). *Toxicology in Antiquity*. San Diego, CA: Academic Press, Inc.

Cilliers, L. and Retief, F. P. 2000. 'Poisons, Poisoning and the Drug Trade in Ancient Rome.' *Akroterion*, 45, pp. 88–100

Cloud, J. D. 1968. 'How did Sulla style his law de sicarus?' *The Classical Review*, 18(2), pp. 140–3

—— 1969. 'The primary purpose of the Lex Cornelia de Sicariis.' *Zeitschrift der Savigny-Stiftung für Rechtsgeschichte: Romanistische Abteilung*, 86(4), pp. 258–86

—— 1971. 'Parricudium: From the lex Numae to the lex Pómpela.' *Zeitschrift der Savigny-Stiftung für Rechtsgeschichte: Romanistische Abteilung*, 88(1), pp. 1–66

Coleman, K. 1990. 'Fatal Charades: Roman Executions Staged as Mythological Scenes.' *Journal of Roman Studies*, 80, pp. 44–73

—— 1998. ' "The contagion of the throng": absorbing violence in the Roman world.' *Hermathena*, 164, pp. 65–88

Cook, J. G. 2002. 'Crucifixion as Spectacle in Roman Campania.' *Novum Testamentum*, 54(1), pp. 68–100

Cooney, M. 2012. *Is Killing Wrong? A Study in Pure Sociology*. Charlottesville, VA: University of Virginia Press

Coulston, J. 2009. 'Victory and defeat in the Roman arena: the evidence of gladiatorial iconography.' In Wilmott, T. (ed.). *Roman Amphitheatres and Spectacula: a 21st-Century Perspective*. British Archaeological Reports, International Series 1946, Oxford, pp.195–210

Crawford, S. 2010. 'Infanticide, Abandonment and Abortion in the Greco-Roman and Early Medieval World: Archaeological Perspectives.' In Brockliss, L. and Montgomery, H. (eds). *Childhood and Violence in the Western Tradition*. Oxford: Oxbow Books

Curran, J. 2018. 'Ius vitae necisque: the politics of killing children.' *Journal of Ancient History*, 6(1), pp. 111–35

Currie, S. 1996. 'The killer within: Christianity and the invention of murder in the Roman world'. *differences: A Journal of Feminist Cultural Studies*, 8(2), pp. 156–70

Dench, E. 2007. *Romulus' Asylum: Roman Identities from the Age of Alexander to the Age of Hadrian*. Oxford: Oxford University Press

Dickie, M. W. 2000. 'Bonds and Headless Demons in Greco-Roman Magic.' *Greek, Roman, and Byzantine Studies*, 40, pp. 99–104

—— 2000. 'Who practised love-magic in classical antiquity and in the late Roman world?' *The Classical Quarterly*, 50(2), pp. 563–83

—— 2001. *Magic and Magicians in the Greco-Roman World*. London: Routledge

Du Plessis, P. J. 2014. 'Perceptions of Roman justice.' *Fundamina*, 20(1), pp. 216–26

Duindam, J. et al. 2013. *Law and Empire: Ideas, Practices, Actors*. Leiden: Brill

Edwards, C. 2007. *Death in Ancient Rome*. New Haven, CT: Yale University Press

Egmond, F. 1995. 'The cock, the dog, the serpent, and the monkey. Reception and transmission of a Roman punishment, or historiography as history.' *International Journal of the Classical Tradition*, 2(2), pp. 159–92

Ellart, C. S.-M. 2012. 'Homicide, Rome.' In *The Encyclopedia of Ancient History*. DOI: 10.1002/9781444338386.wbeah13112

Engels, D. 1980. 'The Problem of Female Infanticide in the Greco-Roman World.' *Classical Philology*, 75(2), pp. 112–20

Evans Grubbs, J. 2011. 'The Dynamics of Infant Abandonment: Motives, Attitudes and (Unintended) Consequences.' In Mustakallio, K. and Laes, C. (eds). *The Dark Side of Childhood in Late Antiquity and the Middle Ages: Unwanted, Disabled and Lost*. Oxford: Oxbow Books

Fagan, G. G. 2016. 'Urban Violence: Street, Forum, Bath, Circus.' In Reiss, W. and Fagan, G. G. (eds). *The Topography of Violence in the Greco-Roman World*. Ann Arbor, MI: University of Michigan Press

Fitzgerald, W. 2004. *Slavery and the Roman Literary Imagination*. Cambridge: Cambridge University Press

Foreman, P. G. *et al.* 2018. *Writing About Slavery / Teaching About Slavery: This Might Help.* Community-sourced document, available at https://docs.google.com/document/d/1A4TEdDgYslX-hlKe-zLodMIM71My3KTN0zxRv0IQTOQs/edit. Last accessed 21 November 2019

Frankfurter, D. 2006. 'Fetus magic and sorcery fears in Roman Egypt.' *Greek, Roman and Byzantine Studies*, 46, pp. 37–62

Friend, C. 2009. 'Pirates, seducers, wronged heirs, poison cups, cruel husbands, and other calamities: The Roman school declamations and critical pedagogy.' *Rhetoric Review*, 17(2), pp. 300–20

Fuhrmann, C. J. 2012. *Policing the Roman Empire: Soldiers, Administration, and Public Order.* Oxford: Oxford University Press

Futrell, A. 2006. *The Roman Games.* Malden, MA: Blackwell

Gardner, J. F. 1993. *Being a Roman Citizen.* London: Routledge

Gardner, J. F and Wiedemann, T. 1991. *The Roman Household: A Sourcebook.* London: Routledge

Garnsey, P. 1968. 'Why Penalties Become Harsher: The Roman Case, Late Republic to Fourth Century Empire.' *Natural Law Forum*, 143, pp. 141–62

Gaughan, J. E. 2010. *Murder Was Not a Crime: Homicide and Power in the Roman Republic.* Austin, TX: University of Texas Press

Gowland, R. L., Chamberlain, A. and Redfern, R. C. 2014. 'On the Brink of Being: Re-evaluating Infanticide.' *Journal of Roman Archaeology Supplementary Series*, 96, pp. 69–88

Granger Cook, J. 2014. *Crucifixion in the Mediterranean World.* Tübingen: Mohr Siebeck

Hallett, J. and Skinner, M. 1997. *Roman Sexualities.* Princeton, NJ: Princeton University Press

Harris, W. V. 2013. *Mental Disorders in the Classical World.* Leiden: Brill

Hengel, M. 1977. *Crucifixion in the Ancient World*. London: Fortress

Hill, T. 2004. *Ambitiosa Mors: Suicide and Self in Roman Thought and Literature*. New York, NY: Routledge

Hillner, J. 2003. 'Domus, Family, and Inheritance: The Senatorial Family House in Late Antique Rome.' *Journal of Roman Studies*, 97(01), p. ix

Hobenreich, E. and Rizelli, G. 2013. 'Poisoning in Ancient Rome: The Legal Framework, the Nature of Poisons and Gender Stereotypes.' *History of Toxicology and Environmental Health*, 84, pp. 487–92

Hoenigswald, G. S. 1962. 'The Murder Charges in Cicero's Pro Cluentio.' *Transactions and Proceedings of the American Philological Association*, 93, pp. 109–23

Holford-Strevens, L. 2001. 'Getting Away with Murder: The Literary and Forensic Fortune of Two Roman "Exempla".' *International Journal of the Classical Tradition*, 7(4), pp. 489–514

Hope, V. 2000. 'Fighting for Identity: The Funerary Commemoration of Italian Gladiators.' *Bulletin of the Institute of Classical Studies. Supplement No. 73: The Epigraphic Landscape of Roman Italy*, pp. 93–113

—— 2007. *Death in Ancient Rome: A Sourcebook*. London: Routledge

Hope, V. M. and Huskinson, J. 2011. *Memory and Mourning: Studies on Roman Death*. Oxford: Oxbow Books

Hopkins, K. 2014. 'Novel Evidence for Roman Slavery.' *Past & Present*, 138(1), pp. 3–27

Horstmanshoff, M. 1999. 'Ancient medicine between hope and fear: Medicament, magic and poison in the Roman Empire.' *European Review*, 7(1), pp. 37–51

Jones-Lewis, M. A. 2012. 'Poison: Nature's Argument for the Roman Empire in Pliny the Elder's Naturalis Historia.' *The Classical World*, 106(1), pp. 51–74

Kuhlmann, P. 2016. 'Fate and Prodigies in Roman Religion and Literature.' *Estudios humanísticos. Filología*, 33(33), p. 15

Kyle, D. G. 1998. *Spectacles of Death in Ancient Rome*. London: Routledge

Kyle, D. G. and Christesen, P. 2014. *A Companion to Sport and Spectacle in Greek and Roman Antiquity*. Chichester: John Wiley

Lachmann, R. 2010. *States and Power*. Cambridge: Polity

Laes, C. 2008. 'Child Slaves at Work in Roman Antiquity.' *Ancient Society*, 38 (April 2007), pp. 235–83

Laurence, R. and Stromberg, A. 2014. *Families in the Greco-Roman World*. London: Continuum

Lintott, A. 1968. *Violence in Republican Rome*. Oxford: Clarendon Press

—— 2008. *Cicero as Evidence: A Historian's Companion*. Oxford: Oxford University Press

Llewellyn-Jones, L. 2011. 'Domestic abuse and violence against women in ancient Greece.' *Sociable Man*, pp. 231–66

May, J. M. 2002. *Brill's Companion to Cicero: Oratory and Rhetoric*. Leiden: Brill

Metraux, G. P. R. 1999. 'Ancient Housing: "Oikos" and "Domus" in Greece and Rome.' *Journal of the Society of Architectural Historians*, 58(3), pp. 392–405

Milner, L. S. 1998. *Hardness of Heart/Hardness of Life: The Stain of Human Infanticide*. Lanham, MD: University Press of America

Minowa, Y. and Witkowski, T. H. 2012. 'Spectator consumption practices at the Roman games.' *Journal of Historical Research in Marketing*, 4(4), pp. 510–31

Morrall, P. 2006. *Murder and Society*. Chichester: John Wiley

Muravyeva, M. and Toivo, R. M. 2018. *Parricide and Violence Against Parents Throughout History: (De)Constructing Family and Authority?* London: Palgrave Macmillan

Nolder, M. J. 2001. 'The Domestic Violence Dilemma: Private Action in Ancient Rome and America.' *Boston University Law Review*, 81, 1119, pp. 8–23

Ogden, D. 2001. *Greek and Roman Necromancy*. Princeton, NJ: Princeton University Press

—— 2002. *Magic, Witchcraft, and Ghosts in the Greek and Roman Worlds: A Sourcebook*. Oxford: Oxford University Press

Oldenziel, R. 1987. 'The Historiography of Infanticide in Antiquity: A Literature Stillborn.' In Blok, J. and Mason, P. (eds). *Sexual Asymmetry: Studies in Ancient Society*. Amsterdam: J. C. Gieben

Pagán, V. E. 2008. 'Toward a Model of Conspiracy Theory for Ancient Rome.' *New German Critique*, 35(1), pp. 27–49

—— 2012. *Conspiracy Theory in Latin Literature*. Austin, TX: University of Texas Press

Phillips, S. 2009. 'Status Disparities in the Capital of Capital Punishment.' *Law and Society Review*, 43(4), pp. 807–38

Plass, P. 1995. *The Game of Death in Ancient Rome: Arena Sport and Political Suicide*. Madison, WI: University of Wisconsin Press

Plessis, P. J. du. 2013. *New Frontiers: Law and Society in the Roman World*. Edinburgh: Edinburgh University Press

Pomeroy, S. B. 2007. *The Murder of Regilla: A Case of Domestic Violence in Antiquity*. Cambridge, MA: Harvard University Press

Porter, J. R. 2018. *A Sampling of Graffiti and Other Public and Semi-Public Texts from Pompeii and Herculaneum*. Available from https://www.academia.edu/36829610/A_Sampling_of_ Graffiti_and_Other_Public_and_Semi-Public_Texts_from_ Pompeii_and_Herculaneum. Last accessed 21 November 2019

Potter, D. 2015. 'Death as Spectacle and Subsequent Disposal.' *Journal of Roman Archaeology*, pp. 478–84

Potter, D. and Mattingly, D. J. 1999. *Life, Death and Entertainment in the Roman Empire*. Ann Arbor, MI: University of Michigan Press

Reiss, W. and Fagan, G. G. (eds) 2016. *The Topography of Violence in the Greco-Roman World*. Ann Arbor, MI: University of Michigan Press

Riggsby, A. M. 2010. *Roman Law and the Legal World of the Romans*. Cambridge: Cambridge University Press

Rives, J. B. 2002. 'Magic in the XII Tables revisited.' *The Classical Quarterly*, 52(1), pp. 270–90

—— 2006. 'Magic, Religion, and Law: The Case of the Lex Cornelia de Sicariis and Veneficiis.' In Ando, C. and Rupke, J. (eds). *Religion and Law in Classical and Christian Rome*. Berlin: Franz Steiner Verlag

Robinson, O. F. 1970. 'Slaves and the Criminal Law.' *Zeitschrift der Savigny-Stiftung für Rechtsgeschichte: Romanistische Abteilung*, 98(1), pp. 213–54

—— 1995. *The Criminal Law of Ancient Rome*. Baltimore, MD: Johns Hopkins University Press

—— 2007. *Penal Practice and Penal Policy in Ancient Rome*. Abingdon: Routledge

Rüpke, J. 2007. *A Companion to Roman Religion*. Malden, MA: Blackwell

—— 2016. *On Roman Religion: Lived Experience and the Individual in Ancient Rome*. Ithaca, NY: Cornell University Press

—— 2018. *Pantheon: A New History of Roman Religion*. Princeton, NJ: University of Princeton Press

Saller, R. P. 1984. '"Familia, Domus", and the Roman Conception of the Family.' *Phoenix*, 38(4), pp. 336–55

Schultz, C. E. 2010. 'The Romans and Ritual Murder.' *Journal of the American Academy of Religion*, 78(2), pp. 516–41

Scott, E. 2001. 'Unpicking a Myth: The Infanticide of Female and Disabled Infants in Antiquity.' In Davies, G., Gardner, A. and

Lockyear, K. (eds). *Proceedings of the Tenth Annual Theoretical Roman Archaeology Conference, London 2000*. Oxford: Oxbow Books

Shuy, R. W. 2014. *The Language of Murder Cases*. Oxford: Oxford University Press

Smith, M. D. and Zahn, M. A. 1999. *Studying and Preventing Homicide: Issues and Challenges*. Thousand Oaks, CA: Sage

Thompson, S. 2006. 'Was Ancient Rome a Dead Wives Society? What did the Roman Paterfamilias Get Away With?' *Journal of Family History*, 31(1), pp. 3–27

Toner, J. 2014. *The Day Commodus Killed a Rhino: Understanding the Roman Games*. Baltimore, MD: Johns Hopkins University Press

—— 2019. *Infamy: The Crimes of Ancient Rome*. London: Profile Books

Tuori, K. 2007. 'Revenge and Retribution in the Twelve Tables: Talio esto Reconsidered.' *Fundamina*, 13(2), pp. 140–5

Vaarhelyi, Z. 2007. 'The Specters of Roman Imperialism: The Live Burials of Gauls and Greeks at Rome.' *Classical Antiquity*, 26(2), pp. 277–304. DOI: 10.1525/CA.2007.26.2.277

Weidemann, T. E. 1980. *Greek and Roman Slavery: A Sourcebook*. London: Routledge

—— 1995. *Emperors and Gladiators*. London: Routledge

—— 1996. 'Single Combat and Being Roman.' *Ancient Society*, 27, pp. 91–103

Wiseman, T. P. 1995. *Remus: A Roman Myth*. Cambridge: Cambridge University Press

Wyke, M. 2008. *Julius Caesar in Western Culture*. Malden, MA: Blackwell

Acknowledgements

I wrote this book while working full time as a bookshop manager and not one word would have been written if it hadn't been for Conor Sally bullying me, cajoling me, poking me and regularly taking my phone away from me and forcing me up the stairs to my office. He spent his evenings and weekends by himself, put up with my whining and huffing, took care of everything and never once complained. He is the greatest cheerleader and taskmaster and partner and I could not be more grateful nor more lucky to know and love him.

The idea for this book came from a conversation with my friend Amy-Elizabeth Manlapas, an incredible history teacher in Atlanta. She mentioned in passing that she used true crime to teach modern history to high school students, and blew my mind and set me off on a path that ended here. The title was the product of the brilliant mind of Sarah Perry and it, like she, is perfect.

This book would not exist without the relentless and proactive belief and support of Scott Pack and Charlie Viney who believe in me much more than I ever believed in myself and spur me on to try to make them proud.

Everyone at Waterstones Belfast (and NI) who have never let me get lost in my research and always keep me on my toes. I hope I made you proud too!

Thank you to my murder pals Jess Vine and Kate Scott (hail yourselves), and my difficult aunts Anna Scott, Eley Williams (who doesn't even know how utterly utterly vital her help was), Alice Tarbuck, Fiona Zublin, Ella Risbridger, Oliva Potts, Kate Young, Isabella Streffan, Marika Prokosh, Sarah Guillick and

Sarah Perry. My god, you are an incredible set of women. Thank you to Janina Matthewson, Jamie Drew, Oliver Kealey, Phoebe Bird, Sian Hunter, Seaínín McCoy, Christine McCurdy, John and Helen Freeman and Helen-Rose Owen just for being great. Alexandra Elbakyan, you are incredible and make my life better. Rachael Krishna for giving me two of the best lines. Dr Sarah Bremner for ace comments.

I am lucky enough to have a lot of family who love and protect and support me: Mum and Tony, Dad and Karen, Gerard and Margaret, Katie and Dave, Lucy and Undi, Millie, Mark and Tracy: thank you and I'm sorry I didn't reply to texts or see any of you for a year.

Finally, infinite and unending thank yous to Sam Carter who was right about everything and pushed me to write not just fun words but good words and reminded me that writing good words was worth all the hard work . . . Any bad words left are my terrible idea.

Notes

Introduction

1. Full disclosure: I use Latin words in this book. The ones I use are mostly in the Glossary so you can check their meaning.
2. According to Wikipedia anyway, based on what appear to be completely imaginary numbers made up by newspapers but let's go with it. She holds this fanciful top spot jointly with William Shakespeare, who was himself also pretty keen on murder as a plot device.

Chapter I

1. That's one story anyway. Livy tells us that other sources thought that Cassius was found guilty in a public court. Livy, *History of Rome* 2.41.
2. Truth be told, the sources don't agree on which way round it was. Plutarch says that the wife's fate was linked to the female snake and his fate to the male, but Valerius Maximus says that the genders were swapped. Take your pick.
3. Appian, *Civil Wars* 1.10.38–42.
4. Plutarch, *Tiberius Gracchus* 9.5–6.
5. Except possibly his sister Clodia, who was divorced by her husband in 66 BCE after he allegedly caught her banging her brother.
6. Cicero, *Philippics* 2.21.
7. Cicero, *Pro Milone*; Appian, 2.21; Dio, 40.48; Cicero, *Philippics* 2.21.
8. Asconius, *On Cicero's Pro Milone* 26KS.
9. To quote his most recent biographer: 'it is fair to say that Clodius did not leave a lasting *personal* impression on Rome.' Tatum, 2014, p. 394.
10. Nicolaus of Damascus, *Life of Augustus* F 130:20.
11. Basically France, Belgium, Switzerland, Lichtenstein and the edges of Germany and Austria. A pretty significant bit of Europe.
12. Parthia was part of the Iranian Empire, which bordered the Roman Empire in the east at the point of modern-day Armenia. The Romans were never able to beat the Parthians and this made the Romans furious.
13. Cicero, *Letters to Atticus* 15.11.
14. Cicero, *Letters to Atticus* 14.21.
15. Cicero, *Letters to Atticus* 14.1.

Chapter 2

1. Corpus Inscriptionum Latinarum (hereafter CIL) III 2399. This can now be found in the Archaeological Museum in Zagreb, Croatia.
2. Prima Florentina: L'Année Épigraphique (hereafter AE) 1987.0177k. Domitilla: Katalog Kaisareia Hadrianopolis no. 38; SGOst 2 no. 10/2/12. Grattius: NotScav 1900, p.578, no. 35. See F. Graf, 'Untimely Death, Witchcraft, and Divine Vengeance. A Reasoned Epigraphical Catalog.' *Zeitschrift für Papyrologie und Epigraphik*, Bd. 162, 2007, pp. 139–50.
3. George Eliot, *Middlemarch*. 2003. London: Penguin. p. 873.
4. Cicero, *Pro Tullio* 51.
5. Cicero, *Topica* 64.
6. Gaius, *Digest* 50.16.236.
7. Gaius, *Digest* 9.2.2.
8. Ulpian, *Digest* 9.2.5.3.
9. Ulpian, *Digest* 9.2.7.2.
10. Ulpian, *Digest* 9.2.11.
11. Ulpian, *Digest* 9.2.7.1.
12. Marcian, *Digest* 48.8.1.3.

Chapter 3

1. Veyne, 1999.
2. Marcian, *Digest* 48.9.1.
3. Modestinus, *Digest* 48.9.9.
4. Seneca, *Controversiae* 5.4, and Juvenal, *Satires* 13.158.
5. In 2012, Adam Lanza murdered twenty-seven people, of which twenty were six- and seven-year-old children, in a mass shooting at Sandy Hook Elementary School in Newtown, Connecticut, before shooting himself.
6. Orosius, *History of the Pagans* 5.16.23–24. 'An unbelievable crime and one never previously experienced among the Romans was suddenly perpetrated at Rome.'
7. For evidence of this, please see the first four paragraphs of his self-published defence speech for Roscius, which consist entirely of boasting about his own bravery and personal virtue in agreeing to take such a dangerous and difficult case.
8. Seneca, *Controversiae* 7.1.
9. Seneca, *Controversiae* 7.1.
10. Valerius Maximus, *Memorable Words and Deeds* 5.8.1.
11. Livy, *History of Rome* 2.5.5. See also Dionysius of Halicarnassus, *Roman Antiquities* 8.79.2.

12. Livy, *History of Rome* 8.7.19; Valerius Maximus, *Memorable Words and Deeds* 2.7.6.

13. There is another version of this story which says that he was publicly prosecuted for treason.

14. Valerius Maximus, *Memorable Words and Deeds* 6.1.3.

15. Livy, *History of Rome* 1.24–6.

16. Basically every day.

17. Cicero, *Against Catiline*, 1.14. Cf Sallust, *War against Catiline* 15.2f., Appian, *Roman History* 2.2 and Valerius Maximus, *Memorable Words and Deeds* 9.1.9.

18. Blanche Taylor Moore is currently on death row for the poisoning of her boyfriend, and is believed to have also poisoned her mother-in-law, her first husband and her father and attempted to poison her second husband.

19. Terry Deary, *Ruthless Romans*. 2003. London: Scholastic. p. 60.

20. The specifics of this story vary wildly across tellings in the ancient world, and the tale is spun with varying degrees of detail and sceptism but those are the basics.

21. Carroll, 2018.

22. Seneca, *De Ira* 1.15.2.

23. Plutarch, *Roman Questions* 102.

24. Hassan *et al.*, 2014. Faerman, *et al.*, 1997.

25. Moore, 2009.

26. The Twinkie defence is named after the defence given by Dan White after he shot the openly gay politician Harvey Milk and San Francisco mayor George Moscone in their offices in 1978. He claimed that he was depressed, evidenced by him eating too many Twinkies, and this led him to murder two men in a planned attack. It was, astonishingly, successful and he was found guilty of voluntary manslaughter.

27. Smaller than it sounds: basically just Turkey.

28. There are approximately seventy-seven possible spellings of Daniel's surname including M'Naughton, M'Naughten, M'Naughtan, McNaugton, MacNaughton, McNaughtan, etc., etc. – you get the picture. As there's no consensus and I don't think Daniel cares, I just picked the one I found easiest to type.

29. Re Daniel M'Naghten, 8 ER 718 (House of Lords, 1843).

30. Africa does not mean the continent of Africa here. The Roman province they called Africa basically consisted of modern Tunisia and the Mediterranean coasts of modern Algeria and Libya.

31. Macer, *Digest* 1.18.14.

32. The distinction between criminally liable and civilly liable is complex, location specific and so ludicrously boring, you'll try to sue me for emotional distress if I try to explain it.

33. These are all real quotes from Reddit users Matrix2002, Agjios and ThrowW_AwayY_Ughhh.

34. On the flip side, using the term clan or tribe here also makes cultures where those terms are used a *lot*, like the Celts or the Ancient Germans or pre-colonisation Africa, much less alien and primitive. A win-win.

Chapter 4

1. Broadly, modern-day Albania and parts of Croatia and Slovenia.
2. Fronto, *Letters to Marcus Aurelius* 3.3.
3. Propertius, *Elegies* 2.8.
4. AE 1987.0177k.
5. CIL 13.2182 (ILS 8512).

Chapter 5

1. Isidorus owned 4,116 enslaved people when he died in 8 BCE and Melania freed eight thousand when she became a Christian ascetic in the fifth century CE.
2. Numbers from Scheidel, 2011. An infinite number of other guesses are available.
3. See Jerry Toner's *How to Manage Your Slaves* (London: Profile Books, 2014), which is a modernised manual for the enslaver written for modern audiences but drawn from Roman enslaver manuals, and which displays the full range of calculated cruelty that such people are capable of.
4. Formia, about halfway between Rome and Naples.
5. This is all recorded in delicious detail in Pliny the Younger's *Letter* 3.14.
6. Though punishing children and enslaved people with disabilities was relaxed in the later Empire.
7. Ulpian, *Digest* 29.5.1.
8. Longinus' entire speech appears in Tacitus, *Annals* 14.43–4.
9. CIL 13.7070.
10. Cicero, *Pro Roscio Comoedo* 10.
11. This is all assuming that the late great Ronald Syme is right that the Vedius Pollio who killed enslaved people horribly is the same P. Vedius Pollio who visited Cicero and annoyed him while Cicero was provincial governor of Cilicia. I have no reason to believe that he isn't. Ronald Syme, 'Who Was Vedius Pollio?' *The Journal of Roman Studies*, 51, 1961, pp. 23–30.
12. Basically the bottom bit of Turkey above Cyprus.
13. Marcian, *Digest* 48.8.11.2.
14. AE 1971.88.

15. Marcian, *Digest* 48.8.1.2. See Robinson, 1970.
16. *Theodosian Code* 9.12.1.
17. Fife, 2016.
18. Seneca, *De Ira* 3.40.
19. The first ever half-time show at the Super Bowl was in 1967 and it featured the University of Arizona Symphonic Marching Band, the Grambling State University Marching Band, and the Anaheim High School Drill Team and Flag Girls.
20. Marcus Aurelius, *Meditations* 8.47 and 4.9 (yes, it is quite a repetitive book!).
21. Marcus Aurelius, *Meditations* 5.8.
22. The thumbs thing comes from a line in a poem by a second-century CE misanthrope called Juvenal who mentioned in Satire 3 that the fates of gladiators were decided by the turning of thumbs, but, crucially and agonisingly, he didn't bother to mention which way the thumb was turned for life or death. I suspect that Juvenal would be delighted by how annoying this is. In the same piece he coined the term 'bread and circuses' because he hated people and fun and, apparently, bread.
23. The internet informs me that the 2008 Detroit Lions are the worst team in NFL history. Blame the internet if that's not true.
24. You can see it in the open-access Corpus Inscriptionum Latinarum online at IV.1474. The Latin, so precise and concise and lovely, reads: 'Spiculus Ner(onianus) v(icit) tiro Aptonetus p(eriit) libr XVI'.
25. Roman literature is absolutely rife with stories of women soaking their knickers at the sight of gladiators but my favourite one comes from Juvenal's misogyny-fest Satire 6. He describes a woman called Eppia who apparently caused a brilliant scandal of the kind that kept people in gossip for months by abandoning her husband and children and running off with a gladiator to Alexandria in Egypt.

Chapter 6

1. Figs are 'a sexual stimulant, as they're high in amino acids, which boost sexual stamina and increase libido' said *Cosmopolitan* in May 2019 to prove my point.
2. These are located in Xama, Tunisia, Bœotia in Greece and Arcadia also in Greece, should you be interested in tracking them down. Pliny, *Natural History* 31.7, 11, 12.
3. Pliny, *Natural History* 28.17.
4. Pliny, *Natural History* 30.7. This is because moles are, according to Pliny, cursed by nature.
5. Cato, *On Agriculture* 157.

6. The giraffe thing, incidentally, comes from, I shit you not, a trashy paper-back called *The Encyclopedia of Serial Killers* by Michael Newton (New York, NY: Facts on File, 2000). It's not included in the 2006 second edition, oddly.

7. Martial, *Epigrams* 4.48.

8. Evans and Gifford, 1881.

9. CIL False inscriptions VI.19.

10. Which broadly corresponds to where modern-day Syria is, plus Lebanon, Israel and Palestine.

11. Tacitus, *Annals* 2.69.

12. Gager, 1992, and Daniela Urbanová, *Latin Curse Tablets of the Roman Empire* (Innsbruck: Institut für Sprachen und Literaturen der Universität Innsbruck, Bereich Sprachwissenschaft, 2018).

13. From North Africa in the late Empire, no. 286B in Audollent, 1904. Translation is from Luck, 2006.

14. Tablet 95 in Gager, 1992, p.194 with my edits.

15. These are from Horace, *Epodes* 3, 5 and 17.

16. Horace, *Satire* 1.8.

17. Tacitus, *Annals* 2.13.

18. CIL 3.2197.

19. Inscriptiones Graecae 12.5784.

20. CIL 6.3.20905.

21. A strigil is a bronze cleaning implement used by Greeks and Romans at the baths. They were rubbed in oil after hot baths and then the strigil, which is a curved bronze or iron instrument, was used to scrape the oil, sweat and dirt off the body. Bracing.

22. Cicero, *In Vatinum* 6.

23. Dio, *Roman History* 74.16.5.

24. Philostratus, *Life of Apollonius* 7.11.

25. Philostratus, *Life of Apollonius* 8.8.

26. CIL 6.19747. The Livia here is not Augustus' wife but the wife of Tiberius' son Drusus and the sister of both Germanicus and the emperor Claudius.

27. So while we count a child's age by how many months or years they have lived (one year old after their first birthday, two years old after their second), Romans counted by the month or year they were in the process of living through. So a Roman baby was in their first year as soon as they were born, in their second year after their first birthday, in their third year after their second birthday, etc.

Chapter 7

1. Tacitus, *Annals* 1.10.

2. Ruth Snyder and Harry Judd Gray murdered Ruth's husband Albert in 1927 by garrotting him and then, very ineptly, tried to pretend that two burglars had done it. They were instantly foiled by Ruth claiming to have been beaten despite having no injuries and the police instantly finding all the jewellery Ruth claimed had been stolen by the imaginary robbers hidden under her bed. The trial was a media sensation, inspired a number of books and films, including *Double Indemnity*, and both were executed. Such was the furore surrounding Ruth, a reporter smuggled a camera into her execution by electric chair and took a photo of her death. It was on the front page of newspapers. It's horrible.

3. The names come from F. Adams, 'The Consular Brothers of Sejanus', *The American Journal of Philology*, 76 (1), 1955, pp. 70 n.2. Junilla's approximate age comes from Tacitus' claim that she was betrothed as an infant to Claudius' son Tiberius Claudius Drusus, who died in 20 CE. Assuming she was no older than two when her betrothed died, she would be no older than thirteen in 31 CE when she was raped and murdered.

4. 'Female impersonator' says Plutarch.

5. According to Plutarch in *Sulla* 36, it was worms leading to terrible leakages which he describes thus: 'This disease corrupted his whole flesh also, and converted it into worms, so that although many were employed day and night in removing them, what they took away was as nothing compared with the increase upon him, but all his clothing, baths, hand-basins, and food were infected with that flux of corruption, so violent was its discharge. Therefore he immersed himself many times a day in water to cleanse and scour his person.' Which he probably deserved.

6. *Scriptores Historiae Augustae*, Hadrian 23.10.

7. I'm so sorry.

8. The standard work on the *consilium principis* is still Crook, 1955. Interestingly, *consilium principis* is an entirely modern term for a relatively informal group of pals but it sounds good, doesn't it.

9. This story appears in *Horrible Histories* series 3, episode 7, aired in 2011 and derives from Suetonius, *Gaius* 27.2. Allegedly Gaius had a man who promised his life in exchange for the emperor's thrown from the Tarpeian Rock.

10. He and his eldest son, Titus, destroyed the Second Temple in Jerusalem, the great centre of Judaism, in 70 CE as punishment for a Jewish revolt. It has never been rebuilt, and its only surviving fragment is now known as the Wailing Wall or the Western Wall.

11. Because of Robert Graves, Claudius is remembered as a 'good' emperor who never killed anyone, but he was actually wildly inconsistent and pretty trigger happy with the executions until he married his niece Agrippina and she put a stop to it. You can read more about that in my book on Agrippina.

12. Twenty thousand is clearly a made-up number by Suetonius, but still.
13. Plutarch, *Cato the Elder* 15.3.
14. Cicero, *Pro Roscio Amerino* 33; Valerius Maximus, *Memorable Words and Deeds* 9.11.2.
15. Obviously, Taylor Swift has never done this and I'm sure she's lovely.
16. Rutledge, 2001.

Chapter 8

1. These numbers are from Retief and Cilliers, 2005.
2. These numbers are from a 2015 paper given by Walter Scheidel titled 'The Lives of the Twelve Hundred Caesars: Roman emperors, global comparisons' as the First Annual Distinguished Lecture in Ancient History, California State University Los Angeles, which used to be available as a recording online but has now disappeared. Thankfully, I had notes.
3. These numbers are mine. I did maths for you.
4. For all the gory details on this one, please see my book on Agrippina. It involves a lot of bodily fluids.
5. For the blissfully ignorant, MKUltra was a series of mind control experiments carried out by the CIA on unwitting and unconsenting US and Canadian citizens between 1953 and 1973, some of which were illegal, leading to several deaths, which was extremely secret but can now be read about on the CIA website. Operation Northwoods was a 1962 proposed, but never carried out, plan to fabricate a *casus belli* for war with Cuba following the establishment of Fidel Castro's communist government. The plan proposed that the CIA carry out a series of terrorist attacks on US soil and frame the Cuban government for the resulting deaths, thus providing a reason for the US to invade Cuba and overthrow Castro. It was soundly rejected by President Kennedy. A related theory beloved by conspiracy theorists is that the CIA assassinated Kennedy as revenge for his rejection of Operation Northwoods.
6. It probably refers to his great love, Berenice, whom he broke up with and banished from Rome when he became emperor because she was Jewish, 'too Eastern' and reminded everyone of Cleopatra.
7. Eutropius, *Abridgement of Roman History* 8.1.
8. Pleasingly, Gaius is properly spelled Caius in Latin (which has no letter G; it's a long story) so the point holds even if we use Caligula's real name.

Chapter 9

1. The concept of social death in the context of slavery is a fascinating one. The seminal text is Orlando Patterson, *Slavery and Social Death: A Comparative Study with a New Preface* (Cambridge, MA: Harvard University Press, 2018).
2. In case you do want to know about it, you can read Zias, 2012.
3. Quintilian, *Major Declamations* 274.13.
4. CIL 9.3437.
5. Martial, *Spectacles* 6(5).
6. Martial, *Spectacles* 9(7). A Caledonian bear is of course a Scottish bear, so it's nice to see some Team GB representation.
7. Foucault, 1977, p. 10. He was describing prisons, which are, to be fair, neither glamorous nor theatrical.
8. Lynch, 2001.
9. For example, Sarat, 2001.
10. *Mola salsa* was made from slightly unripe spelt, harvested between May 7 and 14 each year, and 'boiled salt and hard salt'. It was made only twice a year, on the Vestalia in June, and in September, and was key to Roman sacrifices. See Robin Lorsch Wildfang, *Rome's Vestal Virgins: A Study of Rome's Vestal Priestesses in the Late Republic and Early Empire* (Florence: Taylor & Francis, 2006).
11. Plutarch, *Marcellus* 3.3–4; Pliny, *Natural History* 28.3.
12. Pliny, *Natural History* 30.13.
13. Plutarch, *Marcellus* 3.2–4; Livy, *History of Rome* 22.57.2–6.

Index

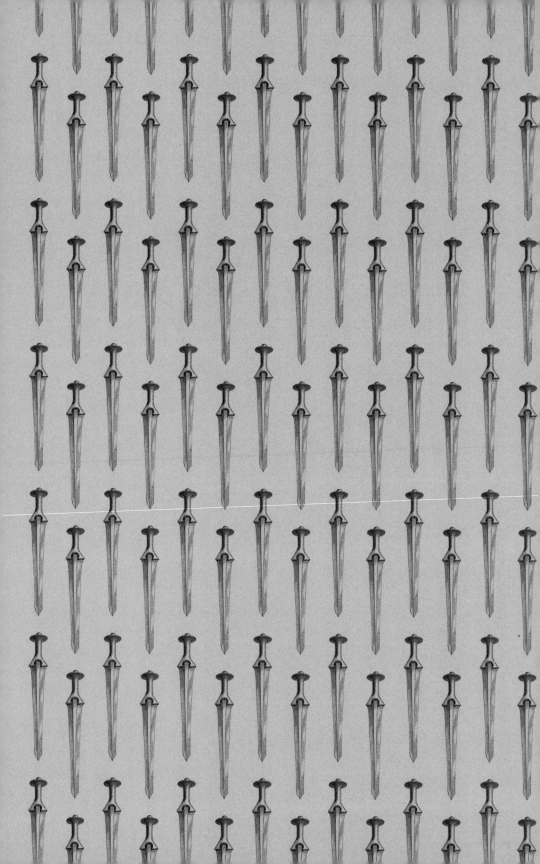